Angry Politics

Angry Politics

PARTISAN HATRED AND POLITICAL POLARIZATION AMONG COLLEGE STUDENTS

Stacy G. Ulbig

University Press of Kansas

Published by the University Press of Kansas (Lawrence, Kansas 66045), which was organized by the Kansas Board of Regents and is operated and funded by Emporia State University, Fort Hays State University, Kansas State University, Pittsburg State University, the University of Kansas, and Wichita State University.

Library of Congress Cataloging-in-Publication Data

Names: Ulbig, Stacy G., author.
Title: Angry politics : partisan hatred and political polarization among college students / Stacy G. Ulbig.
Description: Lawrence : University Press of Kansas, 2020. | Includes bibliographical references and index.
Identifiers: LCCN 2020011853
ISBN 9780700630219 (cloth)
ISBN 9780700630226 (paperback)
ISBN 9780700630233 (epub)
Subjects: LCSH: College students—Political activity—United States. | College students—United States—Attitudes. | College environment—United States. | Polarization (Social sciences)—Political aspects—United States. | Political socialization—United States.
Classification: LCC LA229 .U44 2020 | DDC 378.1/98—dc23
LC record available at https://lccn.loc.gov/2020011853.

British Library Cataloguing-in-Publication Data is available.

Printed in the United States of America

10 9 8 7 6 5 4 3 2 1

The paper used in this publication is recycled and contains 30 percent postconsumer waste. It is acid free and meets the minimum requirements of the American National Standard for Permanence of Paper for Printed Library Materials Z39.48-1992.

Contents

Tables and Figures

TABLES

FIGURES

Acknowledgments

This book has been a long time in the making, and I would like to recognize some of the many who have helped and supported me along the way. Thanks go to Sam Houston State University for supporting this project with a semester-long research leave. Having the leisure to read and think about the many topics on which this books touches, the time to analyze and reanalyze data, and the luxury of writing (and rewriting and rewriting and rewriting) was invaluable. Likewise, I am grateful to the members of the Department of Political Science at the US Air Force Academy for welcoming me as a temporary member among their ranks. The patience the faculty in that department displayed while enduring many conversations about this project stands as testament to their collective intellectual curiosity, creativity, and academic seriousness. Of their continued willingness to speak to me, I can only say I am supremely grateful.

A number of individuals who have stood beside me throughout the lengthy process of writing this book also deserve some recognition. From the time this project was nothing more than an idea, Johanna Dunaway has provided valuable advice and guidance. In the final stages of this project, Lynne Chandler Garcia offered much needed advice and was always able to act excited about the project when I brought it up. In between, Rhonda Callaway, Ken McIntyre, Rich Engstrom, and Shauna Reilly have served variously as sounding boards, counselors, and taskmasters, and the Potato Shack crew provided me with entertaining distractions when I needed to stop thinking too directly about the questions this book tackles. My thanks go to all. Finally, as always, there is Jitterbug—the best (and most expensive) free dog in history. Her remaining days by my side are few, but she continues to remind me at every moment that new challenges should be met with determination and pluck.

1. Incivility and Polarization

> And it's one, two, three shots you're out at the old ball game!!!
>
> —Facebook post (2017)

In the shadow of one of the coarsest and most rancorous presidential elections in US history, an armed sexagenarian Illinois man who had volunteered for the 2016 primary campaign of Bernie Sanders opened fire on a group of Republican Congressmembers practicing for a charity baseball game in Virginia. As the nation reacted to the violence, followers of the Terminate the Republican Party group on Facebook, of which the gunman was a member, celebrated his actions with statements such as the one above. Many were not especially surprised to learn of the attack, seeing it as "a natural, if sick, extension of the virulence that surrounds the country's increasingly tribal politics" (Barabak 2017). The symptoms of such rage have become ever more prevalent in the past decade. The US Senate's 2009 party-line vote on proposed health-care legislation marked what one observer called "the culmination of more than a generation of partisan polarization of the US political system, and a precipitous decline in collegiality and collaboration in governing" (Herszenhorn 2009).

In an era of intense party competition, many of those occupying the halls of Congress seem to agree. In the wake of the 2009 health-care vote, Senator John D. Rockefeller IV observed, "It has gotten so much more partisan. This was so wicked. This was so venal." Several other high-profile Congressmembers further pointed to the rise in partisan rancor as a precipitating factor in their voluntary departures from public office. Citing "campaigns of destruction" that revolved "around destroying the other side" and increased incivility among the senators, Olympia Snowe retired in 2012 (Sharp 2012). Two years earlier, Arlen Specter expressed similar dismay when he delivered his final speech from the Senate floor. In his "closing argument" to his Senate colleagues and the American people, he explained that the collegial debate and bipartisan compromise of three decades earlier had gone by the wayside (Specter 2010). Instead, he said, as more and more senators insisted on ideological purity among party members, "compromising" had "become a dirty word." Many have argued that changes in the "social fabric of Capitol Hill" have impeded the development of cross-partisan personal friendships that support bipartisan trust and civility (Barber and McCarty 2015, 38; Eilperin 2007).

Harkening back to the civility of days when his father served in the Senate, Evan Bayh announced he, too, was leaving it. "When I was a boy, members of Congress from both parties, along with their families, would routinely visit our home for dinner or the holidays. This type of social interaction hardly ever happens today and we are the poorer for it. It is much harder to demonize someone when you know his family or have visited his home" (Bayh 2010). Rising incivility, he argued, impeded bipartisan cooperation when it came to negotiation. After all, as he said, "it's difficult to work with members actively plotting your demise." Bayh also directed his dismay at the US public, saying that elected officials reflect the sentiments of those who continue to elect them to office. From rank-and-file voters to the president, he argued, the "most ideologically devoted elements in both parties must accept that not every compromise is a sign of betrayal or an indication of moral lassitude."

In the years since, US elections have become even more closely divided, with a continued rise of strident partisanship and disrespect across party lines. In 2013 Allegheny College awarded the second annual Prize for Civility in Public Life to Senators Dianne Feinstein (D) of California and Lindsey Graham (R) of South Carolina, in part because many saw them as exemplars of "proud partisans who strive for civility where it is most difficult to achieve, and where it is most dearly needed—on the most contentious political battlefields of our day" (Vucci and Walsh 2013). Response was reported to have been overwhelmingly positive and civil, but, reflecting the state of partisan animosity at the time, some observers contended that one or the other did not merit the award. As Senator Graham remarked upon receiving the award, "It makes news when you're civil in politics, but it's just assumed everywhere else and that has a lot to say about the modern political discourse that we're in" (Allegheny College 2013). Both inside and outside the halls of government, the incivility he bemoaned has become increasingly evident.

When questioned in a recent poll, more than two-thirds of respondents said they believed the tone and civility of political debate in the country was getting worse, and more than three-quarters said they believed such incivility encouraged violence (DePinto et al. 2017). A comparison of polling results from the past decade punctuates the point and illustrates just how far political incivility has spread among the public. Compared with six years earlier, when an overwhelming majority (85 percent) of those interviewed said they thought elected officials should build personal friendships with members of other parties, barely more than a majority (56 percent) held this opinion six years later (Zogby Analytics 2016). The same polling data suggested 10–15-percentage-point declines with regard to beliefs that civility in politics is important for a healthy democracy and that it is even possible to disagree respectfully when it comes to politics. The same respondents did not seem much concerned with reversing this trend. Over the same period, support for teaching respectful political interaction in schools dropped by about 20 percentage points, and compared with six years earlier only about half as many believed that local schools or universities should play a role in making politics more civil in the years ahead. Less than half expressed a desire for elected officials or political parties to take the lead, and less than one-quarter felt the press should work to tamp down political animosities. It is little wonder, then, that headlines proclaiming "Fear and Loathing in American Politics" (Douthat 2015), "Why American Politics Is All about Whom You Hate" (Blake 2016a), "How Politics Became Consumed with Hate" (Antle 2017), and "What Motivated Voters More Than Loyalty? Loathing" (Edsall 2018) have become pervasive.

Perhaps no recent political event epitomizes the incivility and partisan vitriol of contemporary US politics better than the 2016 contest for the White House. From the earliest days of the primary season to Inauguration Day and beyond, candidates from both parties along with their supporters hurled personal insults at their opponents. The public watched as eventual Republican nominee Donald Trump called one of his primary debate challengers a "choke artist" and another "a liar" in a televised debate. Viewing audiences also witnessed one of those challengers suggest to a campaign rally crowd that the eventual president wet his pants during a debate and insinuate that, based on the small size of his hands, he had a small penis—a point Trump would go on to refute in another televised debate (Jaffe 2016; Krieg 2016). Though the Democratic primary saw the two front-runners verbally spar, mostly over specific issue stances or to question each other's knowledge, judgment, and suitability for office, Hillary Clinton held little back when she faced off against Trump in the general election. Asserting that Trump had a history of racial discrimination and that he was "reinforcing harmful stereotypes and offering a dog whistle to his most hateful supporters" at one rally, she went on at another to call half of his supporters "deplorables" who were "racist, sexist, homophobic, xenophobic, Islamophobic" (Blake 2016b; Reilly 2016). Trump said Clinton had "tremendous hate in her heart" (Allen 2016), whereas Clinton contended that Trump was "taking a hate movement mainstream" (Lee 2016). It indeed appears that US presidential elections have become the "swamps of chaotic and confusing name-calling" that Oxford University professor Byron Shafer lamented a decade ago (1997, 3).

It is precisely this sort of hatred and its connections to political incivility and partisan polarization that I scrutinize in the pages that follow. I focus my attention on a particular set of young voters—those enrolled as undergraduates at four-year universities. Not only do today's college students represent tomorrow's voters, activists, and officeholders, but such students also make up the portion of the electorate that might be expected to hold less crystallized political values and be more open to contrary political viewpoints. Thus, gauging the intensity and effects of partisan animosities in this population can offer a glimpse into the prospects for a less rancorous political future. In chapter 2, I review the reasons we might expect the university campus to be a context within which the partisan bitterness witnessed more widely in the nation succumbs less to stirring emotions and more to inquisitive reason, as well as examine the empirical reality on contemporary US campuses. I then leave the college campus to theoretically explore the ways in which partisan hostility can operate in much the same way as ethnic and racial animosities to breed intolerance and disrespect for, as well as violence toward, other groups. Subsequently, I introduce a measure of partisan hatred among college students, investigate the connections between such abhorrence and more global feelings about the two major parties, explore the ways in which media consumption habits might relate to the attitude, and examine some potential social and political consequences of the attitude. Before tackling those tasks, though, I first offer some historical perspective on the contemporary state of the nation's partisan polarization.

PARTISAN INCIVILITY: AS AMERICAN AS BASEBALL, HOT DOGS, AND APPLE PIE

Though some called it "a dirty campaign of historic proportions" (Schrek 2016), the nastiness hurled across partisan lines in the 2016 presidential contest pales in comparison with some of the cut-throat partisan quarrels that took place in the early years of the nation. Conflict across regional, ethnoreligious, class, and economic divides led political actors of the mid- to late nineteenth century to view continuous political conflict as an inescapable aspect of US political life (Shafer 1997, 10–12). With early political parties built upon loyalties to individual leaders, an intensely personal style of politics emerged, bringing with it all the anxiety, distrust, and bitterness such relationships typically embody. Archetypes of political nastiness, the candidates, officeholders, press, and private citizens practiced down-and-dirty politics in their efforts to help their side emerge triumphant from the electoral battlefield. In its infancy, the nation faced political battles of "extremes, in emotion, actions, and accusations" (Freeman 2001, 272), and a quick survey of those contests reveals countless examples of personal animosities, name-calling, raucous rallying, and physical altercations that match or even exceed contemporary practices.

The first contested presidential election, pitting John Adams' Federalists against Thomas Jefferson's Democratic-Republicans, set the precedent for partisan rancor. Jefferson's supporters mocked Adams' large girth and called him, among other things, a "gross hypocrite" and a "hideous hermaphroditical character which has neither the force and firmness of a man, nor the gentleness and sensibility of a woman." Adams' supporters returned the favor by calling Jefferson "a mean-spirited, low-lived fellow, the son of a half-breed Indian squaw, sired by a Virginia mulatto father." Other figures from the era fared little better. Adams referred to Alexander Hamilton as a "bastard brat of a Scotch pedlar," "a Creole bastard," and "a man devoid of every Moral principle." Hamilton called Aaron Burr a "profligate" and a "voluptuary in the extreme." Even Martha Washington got in on the name-calling, saying that Jefferson was "one of the most detestable of mankind." The early candidates disparaged their opposition's supporters as well. Hamilton called Republicans a "detestable faction," and Jefferson's supporters were tagged as "cut-throats who walk in rags and sleep amidst filth and vermin." Alongside this sort of venom, Hillary Clinton's painting of half of Donald Trump's supporters as a "basket of deplorables" and Trump's references to her as "crooked Hillary" appear quite commonplace. And though contemporary campaign rallies might exhibit the same "carnival-type atmosphere, intense partisanship, booing, hissing, and sustained applause" of early rallies, today's political gatherings have only recently begun to recapture the spirit of the past (Herbst 2010, 35). In fact, despite the raucousness, protests, and occasional physical violence witnessed in 2016, modern-day political rallies can appear quite tame when laid alongside some of those from earlier eras. In Abraham Lincoln's time at such events, people engaged in screaming, shouting, cursing, fistfights, attacking horses, and throwing excrement (Krieg 2016). Although today many decry such partisan tactics, Churchill Cambreleng, Martin Van Buren's close ally, saw them as "a noble conflict—of mind to mind, genius to genius" in 1856 (Shafer 1997, 12; US Congress 1856, 1546).

Much like contemporary Americans, nineteenth-century citizens banded together under party labels to fight for their conflicting political ideals, commitments, and policies. As Shafer (1997, 13–16) explains, the major parties worked to align class, religious, ethnic, ideological, and regional identities as well as distinctive worldviews under party labels. From political leaders to the mass public, politics was all about supporting their parties in cut-throat competition against their partisan opponents in a deeply emotional way. The "minds, emotions, and appetites" of the partisan faithful were targeted toward defeating their partisan enemies. Politicians, journalists, and voters alike allowed, and even encouraged, the "raucous and uncouth politics" of the era. Following the Civil War, partisanship remained at the center of US politics as the major parties reflected, and perhaps even exacerbated, the regional identities at the fore of that conflict.

A Brief Respite from the Partisan Storm

Such was largely the state of electoral politics until the late nineteenth and early twentieth centuries, when the rise of the Populist and Progressive movements worked to dismantle the "partisan way of organizing and articulating American political life" (Shafer 1997, 9). Much like Mugwumps and Independents in the 1880s, these reformers viewed parties as a great failures—enemies of the people that stood in the way of the good government and policies to which the US public was entitled (Shafer 1997; see also Hays 1957; Wiebe 1967). To replace the "unresponsive, duplicitous, and corrupt" parties, they sought to build governing institutions that relied on "strong-minded independent people, free from the trammels of party commitment" (Shafer 1997, 18). Bent on modernization and good government, these reformers passed and enforced electoral laws that weakened partisan control of nominations and voting and at the same time provided citizens channels of influence outside the party system (Burns 1984). In contrast with the partisan-based political battles of earlier times, politics in this era were "fragmented, fluid, and issue-focused" (Rodgers 1982, 116), with unelected bureaucratic experts rather than partisan elected officials promoting the general welfare.

Franklin D. Roosevelt's election and the New Deal years precipitated a short-lived revival of partisan conflict as Democrats and Republicans butted heads over welfare policies and government economic intervention. As Roosevelt ran for an unprecedented third term as president, vestiges of the nation's rowdy political beginnings occasionally emerged. Republican presidential candidate Wendell Willkie, for example, had "cantaloupes, potatoes, tomatoes, oranges, eggs, ashtrays, rocks, chairs, [and] a phone book" hurled his way during his campaign against Roosevelt (Cummins 2007, 193). *Life Magazine* reported that Willkie generally "took his beating with a grin." Until, that is, an egg splattered his wife's dress, at which point the candidate "lunged toward the man who threw the egg, his eyes blazing with anger."[1] Still, on the whole, partisan politics became a much less personal activity, especially among the mass public, as "policymaking was more and more removed from the hustings except in the most general way" (Shafer 1997, 23). In support of Roosevelt's efforts to increase the power of the presidency at the expense of strong party organizations, the Democratic Party of the late 1930s has been called "the party to end all parties" (Milkis 1993, 5). New Deal era policies further eroded the emotionally charged two-party system of the nation's earlier years, hampering Americans' ability to make politics coherent through a party-led system (Silbey 1991). Even during the New Deal years, voter turnout failed to reach levels on par with those seen in the viciously partisan nineteenth century.

By 1945, "parties were only a pale imitation of what they once had been, their influence occasional and unsustained" (Shafer 1997, 24). US political life entered a period marked by the "wasting away of parties" (Burns 1984).[2] Though emotional attachments to and identification with party labels did not decline in the electorate, party activity and influence did. The power of party leaders paled in comparison with that they wielded in earlier times. Nonpartisan interest groups increasingly stepped into the partisan void and took control of the policy-making process in the stead of congressional party leaders (see Rodgers 1982; Shafer 1997). The nation's entrance into World War II and the period of postwar domestic peace and prosperity further tamped down much of the ferocious partisanship that had so long defined the US political landscape, but the sounds of rabid partisanship would not remain muted for long.

Returning to Our Rancorous Roots

As the major parties clashed over divisive civil rights issues and foreign policy decisions in the late 1960s and 1970s, candidates and voters alike returned to the angry rhetoric and practices of the past. Portending the sorts of campaigns Senator Snowe would decry decades later, Robert Kennedy was reported to have been focused on the "political destruction of Hubert Humphrey" (Thompson 1973, 159) and, when it came to Michael Dukakis, Republican strategist Lee Atwater allegedly wanted to "strip the bark off the little bastard!" (Cummins 2007, 258). As gonzo journalist Hunter S. Thompson observed, by the 1972 presidential primary season, it had come to a "point where you almost can't run unless you can cause people to salivate and whip on each other with big sticks" (1973, 493). Many might view these sorts of statements as reflective of nothing more than high-stakes presidential campaigns, and that was likely the case to a large degree. Still, the presence of such personal, attack-style politics within, as well as across, parties during this period is telling. After all, this was a time in which many of today's high-ranking officeholders came of political age.

The public name-calling returned to the fore, as well. When Richard Nixon refused to debate Hubert Humphrey, Humphrey taunted him as "Richard the chicken-hearted" (Cohen 2016). Republicans called Bill Clinton a "pot-smoking, philandering, draft dodger" (Cummins 2007, 266) and John Kerry a "flip-flopper." Sarah Palin endured the epithet "Caribou Barbie." In 2016, Trump showed a propensity for assigning nicknames to his political opponents, Republican ("Lyin' Ted" Cruz, "Little Marco" Rubio, "Low Energy" Jeb Bush) and Democratic ("Crooked Hillary" Clinton, "Crazy Bernie" Sanders, Elizabeth "Pocahontas" Warren) alike. Political rallies also brought the reemergence of vitriolic shouts and chants, sometimes urged on by the candidates themselves. The 2008 presidential contest, for instance, brought reports of rowdy crowds urged on by the "red meat" Palin tossed to them, turning angry with shouts of "off with his head" and "kill him" in reference to Barack Obama (Herbst 2010, 43–48). At gatherings in support of Sanders, crowds echoed the "Lock her up!" chants those at Republican rallies hurled at Clinton (Kamisar 2016).

From Words to Actions

For all the partisan animosity displayed by political elites and the mass public over the past half century, contemporary partisan politics have yet to return to the brute physical combat of the founding era, a time when even physical retaliation on one's political opponents rarely met with censure or expulsion from office.[3] In the earliest meetings of the US Congress, southern representatives were known to physically "crowd" New Englanders—bullying and taunting them (Freeman 2001, 169). Political foes commonly engaged in nose-tweakings, canings, and challenges to duel. Incidents such as the brawl that erupted between Representatives Roger Griswold and Matthew Lyon on the House floor in 1798 were not uncommon. Days after Lyon spat tobacco juice at Griswold, the latter took up his hickory walking stick and struck the former with it more than twenty times before "Spitting Matt" was able to run behind the Speaker's desk, grab a pair of metal fireplace tongs, and wield them as a weapon against Griswold. The vote on expelling them from office met with rejection, failing by fifty-one votes. The nineteenth century, after all, was a time in which Vice President Aaron Burr mortally wounded former secretary of the Treasury Alexander Hamilton in a duel.

CONTEMPORARY POLITICAL POLARIZATION IN HISTORICAL PERSPECTIVE

Although partisan political practices in the twenty-first century might bear a striking resemblance to those of the past, we have perhaps not reached the same level of cross-partisan contempt as previous generations. Still, one would have a difficult time claiming that partisan hostilities have not become a prominent feature of recent elections and congressional proceedings, even if they do not rise to the level of physical violence on the chamber floor. As congressional partisan parity became more the norm, procedural strikes at the opposition became more prevalent. Six of the ten longest Senate filibusters have occurred since 1980 (even with a rule change lowering the cloture threshold), and the "nuclear option" has been repeatedly raised in response to presidential judicial nominees in that chamber. Further, beginning with Herbert Hoover, all but two presidents have been threatened with impeachment charges by opposition party members in the House.

Before Hoover, only four presidents, all serving in the rabidly partisan nineteenth century, faced such threats.[4] Presidential candidates, in effigy, have been hanged (Palin and Obama) and decapitated (Trump) and, in reality, targeted with bomb threats (Clinton). Ricin-laced letters (2004) and pipe bombs (2018) have been sent to prominent politicians. Campaign rally attendees have engaged in fistfights (2016) and, as alluded to earlier, some have been motivated to pick up firearms and seek to annihilate their partisan enemies.

Researchers and journalists alike contend that cross-partisan animosity has been rising to levels higher than any in modern memory. As the gulf between partisans of different persuasions widens, the argument goes, we can expect to witness more and more hate-filled campaigns, vicious disagreements about policy goals, and efforts to annihilate and embarrass partisan enemies. Commenting on the state of US politics in 2010, former president Jimmy Carter contended that the "country has become so polarized it's almost astonishing. . . . President Obama suffers from the most polarized situation in Washington that we have ever seen—even maybe than the time of Abraham Lincoln and the initiation of the war between the states" (Lublin 2010). And, similarly, just a month after President Trump entered the White House, opinion about his performance in office showed signs of deep division across party lines (Lauter 2017). Many blame today's uncouth political banter, ideological battles, and an inability to create and implement much needed public policy on a resurgence of political polarization among those holding office as well as the mass electorate.

The Many Shades of Partisan Polarization

Although many are quick to blame polarization for the state of contemporary US politics and often just as swift to point fingers of blame at one target or another, it is important to first understand the varied ways in which the term has been conceived. Several different but interrelated aspects of the phenomenon commonly referred to as political polarization dominate academic and journalist discussions (see Persily 2015 for elaboration). Many view high levels of cohesion within each party, commonly measured as ideological consistency and/or voting tendencies, along with a concurrent divergence between parties in terms of the distance between the median members of each party, as key indicators of polarization. Accompanying the changes in party positions, increased levels of incivility across party lines, discarding of norms that restrict negative political discourse and action with regard to counterpartisans, and stalemates and brinksmanship in policy making have all been viewed as signs of increased polarization in the contemporary period.

When it comes to questions of partisan negativity and political polarization, it is important to consider both those in office and those in the voting booth. Though the partisan sentiments of the mass public and the political elite can be expected to correspond to a large degree, there is a good deal of debate about whether those in office lead their rank-and-file followers toward more extreme positions or whether elites simply responded to mass cries for more extremity from their constituents. There is considerable, though not incontrovertible, evidence that elite polarization has preceded mass movement in the contemporary era—either because of party switching or attitude adjustment in the electorate as a response to elite movement (Barber and McCarty 2015; Fiorina 2013; Lenz 2012; Levendusky 2009; McCarty 2015). At the same time, some contend that polarizing candidates could not win office without a supportive electorate cheering them on (Miller et al. 1976; see also Miller and Miller 1976; Steeper and Teeter 1976). The two likely operate in a reciprocal manner, and establishing a precise causal order, though an intriguing question, matters relatively little in the context of this project. Whether the electorate followed the pied piper of officeholders or those in office rode a wave of constituent sentiment, there is evidence of growing polarization at all levels of US politics.

Polarization of the Political Elite

Although most topics addressed by political scientists exist in a perpetual state of debate, the polarization of US political elites comes as close to being a settled issue as the field can produce (Hare and Poole 2015). By a number of indicators, those holding office, particularly in legislative bodies, have polarized over the past half century. Documenting increasingly frequent bloc voting in Congress and increased levels of disagreement between party caucuses (Hetherington and Rudolph 2014), as well as the recent movement of Republican elites toward more extreme conservative stances (Ahler 2014; Hacker and Pierson 2006; McCarty, Poole, and Rosenthal 2006), existing research establishes the growing partisan and ideological polarization in the US Congress (Garner and Palmer 2010; Poole and Rosenthal 1997, 2001; Stonecash, Brewer, and Marianai 2003). Studies employing the two most common measures of Congressmembers' ideological leanings and voting tendencies, DW-Nominate and ADA scores, both reveal "a significant increase in both party polarization and ideological polarization in both houses of Congress, as well as an increase in party unity" (Paulson 2018, 112). Studies based on both measures consistently illustrate the traditional left-right voting patterns on issues related to government intervention in the economy, as well as a consistent pattern of bloc voting activity on the part of Southern Democrats on a range of issues, primarily those related to race. Qualitative accounts of partisanship and polarization inside the halls of Congress corroborate these quantitative findings (Hacker and Pierson 2006; Mann and Ornstein 2012; Rohde 1991; Sinclair 2006).

Further, the scores indicate that congressional polarization was at its lowest for a forty-year period beginning in the 1930s. Since the 1970s, though, there has been a "steady and steep increase in polarization of both the House and the Senate" (Barber and McCarty 2015, 17). Some have argued that the movement of the Republican Party to the right and the Democratic Party to the left on economic (and some social) issues has contributed a great deal to this trend (Barber and McCarty 2015; Hacker and Pierson 2006; Mann and Ornstein 2012). Additionally, the movement of Southern conservative members from the Democratic to the Republican Party beginning at the end of the twentieth century served to increase both intraparty unity and interparty divergence. Many scholars agree that the years following the 1964 election represented a time of fundamental change in the US political system (see, e.g., Aldrich and Niemi 1996; Schier and Eblery 2013)—a time when the parties "sorted" themselves into ideologically distinct camps.

Between the end of the Civil War and the 1950s, the Democratic Party encompassed both conservative Southerners and liberal Northeasterners. Battles over civil rights issues in the 1960s, though, overlapped with regional identities and fractured the Democratic Party. Prior to that time, a common identity as Democrats helped representatives from the North and the South maintain a great deal of collegiality (Schier and Eblery 2016), but signs of the regional divisions that would cement themselves in the coming decades surfaced in the 1964 presidential election. Despite being a Southerner himself, Democrat Lyndon B. Johnson lost some support in that region and picked up support in the North because of his highly visible support for civil rights legislation. Conversely, Republican Barry Goldwater found success in several Deep South states. Over the following two decades, the share of liberals in the Democratic Party increased as Southerners migrated to the Republican Party. As they did so, the conservative share of members in the Republican Party increased and the liberal share dropped (Reiter and Stonecash 2011; Shafer and Johnston 2009; Schier and Eberly 2013; Stonecash 2015). As the now-familiar pattern of red and blue states emerged, coalitions defined by party labels became galvanized by ideological viewpoints and regionally based cultural divides to produce the polarization we now witness (Noel 2013).

As the parties became more defined along ideological lines, issues that once cut across party lines increasingly came to reinforce the partisan divide (McCarty, Poole, and Rosenthal 1997; Poole and Rosenthal 1997). The intraparty divisions over race and economic issues that existed in earlier years faded as the parties became more internally unified. Concomitantly, regional divides within the parties diminished, resulting in a prevalent overlap in ideological and regional party support. Democratic officeholders came to be predominantly non-Southern and more liberal, whereas their Republican counterparts were increasingly likely to be conservative and Southern. As this partisan reorganization unfolded, members' voting patterns became more and more distinct along party lines. Though interpartisan division with regard to economic issues remained a primary dimension of voting patterns, "other issues—such as social, cultural, and religious issues—[were] absorbed into it" (Barber and McCarty 2015, 21). Members of Congress since this time have exhibited a much stronger tendency toward what Converse (2006) called issue constraint. That is, voting across a range of issues became increasingly unidimensional along party lines (as opposed to previously multidimensional voting patterns that split along regional and ideological lines). In sum, "today's polarization is the product of today's issues and yesterday's realignment" (Stonecash 2015, 70).

As the national parties were transforming, so too were those in the states. Over the past two to three decades, polarization in the states has increased dramatically (Shor 2015). State legislative polarization levels across the nation now look remarkably similar to those in Congress (Barber and McCarty 2015; Shor 2015). In fact, about half of the states appear to be more polarized than Congress, especially California (Shor 2015). And, in Wisconsin, one state supreme court justice was alleged to have put another in a chokehold during a dispute about a case involving collective bargaining for public employees (Stephenson, Spivak, and Marley 2011). Additionally, there is some evidence that we might be "seeing asymmetric polarization," with the Republicans in the states becoming more conservative faster than Democrats are becoming more liberal (Shor 2015, 21).

Some have argued that the actions of the US chief executives have reflected the nation's growing polarization and contributed to partisan and ideological polarization levels (Schier and Eblery 2016). Richard Skinner (2012) contrasts the "modern presidency," which began with the FDR administration, with the "partisan presidency" that currently reigns. The modern presidency era, he argues, was marked by chief executives who worked with Congress across party lines, relied more on nonpartisan experts for policy advice, gained public support from both Democrats and Republicans, had cooperative relationships with the mass media, and played down partisan affiliations to win office. In contrast, partisan presidents, he claims, work closely with congressional members of their own party, rely on ideological think tanks for policy advice, seek (and receive) public support primarily from copartisans, have an antagonistic relationship with the media, and rely on party label references in campaigning. Notably, some argue that the partisan presidency era began with former president Ronald Reagan's administration at the same time the national parties were sorting themselves into more internally cohesive organizations (see, e.g., Bond and Fleisher 2000; Douthat 2010; Klein 2010; Milkis and Rhodes 2007; Pfiffner 2006; Skinner 2012).[5]

Taken together, the evidence supports the argument that the nation is now experiencing political polarization at a level unheard of in modern memory. But it is important to remember that party polarization has been a part of US politics throughout our history (Carsey and Layman 2015). In fact, a quick glance at congressional voting patterns over the course of our nation's history reveals that our founding era set the standard of polarization, much as it did for incivility. Recognizing that it is not the only (or necessarily ideal) method, I turn to a commonly used, DW-Nominate score-based measure of the relative distance between congressional Republicans and Democrats to place contemporary political polarization levels in historical context.[6] As illustrated in Figure 1.1, the measure ranges from zero to one, with higher scores indicating more party-line voting, and thus, a larger difference between the voting behavior/ideology of congressional Republicans and Democrats. Since 1879, polarization levels in the US House have typically been higher than those in the Senate, as is the case now.[7] The overall trend is one of extremely higher polarization levels throughout the nineteenth century. Following this era, also marked by rancorous and sometimes violent political exchanges, polarization levels declined in the early twentieth century as nonpartisan, good government reforms made an impact. The subsequent Great Depression and World War II years marked the nadir of congressional divisiveness, followed by a distinct and extreme upward trend in polarization beginning in the late 1950s and continuing through today. Overall, then, the recent period is, indeed, highly polarized, but so was the period of the nation's founding (Noel 2013).

As Brady and Han (2015) observed, "The present period of polarization is akin to the polarization we had for much of the nineteenth and early twentieth century" (138). Still, our current state of polarization might differ from that era in some respects. First, as some have argued, the role of ideology in polarization might be more prevalent than in the past (Noel 2013). Carsey and Layman (2015), for instance, argue that "conflict extension" marks today's polarization to a much stronger

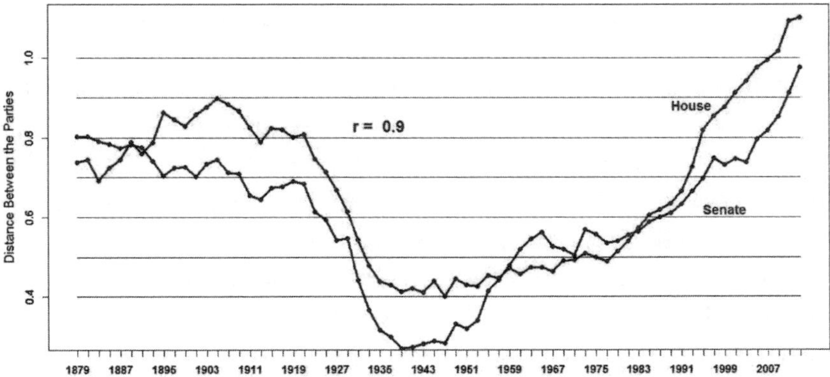

Figure 1.1 Political Polarization, 1879–2015

Source: Vote View Blog, https://voteviewblog.com/category/114th-congress/.

degree than we have previously witnessed. Although major US parties have historically split over policy issues, party polarization tended to focus on one general policy area at a time, with divisions over one issue receding as new issue disagreements arose (Sundquist 1983). In contrast with such "conflict displacement," Layman and Carsey (2002) argue, today's conflicts are extended—"divisions on multiple issues fall along the same partisan/ideological lines." Thus, today's polarization might be even more intense than that of our founding era, a speculation corroborated by the polarization scores reported in Figure 1.1, in which the last three measures of polarization in the United States are estimated to be at least equal to, and perhaps higher than, the zenith point of similar polarization in the nineteenth century (and trending upward still).

Taken on the whole, a strong consensus of scholarly opinion arises in response to the question of polarization among those in office. The political elite has been polarizing for decades; its members have reached heights of alienation from those opposing their views and are more willing than ever to hurl uncivil insults across the partisan or ideological divide that far surpass those of their predecessors of the past half century. And, in many ways, contemporary officeholders and those from our nation's earliest days bear a remarkable resemblance.

Polarization of the Mass Electorate

Although there is widespread agreement that the contemporary US electorate is more divided in a number of ways than it has been in the past, there has still been some debate about the extent and timing of mass polarization. Some studies investigating the partisan movement of the mass electorate conducted through the early twenty-first century, a time when elite polarization was reaching modern heights, pointed to small fractures among the public, at best. Many researchers contended that the public remained largely centrist in their issues stances and that the degree to which the masses reflected elite polarization remained minimal through the beginning of the twenty-first century (DiMaggio, Evans, and Bryson 1996; Evans, Bryson, and DiMaggio 2001; Fiorina, Abrams, and Pope 2005). Studies revealed that more people, including (somewhat surprisingly) almost half of self-identified Democrats and Republicans, still considered themselves middle of the road ideologically (or nonideological) rather than extremely liberal or conservative (Hetherington and Rudolph 2014). And residents of red and blue states were shown to share many issue opinions, even on seemingly controversial issues (Brownstein 2007; Fiorina and Abrams 2009; Fiorina, Abrams, and Pope 2005; Garner and Palmer 2010; Hunter 1995). Overall, these researchers often contended that, in many ways, the contemporary electorate looks much like it did forty years ago, continuing to maintain somewhat of a centrist shape (Fiorina and Abrams 2015). Some point to evidence of little increase in the degree of ideological coherence in public opinion since Converse (1964) alerted us to the dearth of it more than fifty years ago (Fiorina and Abrams 2009), and others point out that even on issues where we would expect ideological divides, such as abortion, the distinctions are somewhat muted (Schier and Eblery 2016).

Others, however, noted a growing ideological awareness among partisans and the increasingly distinctive issue stances taken by Democratic and Republican voters have taken over the same period (Abramowitz and Saunders 2005, 2008; Brewer 2005; Fleisher and Bond 2001; Hetherington 2001; Jacobson 2004; Layman and Carsey 2002; Levendusky 2009; Lindaman and Haider-Markel 2002; White

2003). Alongside the growing divisions among political elites, they argued, the chasm between Democrats and Republicans in the electorate was increasing over time as well. As one scholar observed, a decade into the twenty-first century, voters were just "beginning to show the polarization that pundits and politicians developed earlier. But they [were] showing it" (Noel 2013, 173–174).

Some argue that political activists, who tend to support more extreme positions on issues, have been key catalysts in the polarizing tendency of the mass electorate (Abramowitz 2010; Barber and McCarty 2015; Carsey and Layman 2015). With party system changes that gave primary and caucus participants more power, activists have become increasingly able to influence both the party nominations and party platforms. As William Crotty (2013) concluded, "On one issue there is no disagreement: the critical importance of core activists in shaping the parties' message, clarifying their appeals to voters and choosing candidates for office who share their beliefs" (346). Party nominations have become more extreme, especially since 1972 (Schier and Eblery 2016). Advocates of the activist-led mass polarization perspective argue that over the past four decades, the two parties, dominated by ideologically motivated activists, have offered the public a choice between increasingly extreme candidates. And the parties then work to "get the voters to go along" (Bawm et al. 2012, 572). Accordingly, such theorists believe activist influence on the party platforms helps to explain the recent uptick in mass ideological polarization as well as the tendency of voters to remain engaged in the electoral process. In support of their view, they point to evidence that as early as 1972 ideological activists within both parties have acted to alter platform planks on salient and controversial policies such as abortion, race, women's rights, and others (Noel 2015; Peters 2012; Schier and Eblery 2016). And, they argue, the same conflict extension occurring in Congress affects activists at the national conventions, suggesting that activist influence on platform stances is likely to spread (Carsey and Layman 2015).

Still, if voters remain more moderate in their policy stances than activists and those in office, they might simply choose to abstain rather than support a party candidate espousing extreme positions. Yet, we have seen no downward trend in voter turnout in recent elections, and, in fact, have seen a slight increase in turnout for presidential elections since 2000. Voters, then, appear to be willing to support the more extreme activist-chosen candidates. As the candidates move further apart, the voters follow. This might be the case because many Americans, especially those who consider themselves moderates, are not entirely ideologically consistent but rather what some have called "conflicted" (Broockman 2015). That is, they agree with each party on some issues and might be even more extreme than either party on others, especially those most salient to them. So when parties offer a range of extreme policy stances and the winds of the campaign stir up passions related to even a single issue about which voters care deeply, voters can still identify at least one appealing reason to support a candidate they might not especially admire. And, interestingly, this effect appears to hold even for less frequent voters, who are typically less political engaged (Broockman 2015). Such evidence has led some to argue that party identifiers, and even those claiming to be Independents, more and more simply "'echo' the choices on issues presented to them and support the candidates chosen" by the party activists (Crotty 2013, 346).[8]

Such arguments can lead to the bleak conclusion that "the country is polarized because we have two ideologically coherent parties, and political activists continue to pull them apart" (Noel 2013, 178). Although party activists might bear some responsibility for the increasing polarization of the US public, it would be somewhat unfair to blame the activists for singlehandedly engineering such a shift. Along with the actions of party activists, the electorate went through what many have termed a "sorting out" period in which voters adjusted their partisanship to match their ideological stances on salient issues. Considering a bottom-up causal influence, the actions of activists might merely be a representation of mass demands rather than a mobilizing agent of polarization among the general public. Examining elections of that era, Nie, Verba, and Petrocik (1976) documented a rise in issue voting and increased ideological polarization of the electorate between 1956 and 1972.[9] In the same era, others reported evidence of increased attitude constraint among the mass electorate, suggesting the "growth of a more ideologically oriented mass public" (Nie and Andersen 1974, 580). Contemporaneously, increasing segments of the public dealigned with political parties and began splitting their tickets (see, e.g., Beck 1977; Boyd 1972; Norpoth and Rusk 1982). Suggesting electorate-driven polarization, scholars pointed out the ways in which each party had failed "to cope with the polarization of policy demands among its supporters in the contest for the presidency" in elections as early as 1968 (Miller et al. 1976; see also Miller and Miller 1976; Steeper and Teeter 1976). Such evidence might suggest voter attitude change may have preceded elite-level movement, though, as some have recently asserted, "it is unlikely that changes in public preferences alone explain the widening gulf between the two parties in Congress" (Hill and Tausanovitch 2015, 1058).

Although it might remain true that, on the whole, many voters still express the relatively moderate policy positions of nearly four decades ago (Ansolabehere, Rodden, and Snyder 2006; Bafumi and Herron 2010; Fiorina and Abrams 2008; Fiorina, Abrams, and Pope 2005; Levendusky, Pope, and Jackman 2008), it is important to remember that the most engaged and knowledgeable voters in the mass electorate show a more polarized distribution akin to that of party activists who participate in party organizational activities, though they are not as extreme (Hare and Poole 2015). And even the less engaged are likely to hold strong, and perhaps more extreme, views on issues they find salient. Still, even if the public is no more ideologically polarized than it has historically been, there is little doubt that "the two political parties are much more divided and that division defines contemporary politics and discourse" (Schier and Eblery 2016, 40). The process of partisan sorting in the electorate that occurred over the latter half of the twentieth century can help reconcile these two seemingly contradictory claims that the electorate is both more and no more polarized than it has ever been (see, e.g., Hill and Tausanovitch 2015).

US political parties comprise coalitions of interests, but those interests need not necessarily be based on ideological viewpoints (Noel 2013). In the post–Civil War era, for instance, the coalitions within each party were not aligned along ideological lines. As discussed previously, the Democratic Party housed the rather odd coalition of Northeastern liberals and Southern conservatives. Although those from the Northeast could arguably be drawn to the party by ideological concerns, the

Southerners held ideological viewpoints that clashed with many of the party's stances. The Republican Party, too, faced internal ideological divisions, though perhaps not as stark as those in the Democratic camp. And these patterns were prevalent in the electorate as well (McCarty 2015). Beginning in the 1960s, however, voters began sorting themselves into parties along ideological lines in much the same way members of Congress did, though perhaps not as quickly. The resultant party composition on display in the contemporary United States exhibits far fewer internal ideological divides among officeholders, activists, and voters alike.

As McCarty (2015) points out, the timing of increased political polarization is "consistent with explanations based on large historical trends such as the post–Civil Rights realignment of southern politics and increased levels of economic and social inequality" (3). The realignment of large portions of the Southern electorate from the Democratic to Republican Party represents perhaps the clearest example of the mass electorate shifting in such a way that ideological leanings and partisan identifications became much more closely aligned. Always conservative on race issues and sympathetic to conservative economic positions, Southerners en masse migrated to the Republican Party following the Democratic Party's endorsement of civil rights legislation. In effect, the party system finally caught up with the mass ideological system already in place (Noel 2015).

The secular realignment that began in the late 1960s shifted the party system from one of "umbrella" parties that housed ideological diversity to one in which the parties are internally unified along ideological lines (Paulson 2018). Beginning with the Johnson-Goldwater contest of 1964 and rejuvenated by the 1994 election of Newt Gingrich to the position of speaker of the House, the South transformed. By 1994, voters whose demographic profiles suggested they were likely to have been Southern conservative Democrats previously were likely to report as Republicans (Paulson 2018). Over time, voters increasingly came to hold political views that aligned with their parties' platform stances, even as activists pushed the platforms in divergent directions (Barber and McCarty 2015; Layman and Carsey 2002; Levendusky 2009). Much as in Congress, conservative Democrats and liberal Republicans in the electorate are a rarer and rarer breed (Noel 2015) as fewer partisans "hold a mix of Democratic and Republican positions" (Barber and McCarty 2015, 22). Since 1992, the correlations between party identification and issue positions "have been big and getting larger" (Gelman 2015, 91). In fact, the Pew Research Center (2014) reported, "The share of Americans who express consistently conservative or consistently liberal opinions ha[d] doubled over the past two decades, from 10 percent to 21 percent." And about 70 percent of the most highly engaged members of the electorate now hold policy positions in line with those of their party. As a consequence, the median Republican voter is now more conservative and the median Democratic voter more liberal than 90 percent of the opposing party's supporters (Doherty 2014). In effect, "self-identified Democrats [are now] more homogeneously liberal and self-identified Republicans more homogeneously conservative" (Fiorina and Abrams 2015, 42) than in the modern past.

Concomitant with mass partisan realignment, changing social conditions and increasing levels of economic inequality have precipitated intense battles over the proper scope of governmental authority (Stonecash 2015). And as candidates now face more ideologically consistent primary constituencies across the nations, they espouse their parties' increasingly differentiated stances more vociferously than ever. After they are in office, their voting behavior more and more closely toes the party line. Thus, arguments of a disparity between party leaders and their constituencies might be somewhat misplaced; "today's elite polarization is not imposed on a centrist electorate" (Abramowitz 2015, 87).

Whether political polarization has been driven by elites at the top, activists in the middle, or voters on the ground, the contemporary era, in many ways, mirrors that of our nation's early years. Major parties offer distinct policy choices to the public. Candidates, officeholders, and voters alike hold stances on key issues of the day that directly conflict with those of their partisan opponents.[10] Campaign rhetoric takes on rancorous tones as candidates and their supporters hurl insults across party lines, and public rallies occasionally become violent. So although many people decry the hyperpartisanship and incivility pervading contemporary politics, what we are witnessing might be merely a return to earlier norms. Some, though, see something unique about politics today. They point out that "what seems particularly significant about the modern era is that ideology and party voting have come together, perhaps for the first extended period in U.S. history" (Noel 2013, 173). Others have commented that many issues and attitudes once independent of party conflict now show an increasingly strong relationship to it (McCarty 2015).

IT FEELS LIKE POLARIZATION

Although the empirical research substantiates such an argument to some degree, an increasing number of political observers and scholarly researchers alike have turned their attention to a striking, and to many alarming, rise in a less issue-based type of mass polarization. Such scholars argue that Democrats and Republicans quite simply dislike each other, regardless of the issue positions each side takes. Consequently, they say we should be looking for evidence of mass polarization in emotional responses to counterpartisans rather than seeking to distinguish differing issue stances across the partisan divide.

In the past decade, a good deal of scholarly and journalistic attention has focused on a partisan divide "rooted in how people feel rather than where they stand" (Hetherington and Rudolph 2014, 17). When queried by researchers, self-identified partisans more and more frequently offer negative opinions about the opposite party. When given the task of rating the opposite party on a "thermometer" scale ranging between 0 and 100, partisans' ratings of the opposite party have become increasingly negative over time (see, e.g., Hetherington and Rudolph 2014). Between 1994 and 2014, the share of Republicans who reported unfavorable opinions of the Democratic Party rose by more than 25 percent (from 17 percent to 43 percent); the rise in Democratic negativity toward the Republican Party went from just 16 percent to 38 percent (Doherty 2014). A snapshot of the US public in summer 2017 suggests that sentiments continue to sour. About half of each party's adherents (50.3 percent of Democratic and 49.8 percent of Republican respondents) registered very unfavorable opinions of their partisan enemies when asked by pollsters. And as indicated in Figure 1.2, nearly

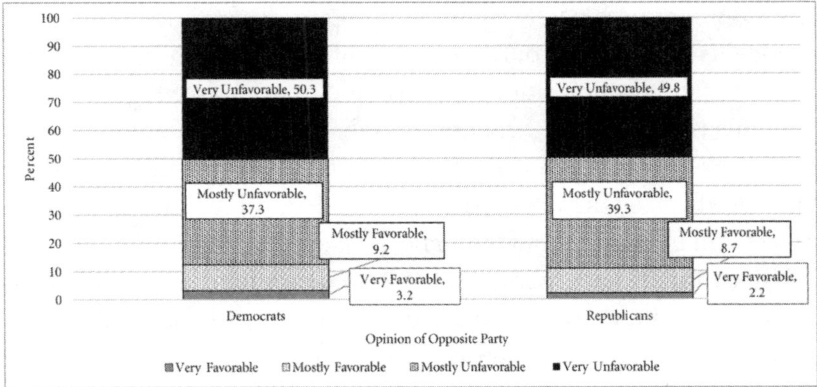

Figure 1.2 Opinions of Opposite Political Party

Notes: Results based on data from the Pew Research Center, Political Typology Survey, conducted June 8–18 and June 27–July 9, 2017.

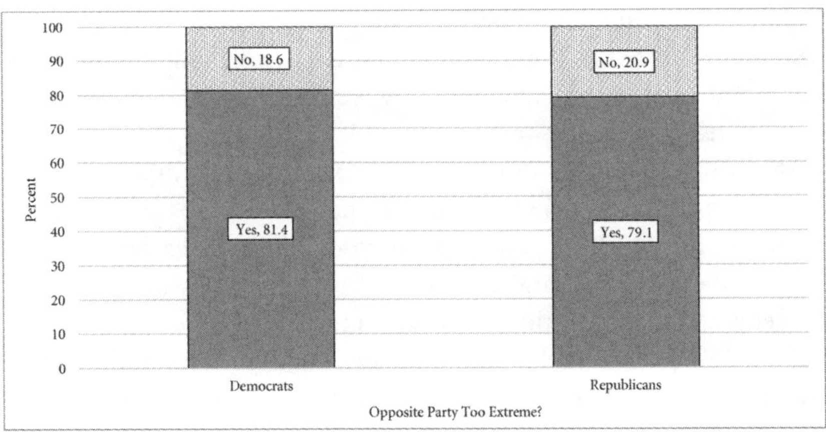

Figure 1.3 Views of Opposite Party Extremity

Notes: Results based on data from the Pew Research Center, Political Typology Survey, conducted June 8–18 and June 27–July 9, 2017.

eight in ten self-proclaimed partisans viewed the opposite party in an unfavorable way.[11]

Some of this negativity likely resulted from conflicting views on the fundamental role of government when it came to policy areas that touched on issues of race, immigration, national security, and gender, among others, with nearly equivalent proportions of those partisan respondents (81.4 percent of Democrats and 79.1 percent of Republicans) claiming that the opposition party was too extreme (see Figure 1.3). At the same time, though, there are signs that ideology differences might not be the only factor at play. Whereas more than two-thirds of partisan identifiers felt their own party had high ethical standards, a quarter or less said the same about the opposite party (see Figure 1.4).

Given the growing sentiment that closed-minded, immoral, lazy, dishonest, and unintelligent individuals support and represent the opposite party, it is perhaps not surprising that even our social lives have become arenas for partisan battle (Scott 2018). Party identifiers more readily report that they dislike each other than they did a generation ago (Shaw 2012). People have become increasingly likely to say they would be upset if their child married someone from the other party (Iyengar, Sood, and Lelkes 2012) and to express a preference for living in a place where most people share their political views (Pew Research Center 2014). Returning to Pew data from summer 2017, the current state of the potential voter sentiment looks little different. Sizable shares of each party admitted that if they found out a friend had cast a ballot in support of the opposite party's presidential candidate in 2016, it would have put a strain on the friendship (see Figure 1.5). However, overwhelming majorities of respondents gave what could be seen as the socially desirable answer that such a vote would not have any effect. Almost one-third of those on the left admitted that a friend supporting Trump in the voting booth would hurt the relationship. Though far fewer Republican adherents said the same about a friend's vote for Clinton, about 12.6 percent admitted that it would be taxing on the friendship.

Taking my launching point from recent investigations into the contempt with which partisans hold their political counterparts, the research I offer in this treatise speaks to variations in negative partisan affect across generations, the potential sources and consequences of such attitudes, and the prospects for the future civility of US political discourse. I focus my analyses on today's nascent political actors—college students—for a number of reasons on which I elaborate more fully in chapter 2. First, as Nelson Mandela stated, "The youth of today are

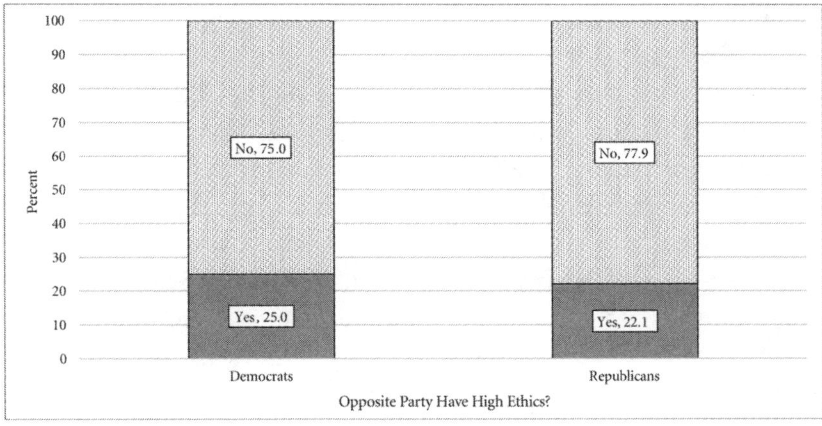

Figure 1.4 Views of Party Ethics

Notes: Results based on data from the Pew Research Center, Political Typology Survey, conducted June 8–18 and June 27–July 9, 2017.

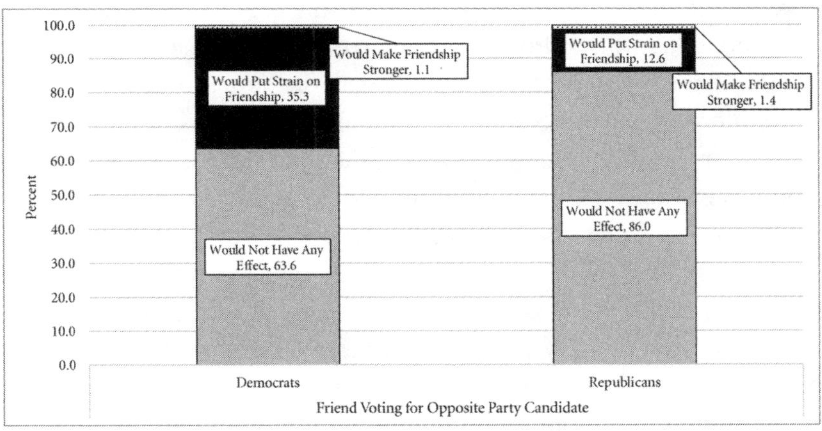

Figure 1.5 Effect of 2016 Presidential Votes on Friendships

Notes: Results based on data from the Pew Research Center, Political Typology Survey, conducted June 8–18 and June 27–July 9, 2017.

the leaders of tomorrow." If today's college students spew less partisan venom than their elders, they might hold the greatest hope for reversing the polarizing trend or at least countering the deleterious effects of such polarization. Some might argue that traditionally aged college students bring partisan baggage to campus along with their laptops and cell phones. Even if this is so, the college years have been shown as a period when notoriously stable political attitudes are most likely to be mutable (see, e.g., Dinas 2013; Miller and Sears 1986; Sears and Funk 1999). Consequently, the college graduates who will likely fill political positions in the future might be learning to lay aside their partisan goggles. Unfortunately, popular journalistic accounts and scholarly research alike increasingly offer evidence that political interaction on campuses across the nation has become more combative in the past four decades. At the same time, student tolerance for contrary political viewpoints has been shown to be on the decline, and campus-based political animosities have been on the rise, with neither showing signs of reversing course. Thus, I seek to explore the depths of these animosities among a group of undergraduate students in order to gain some perspective on the prospect for a depolarization movement led by postmillennial generations.

In chapter 2, I present an argument that mass affective polarization operates in much the same way interethnic animosities do, breeding intolerance and disrespect for, as well as violence toward, opposition groups. I explain in chapter 3 the research approach that informs the remainder of this tome, discuss the importance of studying college students, and describe my primary measure of partisan hatred, paying particular attention to the ways in which partisan hatred resembles ethnic hatred, and, important differences between the two. Chapter 4 offers a descriptive look at the demographic and attitudinal characteristics most associated with college students' reported feelings of partisan animosity. Chapter 5 explores the connections between the media consumption habits of university students and their feelings of out-party loathing, considering both the possibility that media content might play a role in breeding such sentiment and that such ire might be feeding media consumption. In particular, I examine online media consumption and contrast its relationship to feelings of partisan hatred with that of more traditional print and broadcast media sources. Chapters 6 and 7 answer the perennial "So what?" question, examining potential consequences of affective polarization and partisan hatred. The social (chapter 6) and political (chapter 7) ramifications of partisan hatred come under the microscope as I show that college students who expressed more partisan animosity hold very different feelings about living near members of the opposite party or the idea of a family member marrying a member of the opposite party than those with more generous feelings toward their partisan opposites. And, as some have worried, those who expressed more bitterness toward their partisan opponents exhibited less willingness to compromise with those on the other side of the aisle. In the grand tradition of political science offerings of this type, I conclude in chapter 8 by speculating about the future of affective polarization and partisan hatred in US politics, along with prospects for a pendulum swing back toward partisan civility.

2. Affective Polarization and Social Identities

People hate as they love, unreasonably.

—William Makepeace Thackeray

Politics "are emotional attachments that transcend thinking."

—Christopher H. Achen and Larry M. Bartels (2016)

Like scholars before me, I argue that much of the polarization we see in the mass electorate relates less to cross-party disagreement about the proper scope of governmental authority and/or policy goals and more to ingrained emotional reactions to counterpartisans (see, e.g., Hetherington and Rudolph 2014; Huddy, Mason, and Aarøe 2015; Iyengar, Sood, and Lelkes 2012; Iyengar and Westwood 2015; Mackie, Devos, and Smith 2000; Mason 2015a; Tajfel 1981). I contend that much of the growing polarization we see across partisan lines in contemporary US politics results from the strong social affiliations individuals feel with their own party in contrast with what they feel toward the opposite party. As Mason (2018) argues, "Affective polarization is particularly driven by social identities (more powerfully than issue positions) because social identities have repeatedly been found to generate in-group privilege and outgroup derogation" (284). And, in much the same way ethnic/racial identities feed animosities that can breed intolerance and disrespect for, as well as violence toward, other demographic groups (Haidt, Rosenberg, and Hom 2003; Mullen and Skitka 2006; Parker and Janoff-Bulman 2013; Skitka, Bauman, and Sargis 2005), partisan identification can lead to denigration of partisan opponents and unwillingness to engage the other side in a meaningful way.

Social identity theory argues that deeply held intergroup prejudices spring from the human instinct to define both ourselves and others in terms of the social groups with which we most closely identify. Tajfel and Turner (1979) offer a three-stage process by which social identities form and operate. According to their theory, we first process the world we encounter by placing both ourselves and others into social categories based on recognizable characteristics such as race, gender, and socioeconomic status. In doing so, we then create social identities for ourselves and others (see, e.g., Brewer 2001; Tajfel 1978; Tajfel and Turner 1979, 1986). Finally, in much the same way groups might fight over tangible resources such as food or water, rival social group members contend with each other to maintain self-esteem. Individuals compete by using their social identities to compare themselves with others, focusing on the positive aspects of the in-group to which they belong and the negative aspects of the out-group with which they compare themselves (e.g., Brewer 2001; Gibson 2006; Wilmer 2002).

Experimental research has long established the strength of in-group/out-group classifications, even distinctions made along arbitrary lines and in situations where the participants have no preexisting common interests (Billig and Tajfel 1973; Tajfel et al. 1971; see also Allen and Wilder 1975; Brewer and Silver 1978; Doise and Sinclair 1973). When assembled as a nominal group, people rather quickly start saying they think of themselves in terms of the group and believing their own group members are superior to those identified with other groups (see, e.g., Devine 2015). Outside the laboratory setting, the social identity process can be expected to have even more influence over perceptions and attitudes. For, as some have argued, the development of social identities serves as a primary means of childhood and cultural socialization (Weldon 2006). Hence, social identities are likely to form early in the life span and endure over a lifetime, gaining reinforcement from repeated favorable comparisons with out-groups, and frequently lead to prejudice and discrimination against out-group members (Tajfel and Turner 1979).

PARTISANSHIP AS A SOCIAL IDENTITY

The development and persistence of partisan identification in both the United States (Gerber and Green 1998; Green, Palmquist, and Schickler 2002; Greene 1999) and abroad (Abrams 1994; Abrams and Emler

1992; Duck, Hogg, and Terry 1995; Kelly 1988, 1989, 1990a, 1990b) have been described in much the same manner. An emotional attachment, partisan identification develops through early childhood socialization and tends to persist over a lifetime (Campbell et al. 1960). In the same way comparisons of social identity frequently lead to negative feelings toward an out-group, comparisons based on partisan identities result in negative affect toward the opposing party. Even those who identify as nonpartisan (purely Independent) express negativity about the competing partisan groups of Democrats and Republicans (Greene 1999).[1] Just as repeated biased comparisons to out-groups work to strengthen social identities, partisan identities have been seen as becoming more stable over the life span as a result of continued social reinforcement (see, e.g., Alwin, Cohen, and Newcomb 1991; Krosnick and Alwin 1989; Sears and Funk 1999). Further, the very issues that animate much of the US political scene—fights over relative partisan power, economic issues, and moral/cultural battles—have been said to underlie many social identity group conflicts (Esman 2004; Jesse and Williams 2011). Thus, there are good reasons to believe partisan identification operates in much the same manner as social identification to create the sort of affective mass polarization and cross-partisan disrespect recently highlighted. After all, "politeness is the practice of respecting that part of a man's beliefs which is specifically concerned with his own merits or those of his group" (Russell 1928).

Recent research has highlighted the ways in which identities primed by context and cues can operate in an especially powerful manner by raising the salience of and concerns related to group identities (Klar 2013; McLeish and Oxoby 2008). The mention of an identity group has been shown to correlate with attitudes and behaviors that reflect stereotypes related to primed social groups (Steele 2010), and a focus on the policy relevance of group identities has been linked to feelings of efficacy, both internal and external, that increase the salience of identity groups (Van Zomeren, Leach, and Spears 2010). Building on such research, Klar (2013) experimentally verified these effects and most importantly demonstrated the way perceptions of threat exert an even more powerful effect. She and others (Brader 2006; Steele 2010) argue that the negative emotions associated with threat shape preferences.

Contemporary political practice certainly operates to make partisan (and ideological) identities highlight salience. Candidates and the media alike call on partisanship and ideology frequently and often highlight the policy relevance of these identities. Further, and perhaps most importantly, political conversations are often framed as battles in which one side of the political spectrum threatens the other. In fact, there is even some evidence that partisan biases might influence decision making more than racial and gender biases (Iyengar and Westwood 2015), perhaps because more salient identities might supersede less salient ones (see, e.g., Klar 2018). It is little wonder then, that when partisan identities come under threat, civility toward counterpartisans falls by the wayside.

Such an argument does not necessarily exclude the possibility that Democrats and Republicans disagree about prominent political issues of the day based on differing ideological viewpoints. Rather, a social identity perspective can help to explain why such divisions have become increasingly prevalent in the mass electorate. As Bertrand Russell (1928) noted, "Every man, wherever he goes, is encompassed by a cloud of comforting convictions, which move with him like flies on a summer day" (28). Reassuring partisan convictions have been shown to affect the perceptions many have of counterpartisans, with motivated reasoning leading to perceptual biases favoring the in-group (e.g., Bartels 2002; Jerit and Barabas 2012; Nicholson 2005; Pettigrew 1979; Redlawsk 2002). Recent research further suggests that such "automatic association is very much related to the ways in which voters evaluate and interpret the political world" (Theodoridis 2017, 1264). For instance, partisans greatly exaggerate (by about 300 percent on average) the degree to which stereotypical groups support both major US parties (Ahler and Sood 2018)—reporting, for example, that there are far more lesbian, gay, bisexual, and transgender (LGBT) supporters in the Democratic Party and more wealthy people in the Republican Party than is the case. Such tendencies can lead to similar distortions of the typical ideological positions of both parties, and, interestingly, these effects have been observed for perceptions of both one's own party as well as the opposite party (see Ahler 2014; Gelman 2015). Coupled with ideological sorting along party lines over the past five decades, such socially based inclinations have resulted in a stronger connection between issue stances and partisan identities. At the same time, and perhaps more importantly, preexisting partisan identities have led to exaggerated perceptions of the ideological distance between parties and misperceptions about the ideological diversity that actually exists within parties.

VIEWING IDEOLOGY THROUGH A SOCIAL LENS

When it came to political identities before 1964, people primarily thought of themselves as a Republican or a Democrat rather than a conservative or a liberal. As Dalton (2013) suggested, "People did not just vote for the Republican or the Democratic candidate, they considered themselves to be a Republican or a Democrat" (3). Such identification brought a "sense of belonging" that conferred "affective social benefits" (Schier and Eblery 2016, 32; see also Gerber et al. 2012). So people remained incredibly loyal to their partisan identities, and ideological differences both within and between the parties meant far less. Hence, when Converse (1964) examined ideological stances and self-professed partisan identity, he found little evidence of ideological consistency along party lines. Socially based partisan identities took precedence over rationally based issue stances.

As the two major parties realigned over civil rights–related issues during the latter part of the twentieth century, partisan elites, the media, and the electorate began linking more conservative stances with the Republican label and more liberal stances with the Democratic label. Whereas previously voters, especially those in the South, did not strongly associate the party names with consistently liberal or conservative positions, members of the public gradually shifted their partisan affiliations to align with their ideological stances. As demographic groups moved their support from one party to the other in response to the changes in the party platforms, rank-and-file Republicans and Democrats increasingly perceived "the ideological difference between 'us' and 'them' [as] much more significant than it once was" (Noel 2013, 165). In fact, some have argued that the public is not actually much more divided along issue lines than before the 1960s. But as partisan and ideological identities increasingly showed more alignment in the public's mind, subjective perceptions of the ideological distance between typical Democratic and Republican voters accelerated (Stoker and Jennings 2008; see also, e.g., DiMaggio, Evans, and Bryson 1996; Fiorina, Abrams, and Pope 2006) even when the actual issue stances of typical party voters were not necessarily extreme.

An identity-based approach to self-professed partisanship and ideology helps to reconcile the fact that even though a great deal of partisan sorting along ideological lines has occurred, the two still do not align entirely (Mason 2018, 281; see also Grossman and Hopkins 2016; Kinder and Kalmoe 2017; Mason 2015a). For, as Theodoridis's (2017) recent implicit association test research showed, "Many Americans associate themselves with their party at a deep, visceral level, sometimes in a more or less pronounced way than they realize or report in explicit measures" (1264). Such deeply meaningful attachments to partisan group identities work to influence political judgments about a range of phenomena, including the ideological commitments of both in-group and out-group members (e.g., Devine 2015; Ellis and Stimson 2012; Malka and Lelkes 2010). In fact, there is even evidence that some might alter their issue stances and ideological identifications in response to their increasingly stronger partisan identifications. Studies suggesting that individuals often change their beliefs and actions to match those of a perceived in-group majority support this contention (see Asch 1951; Berelson, Lazarsfeld, and McPhee 1954; Sherif 1966; Turner 1991).

Further, when it comes to ideology, researchers since the 1970s have contended that ideological self-placements, at least to some degree, reflect socially based identities rather than issue-based positions (Conover and Feldman 1981; Devine 2015; Ellis and Stimson 2012; Levitin and Miller 1979; Malka and Lelkes 2012; Mason 2018). Viewing ideological labels as identities that have "largely symbolic meanings" connected to other social identities reflecting dominant cleavages (such as partisanship and race) in the United States (Conover and Feldman 1981, 617, 643), these scholars tend to make a distinction between ideology as a social identity and as an operational expression of principled beliefs (Claasen, Tucker, and Smith 2015; Ellis and Stimson 2012;

Mason 2018; Noel 2014; Popp and Rudolph 2011). Such scholars argue that ideological self-placements represent less rational, issue-based classifications and more feelings of kinship with similarly labeled others "even when this is not true in terms of actual opinions" (Mason 2018, 281). Rather than a coherent set of issue positions, then, the terms *liberal* and *conservative* represent more of a group identity that serves to separate "us" from "them" in the political world (Kinder and Kalmoe 2017; Mason 2018). And as an identity-based conception, ideological labels do not necessarily have to align with political values and policy stances. Instead, such group identities only need to offer a sense of attachment and a sense of exclusion (see, e.g., Brewer 2001).

Taken together, the arguments and evidence in favor of viewing partisanship, and increasingly ideology as well, as socially based identities rather than issue-based calculations go a long way toward explaining the political polarization of contemporary US politics. Because ideological perceptions of both oneself and others likely have some of their origins in partisan social identities, it is perhaps not surprising that many voters, despite reporting stronger ideological commitments, continue to hold relatively unconstrained issue positions in many ways similar to those observed more than a half century ago (Converse 2006; see also Achen and Bartels 2016; Kinder and Kalmoe 2017; Mason 2018). Additionally, the growing bitterness targeted at political opponents by ideologues from both the left and the right can be better explained. Like partisan identities, ideological self-perceptions can work to increase "affective polarizations against outgroup ideologues, even at low levels of policy attitude extremity or constraint" (Mason 2018, 280). Instead of acknowledging the issue positions they realistically have in common, ideologues from both sides tend to employ ideological labels to denigrate and vilify their political adversaries. As a result, liberals and conservatives show a tendency to socially distance themselves from each other in much the same way partisans do—expressing a significantly lower willingness to marry, be friends with, live next to, or even occasionally socialize with those holding a different ideological identification (Mason 2018). A social identity approach to partisanship, then, helps account for much of the ideological and affective polarization evident in contemporary US politics.

THE EMOTION OF SOCIAL IDENTITIES

Viewing partisanship from a social identity perspective also helps to better explain the ways in which interpartisan disagreement can generate anger and lead to increased incivility or even physical attack of political opponents (Banaji and Heiphetz 2010; Huddy, Mason, and Aarøe 2015; Mason 2018; Rokeach 1973). Following the 2017 congressional baseball practice shooting, a *Los Angeles Times* journalist observed, "People today don't just disagree. They've grown to hate the other side, from President Trump on down. Not necessarily over issues or ideology, which can be debated or leavened by compromise. But rather as an outgrowth of a deeper pathology, a contempt toward people for merely existing" (Barabak 2017). Research findings from a number of sources corroborate his point, reporting that nearly half of participants in a study said that personal insults are "fair game" in politics (Pew Research Center 2016). And substantially more people viewed interrupting a political opponent in a public forum, belittling or insulting a political adversary, making personal attacks, or questioning the patriotism of someone holding a differing opinion as acceptable political actions than did so about a half decade earlier (Zogby Analytics 2016).

A social identity perspective on partisan polarization would suggest that such sentiments spring "from threatened group status and interparty competition." (Huddy and Mason 2010, 5). As outlined by many early social identity theorists, social group identities serve to maintain self-esteem by distinguishing in-group members as separate from and superior to out-group rivals. Threats from out-group members coupled with assurances of superiority from in-group members have been shown to generate intense emotional responses (Huddy, Feldman, and Weber 2007; Huddy and Mason 2010; see also Coser 1956; Jetten et al. 2001; Lerner and Keltner 2000; Levine and Campbell 1972; Marcus, Neuman, and MacKuen 2000; Rothgerber and Worchel 1997). These tendencies can be so strong that group identities are sometimes experienced "as an extended part of the self," such that brain activity responses to pain and suffering of in-group members resembles that of personal physical pain (Ellemers and van den Bos 2012, 879).

Though some argue that feelings relying on socially based partisan identities tend to result in increasingly negative perceptions of political rivals (Hetherington and Rudolph 2014; Tajfel 1978; Tajfel and Turner 1979, 1986), others contend that a social identity operates to satisfy psychological needs for inclusion in the favored group as well as exclusion from rival groups (Brewer 2001; Suhay 2015). Self-categorization theorists believe social identities help account for intragroup as well as intergroup dynamics—helping to explain both the cohesion within parties and the polarization between them others have pointed out (Suhay 2015). This is said to occur because salient social identities cause individual group members to strive to become the "prototypical" in-group member (Abrams et al. 1990; Turner 1985, 1991; Turner et al. 1987). That is, they will overtly shift their attitudes and behaviors away from those held by an out-group (Clark and Maass 1988; Nelson, Dunn, and Paradies 2011; Wood et al. 1996) to receive validation from the in-group (Suhay 2015, see also Theiss-Morse 2009; Turner 1985; Turner et al. 1987). Conversely, even suggesting that in-group members might share beliefs or actions with out-groups, especially intensely despised ones, can lead to negative in-group social treatment (i.e., derogation or shaming as per Marques, Abrams, and Serôdio 2001). It would seem that as de Tocqueville observed, when one contravenes group opinion, "you are free not to think as I do . . . but from this day on, you are a stranger among us."[2]

Importantly, there is also evidence that the most strongly identified group members will be influenced to a greater degree (Cassese 2019; Terry and Hogg 1996; Terry, Hogg, and White 1999), and thus have stronger emotional reactions to out-group threat (Cadinu and Cerchioni 2001; Mackie, Devos, and Smith 2000). Thus, "strongly identified group members are more inclined to feel angry when threatened by an out-group because they believe they can prevail in an intergroup competition" (Huddy and Mason 2010, 5). Further, as both those in office and in the electorate increasingly sorted themselves along ideological lines, the overlap between partisan identity and ideological identity strengthened. And the partisan realignment of the mass electorate led to long-standing sociodemographic group cleavages along class, gender, and race lines aligning more directly with partisan identity as well. In short, the United States "has gone from being a nation of cross-cutting political identities to a nation of highly aligned political identities" (Mason 2015b, 59).

The overlapping of social identities in this manner has been shown to strengthen preexisting identities (Mason 2015a). So, as partisan identities came to align with other politically relevant identities, cross-partisan animosities rose. As Roccas and Brewer (2002) observed more than a decade ago, intolerance, biased group assessments, and anger tend to accompany the alignment of social identities (see also Schlueter, Schmidt, and Wagner 2008; Iyengar, Sood, and Lelkes 2012; Sherif et al. 1961). After all, in such a political cosmos, an invective hurled across party lines is an insult not only to one's partisan social identity but to one's ideological, racial, sexual, and class identities as well. And, according to social identity theory, the reaction to an out-group threat is typically to identify with the in-group more strongly. As a result, even minor out-group insults become magnified into serious threats that justify more immediate and virulent counterattacks (see, e.g., Mason 2015b; Sowell 2007).

Group threat has also been linked to increases in anxiety levels, "which incline partisans towards heightened . . . anger, which promotes action" (Huddy and Mason 2010, 4). Consequently, instances of incivility make more frequent appearances on the political landscape. As partisan emotions have spiraled ever higher in recent years, some have noted an increase in "oversimplified, inaccurate and derogatory beliefs concerning the other [partisan] group that are identified as the enemies" (see Edsall 2018). Consequently, even less engaged and committed partisan identifiers can more easily distinguish themselves from their perceived political enemies and have their passions inflamed by insults hurled across the partisan divide. Thus, partisan elites find themselves leading increasingly committed mass armies into war on the electoral and policy-making battlefields of contemporary politics.

The Abyss of Total Devaluation

Still, many would question the ability of emotional attachments to a political party, even intense ones, to drive individuals to physically assault members of the opposing party. To understand how this could feasibly be the case, we might begin with a perspective offered by German philosopher Carl Schmitt (1963) when he wrote of the "inevitability of a moral compulsion" (67). Like social identity theorists, he focused on in-group bias and out-group denigration, arguing that combatants in intergroup rivalries must "consider the other side as entirely criminal and inhuman, as totally worthless. Otherwise, they are themselves criminal and inhuman." Such group dynamics, he contended, "compell[ed] ever new, ever deeper discriminations, criminalizations, and devaluations to the point of annihilating all unworthy life." US political discourse in recent years provides ample evidence of such interpartisan attitudes as well as the "absolute enmity" Schmitt sees as a predecessor to physical annihilation of the out-group.

The words of modern scholars echo Schmitt's eerily, with some claiming that identity with social groups "represents a process of depersonalization" (Devine 2015, 512) in which partisan opponents are "defamed, delegitimized and dehumanized" (Edsall 2019). According to recent research from the field of social psychology, decreased social engagement and acceptance of violence against groups viewed as less than fully human accompany the dehumanization of out-groups (Andrighetto et al. 2014; Ellemers 2017; Viki, Osgood, and Phillips 2013). And such processes appear to be at work in contemporary US politics, with partisans on both sides of the aisle viewing the opposing party as significantly less human and more mechanistic than their own party (Cassese 2019). The analyses that follow suggest similar attitudes might be present on college campuses. Correspondingly, those who more strongly rated the opposition party as less human also expressed a desire to socially and morally distance themselves from out-party members. The latter, moral distancing, suggests that political identities have become "a marker for basic decency," and partisan opponents "are deemed to lack basic compassion, or basic loyalty to the country" (Brooks 2014; see also Kalmoe and Mason 2018). The very motives and integrity of counterpartisans are questioned, and a "primal sense of 'us against them' makes partisans fixate on the goal of defeating and even humiliating the opposition at all costs" (Iyengar and Krupenkin 2018, 215; see also Theriault 2015, 12–13). Thus, as some have argued, dehumanization and moral judgment are intricately linked (Cassese 2019;

Ellemers 2017) and can lead to a heightened sense of threat and lowered sense of empathy toward partisan opponents (Andrighetto et al. 2014; Haslam and Loughnan 2016; Leach, Ellemers, and Barreto 2007; Nagar and Maoz 2017). This seems to especially be the case when groups are actively engaged in conflict (Bandura 2016). In fact, Kteily and Bruneau (2017) find a connection between blatant dehumanization and aggression in the context of a political campaign, and Kalmoe and Mason (2018) find that between 5 and 15 percent of the partisans they surveyed endorsed violence against their political opponents.

Such arguments fit well with the view that political passions in the United States run so deep because of differing "worldviews" or "visions" that extend beyond traditional culture war issues (Hunter 1991; Sowell 2007). Partisan polarization and the cross-partisan negativity resulting from beliefs that those on "the other side are personally flawed, that they do not possess the right values and goals" (Hetherington and Rudolph 2014, 15–16). In fact, research by Jonathan Haidt and his colleagues suggests that those on opposite sides of the aisle might indeed hold different moral preferences (see, e.g., Graham, Haidt, and Nosek 2009; Haidt 2012). And as some have pointed out, if "you sincerely believe that you have a . . . superior life philosophy, you're more willing to pull out all the stops to ensure your party wins" (Cummins 2007, 9).

In such a political climate, even when positions are overtly defended as sincere and rational, issue-based decisions have been argued to instead be motivated by an "automatic, basic need to defend our social group" (Mason 2015b, 58) and maintain individual self-esteem. In effect, the conflict extension Carsey and Layman (2015) argued with regard to different policy areas seems to exist between partisanship and issue positions. Although partisans might believe they take policy stands based on more objective reasoning, they are to a large degree driven by a desire to protect their party, and in doing so they defend themselves (see Brooks 2014). A Democrat who defends her party's stand on immigration and a Republican who defends his party's stance on gun rights are, in effect, defending their own identities as members of their parties (and of the ideological and sociodemographic groups that make up that party). Even those with little substantive political knowledge can be expected to respond in this manner. After all, party labels and all the group identities they entail represent perhaps the archetypal easy, symbolic issue (Carmines and Stimson 1989)—operating on an emotional gut level that requires little cognitive effort (see Hetherington and Rudolph 2014). Because many issues that animate contemporary political debates activate the ideological and sociodemographic group allegiances encompassed by partisan identities, policy battles frequently focus less on actual policy outcomes than on defeating the partisan enemy.

THE LESSER OF TWO EVILS

The recent rise of what some have termed "negative partisanship" suggests how strong such a tendency has become (Abramowitz and Webster 2016). As hatred of the out-party rises, some argue that negative sentiments about counterpartisans have come to be a "prime motivator in partisans' political lives" (Iyengar and Krupenkin 2018, 211), with out-party loathing being more powerful than in-party loyalty (Edsall 2018). Ratings of the two major political parties provide some evidence of such a phenomenon. Although partisans' feelings about their own parties have remained remarkably stable over the past four decades, sentiments against the opposing party have grown much more negative (Hetherington and Rudolph 2014). Partisan antipathy has been argued to drive voters to the polls to defeat partisan enemies even when their own party's candidates offer little appeal (Abramowitz and Webster 2016; Edsall 2018). With two of the most unpopular major party candidates in US history, the 2016 presidential election showcased such voting tendencies. About half of each party's supporters were estimated to have been driven to the polls to vote against the opposition candidate rather than to cast ballots because they wanted to elect their own party's nominee (Geiger 2016).

Social identity theory provides a ready explanation for such behavior. Group threat acts as a highly mobilizing force that spurs voters to act as members of their partisan team rather than as individual citizens. As Tajfel and Turner (1979) argued, "A threat to our group's status also causes us to think, feel, and act defensively. We are hard-wired to feel like losers if our group loses, and to feel like winners if our group wins" (Mason 2015b, 58; see also Tajfel and Turner 1979, 33–47). And feeling like a loser might not be merely an emotional response but a physiological one as well. Men's testosterone levels have been shown to drop following experiences of political loss (Stanton et al. 2009). Even though the in-party candidate might not be overly attractive to a voter, he or she might be moved to support the nominee to defend the in-party against attack. All the emotion that accompanies intergroup competition, then, gets translated into behavior on the political stage (Hunter 1991). It is no wonder, then, that Steve Bannon, Donald Trump's former chief political strategist, commented, "Anger and fear is what gets [*sic*] people to the polls" (Edsall 2018).

SOCIAL IDENTITIES AND POLITICAL HATRED

A somewhat dismal prospect, Bannon's words echo those of Hunter S. Thompson (1973) in the wake of the 1972 presidential primary season when he observed that a candidate has to "cause people to salivate and whip on each other with big sticks" (493; see also chapter 1 of this book) to run a winning campaign. And though such campaign tactics had largely fallen out of practice in the post–World War II period, our nation's first politicians linked their political identities closely to their other social identities. During the Republic's earliest years, Freeman (2001) argues, "honor was the core of man's identity," and politics of the time were so nasty precisely because an individual's "very identity was up for grabs" (xvi). The focus on personal honor imbued politics of the time with an emotional intensity and sense of morality akin to that on full display in contemporary politics. Though initially centered on support for particular political leaders, the institutionalization of the original political parties led to attacks being increasingly tied to partisan labels, and "politics became a war between opposing armies rather than a personal contest of reputations" (Freeman 2001, 261). During the founding era, other social identities, especially those associated with regional loyalties, increasingly reinforced partisan allegiances, adding strength to partisan identifications. When Freeman observes of the political landscape of the late nineteenth century that "party bonds were personal above all else . . . eliciting a level of fear, suspicion, and rancor that often seems exaggerated or delusionally 'paranoid'" (259–260), she could just as well have been discussing the early twenty-first century.

Identities, Group Rivalry, and a Bloody Beating

The 1856 attack on a US senator by a member of the House on the Senate floor illustrates the ways in which partisan social identities can generate negative cross-partisan sentiments intense enough to lead to near-fatal physical violence perhaps better than any other. Following his "Crime Against Kansas" speech, Senator Charles Sumner, an antislavery Republican from Massachusetts, was beaten nearly to death by South Carolina Democratic representative Preston S. Brooks for insults the former had levied against the latter's uncle, his state, and his party (Benson 2004). In his acrimonious two-day speech, Sumner denigrated Brooks' uncle, Senator Andrew P. Butler (D-SC) by mocking his chivalry, comparing him to Don Quixote, and saying that Butler had "a mistress . . . who, though ugly to others, is always lovely to him; though polluted in the sight of the world, is chaste in his sight—I mean, the harlot, Slavery" (US Senate 1856, 9). Taking offense, Brooks sought to defend his family's honor. After rejecting the idea of challenging Sumner to a duel because he felt the Republican was not enough of a gentleman to merit it, Brooks decided to whip Sumner instead. He first considered using a horsewhip but settled on a lightweight gold-handled cane. Two days after Sumner's speech, as the Senate adjourned, Brooks walked up to Sumner, who was seated at his desk on the Senate floor addressing envelopes. The Southerner beat his political rival into unconsciousness for "gross insult to my State . . . and uncalled for libel . . . on my blood" (Puleo 2012, 109). Brooks struck Sumner mercilessly, splintering his cane and leaving the Republican covered in blood from gashes that opened his scalp to the bone.

Some in the chamber stood by in silent approval, others shouted encouragement for Brooks, and still others attempted to intervene and help Sumner, only to be initially prevented from doing so by those sympathetic to the attacker. After Brooks finally relented and Sumner had been carried out of the chamber, some of those present picked up pieces of the broken cane and proudly displayed them as a sign of support. In the wake of the incident, partisan and regional identities came to the fore inside the chambers of government and across the nation.

Rank-and-file members of the electorate rallied in support of their respective parties. Sumner, who was left permanently incapacitated, became a martyr in the North, and Brooks was received as a hero across the South. Stephen Puleo's (2012) description of "outrage in the North; jubilation in the South" and the ways in which the attack "established Sumner and Brooks as Antichrist figures to their opposing sides" (116) illustrates well the ways in which social identities operate in the political sphere. The public's reaction was filled with examples of in-group loyalty and moral superiority, out-group vilification, and calls for defeat of the other side. In the South, "glee and righteousness" was widespread (Puleo 2012, 119). Northerners were "horrified and angry," and even those who disliked Sumner's aggressive style rallied to support him against the "sneaking, slave-driving scoundrel Brooks" (Puleo 2012, 125). The partisan newspapers of the day expressed ever-stronger endorsements of their respective champions. Across the South, journalists expressed their approval with phrases such as "well done" and "hit him again," proclaiming Brooks a "chivalrous" figure worth emulating. Conversely, Northern papers portrayed Brooks as a "cowardly scoundrel" who should have been "mercilessly kicked from one side of the continent to the other." Members of the mass public expressed similar sentiments and called for harsh retribution against their opponents. Southerners commented to friends that "you can reach the sensibilities of such dogs only through . . . their heads and [with] a big stick" and that "such wretches must be hung or put in the penitentiary." They complimented Brooks on his "cool, classical caning of Mr. Sumner" and told him that his political opponents would be tarred and feathered, horsewhipped, and expelled by the people of the South (Puleo 2012, 123–124). Meanwhile, Northerners lauded Sumner, expressing affection and admiration, explaining how even their children understood the injustice done to him and telling him that he "could rally the North to destroy the South once and for all" (Puleo 2012, 130–131).

The caning has been argued to be the spark that ignited the Civil War (Benson 2004; Hoffer and Hull 2010; Puleo 2012). The public's reaction certainly supported all-out warfare and defeat of partisan enemies. The *New York Times* called for the defeat of the South, Brooks was burned in effigy at public rallies, and some felt that the "cut-throat Southerners [would] never learn to respect Northern men until some one of their number has a rapier thrust through his ribs, or feels a bullet in his thorax" (Puleo 2012, 126–127). "Sectional clouds, already dark, thickened ominously as word of the caning spread. The steady chill in North-South relations over the years suddenly intensified, fostering extremism and obliterating compromise" (Puleo 2012, 117). Subsequent to the caning, John Brown led a raid that ended with the murder of five proslavery men in Kansas. The violence and deaths of several hundred people across Kansas further alienated the North from the South and drove the two major parties, and their supporters, further apart. With little hope or even attempt at resolving the debates over the issue of slavery peacefully, the nation plunged into the Civil War.

Civil War Redux?

In much the same way regional identities combined with debates over slavery to strengthen partisan animosities that would define US politics for generations to come, regional, social, and economic identities have combined with key issues on the political agenda over the past half century to shape contemporary partisan hatred. Partisan identity has become a low-cost, and highly emotional, way of "telling political actors who is their ally and who is their enemy" (Noel 2013, 2). And like our ancestors, "the more sorted and powerful our political identities become, the less capable we are of treating our political opponents with fairness and equanimity" (Mason 2015b, 60). With self-perceived partisanship and ideology strongly aligned, even the less interested and informed are "more likely to be angry" at their political opposition and find themselves motivated to become involved in political activities

(Mason 2015b, 57). Even with little understanding or commitment to particular issue stances, Americans are increasingly driven to aggressive activism in an effort to see their own side win and the other side lose.

POLITICAL TOLERATION ON AND OFF CAMPUS

Although ominously telling, much of what we know about the ways in which social identities and affective political polarization operate comes from research based on samples of adults of all ages. Because the US public at large constitutes the electorate, studying such samples is certainly reasonable. Still, if we are interested in learning more about how interpartisan animosities develop and operate, investigating the attitudes of voters aged eighteen to eighty (or more) might not be the best approach. After all, work on the development of both partisanship and social identities more generally suggests that reinforcement of positive in-group and negative out-group affect over the life span should act to further solidify such associations. Among the older segments of the electorate, then, we could expect virtually reflexive negative judgments of the opposition and attitudinal defensiveness regarding the preferred party. Further, if we are interested in the prospects for a more civil political future, it seems unlikely to expect those with deeply entrenched partisan-related attitudes to exhibit much change. Thus, focusing investigative attention on those members of the electorate holding weaker partisan social identities and thus being more amenable to attitude change offers a more fruitful research avenue to explore.

Although younger voters cannot be expected to be completely devoid of partisan social identities, they can be expected to hold weaker attachments to social groups, especially political ones. Political scientists have long argued that even the youngest members of the electorate have a sense of partisan identification, even if it is not an especially informed one (see, e.g., Sears and Valentino 1997). The influences of both childhood socialization (see, e.g., Campbell et al. 1960; Hyman 1959) and inherited biological predispositions (see, e.g., Hibbing, Smith, and Alford 2014) suggest that by adulthood most people possess a partisan identity of some sort, even if it is an identity as a political Independent. Still, new voters have a shorter history of identity reinforcement, especially political ones, than their elders. Younger potential voters have historically been shown to express weaker partisan attachments, report paying less attention to politics, and show higher levels of political apathy. Further, the experiences of early adulthood have been shown as influential in shaping, and potentially changing, political attitudes held in the preadult period (see, e.g., Dinas 2013; Miller and Sears 1986; Sears and Funk 1999).

The college environment, in particular, might be expected to serve as a catalyst for attitude change. University campuses, particularly those of public, state-supported institutions, typically expose students to a more diverse community of peers. In addition to interacting with individuals from varied socioeconomic, racial, ethnic, cultural, and religious backgrounds, students also likely encounter others with dissimilar attitudes about a range of topics. Because their daily academic and social activities can require interaction across groups, they cannot as readily isolate themselves from this heterogeneity as older adults can. In such an environment, preexisting beliefs are more likely to meet challenges from those holding alternative viewpoints. Research examining social (and media) network diversity suggests that those exposed to a diversity of opinions tend to hold less hostile partisan attitudes (see chapter 5). Additionally, one of the core values associated with the pursuit of higher education has traditionally been openness to and toleration of new ideas, even when those ideas conflict with personal beliefs. Researchers have long documented the connection between higher levels of education and lower levels of prejudice (Allport 1954). Education shows a connection with higher levels of tolerance for racial and ethnic minorities, immigrant groups, religious outgroups, sexual minorities, people who are obese, people experiencing homelessness, and people with disabilities (see Henry and Napier 2017, 931) as well as support for allowing those with nonconformist ideas or lifestyles to speak or teach publicly or have their books circulated by a public library (Chong 2006).[3] Further, there is some evidence that levels of symbolic racism among students declined between their first and last years in college (Sidanius et al. 2008). These findings have generally been based on arguments that education, either though knowledge (Jenssen and Engesbak 1994) or cognitive competence (Bobo and Licari 1989; Nie, Junn, and Stehlik-Barry 1996) socializes people to be more tolerant of those who differ from them (Carvacho et al. 2013; Henry and Napier 2017; Jenssen and Engesbak 1994; Sidanius et al. 2008). If college students demonstrate similar toleration of those they view as partisan opponents, it might bode well for a return to civil political discourse and bipartisan compromise as these students age.

Over the past four to five decades, however, the level of support among college students for the expression of some controversial ideas and lifestyles seems have decreased (Sides 2017; Villasenor 2017). Examining longitudinal trends, researchers have documented a decline in support for the expression of conflicting opinions on college campuses among those who entered college since the late 1980s. College students in the millennial generation, and especially those in the iGen cohort (those entering college in about 2013), report being less willing to let a controversial speaker express opinions on the college campus (Poushter 2015; Sides 2017).[4] Since 2015, university students report feeling less comfortable speaking up inside or outside the classroom (Stevens and Haidt 2018) for fear of suffering negative judgments from friends or retaliation from professors. Nearly a decade ago, students reported that their peers were arrogant, believed "they [were] always right," and had no respect for views different from their own (Herbst 2010, 109–111). More recently Henry and Napier (2017) documented a connection between higher levels of education and higher levels of ideological prejudice from liberals/progressives and conservatives. When asked whether it was more important for colleges to "create a positive learning environment for all students by prohibiting certain speech or expression of viewpoints that are offensive or biased against certain groups" or to "create an opening learning environment where students are exposed to all types of speech and viewpoints, even if it means allowing speech that is offensive or biased against certain groups of people," a bare majority of the college students asked said they preferred the former (Villasenor 2017).[5]

So although there is good reason to believe today's college students might express more tolerance of political opponents, and thus less cross-partisan bitterness than other members of the electorate, there is also good reason for concern that the same negative partisan affect suggested by recent findings with regard to the electorate more broadly might also be lurking on college campuses. This could paint a rather dire outlook when it comes to forecasts of affective partisan polarization in the nation.

Affective Polarization Across the Generations

I begin my investigation into the state of partisan attitudes on college campuses by revisiting the brief analyses of the 2017 Pew Research Center data I presented in chapter 1, with an eye toward determining whether younger, college-educated members of the electorate exhibit lower levels of affective political polarization than do other potential voters.[6] Turning first to views of partisan opponents, Figure 2.1 shows that younger survey respondents who reported having spent at least some time in the college environment appear just as, if not more, likely to express negative opinions about their partisan rivals. This finding comports well with the research (reviewed above) that documents a decline in tolerance of contrary opinion over the college years. Interestingly, there is some variation across the partisan spectrum. Fewer young, college-educated individuals who professed an affinity for the Republican Party reported unfavorable opinions of the Democratic Party than either their similarly aged, noncollege peers or more mature adults. Conversely, young, college-educated Democrats expressed more highly negative views of the Republican Party than the comparison groups. For their part, young, college-educated, nonpartisan (Independent) identifiers showed a tendency to disfavor the right more than the left—with 85 percent of them assigning the Republican Party unfavorable ratings and 61.5 percent doing the same for the Democratic Party.

When it came to views of party extremity, college-educated young respondents offered opinions remarkably similar to those of the older electorate, with about eight in ten partisans expressing unfavorable views of their partisan opposition. At the same time the non-college-educated, young partisans were the least likely to say either party was

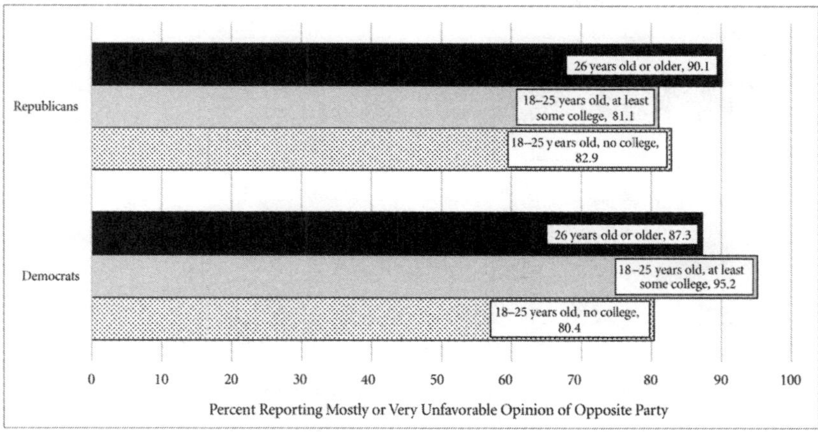

Figure 2.1 Unfavorable Opinion of Opposite Political Party, by Age and Education
Notes: Results based on data from the Pew Research Center, Political Typology Survey, conducted June 8–18 and June 27–July 9, 2017.

too extreme (see Figure 2.2). The same cannot be said of the young nonpartisans with college experience. Almost two-thirds (64.5 percent) of those respondents said they felt that the Democratic Party was too extreme, but only about 23 percent said the same of the Republican Party.

In contrast, however, these same nonpartisan, college-educated, young voters viewed the Republican Party's ethical standards with lower regard than they did the Democrat's (see Figure 2.3). Whereas nearly 87 percent of that subsample said the Grand Old Party (GOP) did not have high ethical standards, only 26 percent said that about the Democratic Party. It is important to keep in mind the political context within which these survey data were collected when interpreting these results. Collected just months after the 2016 presidential election, the attitudes of Independents, like partisans, were likely influenced by the events of that contest. Together, though, these two findings might help explain both the appeal Bernie Sanders held for many college-aged voters in the 2016 Democratic presidential primaries and the slight decline in young voter turnout. The youngest college-educated Independents might have found themselves orphaned by both parties. Turned off by their impressions of the Republican Party's ethics and repelled by the

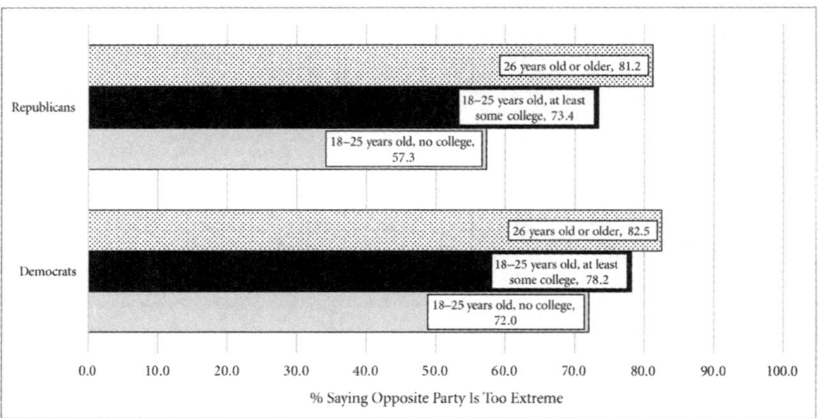

Figure 2.2 Views of Opposition Party as Too Extreme, by Age and Education
Notes: Results based on data from the Pew Research Center, Political Typology Survey, conducted June 8–18 and June 27–July 9, 2017.

Democratic Party's policy stands, they simply chose to forego the election altogether.

Meanwhile, young, college-educated partisan's views of the opposition party's ethical stands aligned with their views about that party's extremity. A majority of Republican and Democratic identifiers said that the other party had poor ethical standards. Again, however, there is some evidence that those on the left were harsher in their assessments of their partisan competition than those on the right. Whereas about 54 percent of Republican, college-educated, young respondents said they felt the Democratic Party had poor ethical standards, about 75 percent of their Democratic counterparts said the same about the GOP.

This same tendency revealed itself when young, college-educated partisans were asked about a having a friend who voted for the other party's presidential candidate in 2016 (Figure 2.4). Whereas slightly more than half of Democratic respondents said a friend's vote for Trump would strain the friendship, only about 8 percent of Republicans said the same of a friend's Clinton vote. At the same time, neither side of the partisan aisle reported a friend voting for their own party's candidate to be much of a bonding exercise. Only about 6 percent of Democratic

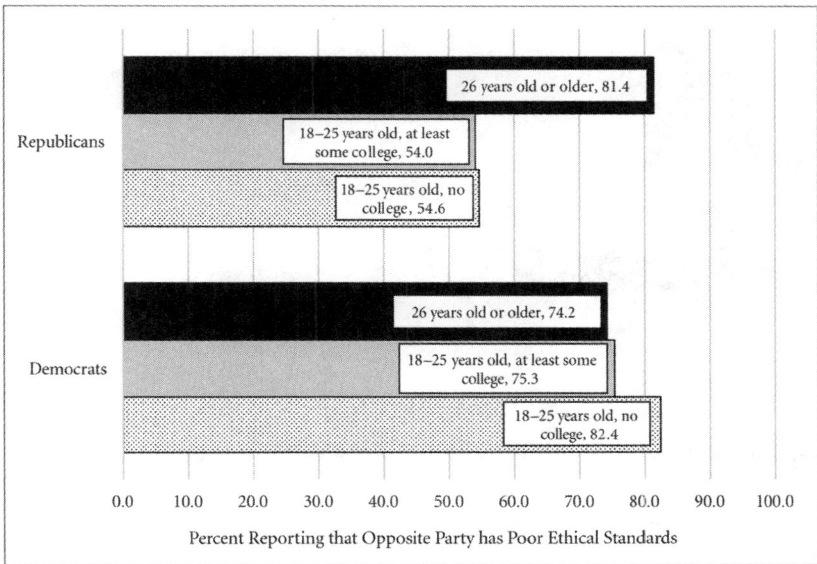

Figure 2.3 View That Opposition Party Has Poor Ethical Standards, by Age and Education

Notes: Results based on data from the Pew Research Center, Political Typology Survey, conducted June 8–18 and June 27–July 9, 2017.

and 7 percent of Republican, college-educated, young people said that a friend voting for Clinton or Trump, respectively, would strengthen the friendship. This finding might indicate that out-party negativity drives the partisan affect expressed by young, college-educated partisans more than in-party favoritism does, as it has been argued to do among broader samples of the electorate.

This brief look at the partisan attitudes of the youngest segment of college-educated voters suggests that although negative partisan affect and partisan polarization might exist on campus in ways similar to off campus, it is limited in important ways. Perhaps most importantly, the data do not allow me to determine which respondents were college students at the time they were asked these questions. Neither am I able to discern the potential diversity, political or otherwise, of the respondents' college experiences. Further, I am limited to examining attitudes about overall opinions of the parties, views of party extremity and ethical standards, and perceptions of a rhetorical friend's vote

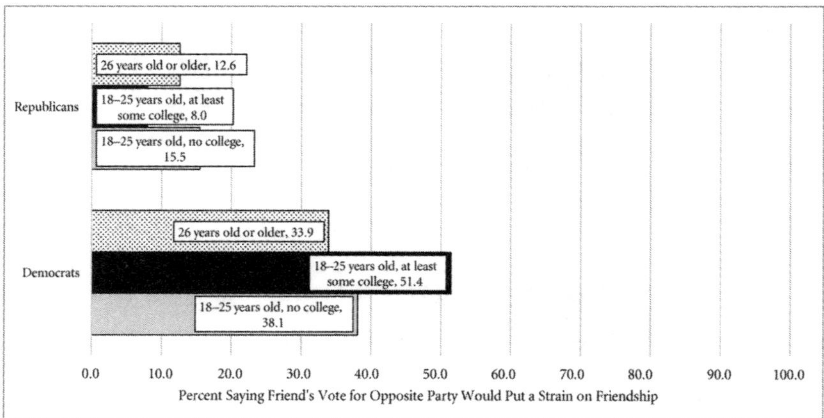

Figure 2.4 Percent Saying Vote Would Put a Strain on Friendship, by Age and Education

Notes: Results based on data from the Pew Research Center, Political Typology Survey, conducted June 8–18 and June 27–July 9, 2017.

for the opposing party's candidate. Unfortunately, data limitations prevent me from studying more specific opinions about what aspects of the opposition party the respondents found most repellant and/or whether they expressed the same negativity toward rank-and-file out-party members as well.

To address some of these data shortcomings, I undertook a study of a diverse set of college students on a large, state-university campus. My goal was to get a better idea about the existence and extent of partisan animosity and affective polarization among the youngest members of the electorate, who might be expected to be most tolerant of contrary political views. Though I harbored no illusions that my research would uncover a method for quelling some of the partisan vitriol so many have decried, my findings, I thought, might help inform conversations about the current and future state of political civility and compromise. With that goal in mind, I focus my attention on feelings of negative partisan affect that theoretically plant their roots in partisan social identities. To the task of measuring negative sentiment of this sort, I dedicate chapter 3.

3. Studying Partisan Hatred on the College Campus

I approach my investigation of possible connections between partisan disaffection and political polarization among young voters using a survey research approach. Because young, likely voters are my population of interest, and US Department of Education reports show that most undergraduate students are enrolled at public colleges and universities, I chose to study a diverse sample of students currently enrolled at a large public university.[1] I conducted my study on the Sam Houston State University (SHSU) campus, a university typical of many state universities in the nation. It is a large public university seventy miles north of Houston in Huntsville, Texas, and draws students mostly from the rural areas of East Texas and the Houston and Dallas metropolitan areas. The student body is racially/ethnically diverse, with students generally coming from modest financial backgrounds, many representing the first in their families to attend college. According to the SHSU Fall 2016 *Institutional Handbook* (produced by the SHSU Office of Institutional Effectiveness), the university had a fall 2015 enrollment of 17,421 students, with an undergraduate student population about two-thirds female and racially diverse. Just more than half (52.5 percent) of the students were Anglo. African American (18.5 percent) and Hispanic (20.4 percent) students constituted sizable minorities, and smaller proportions of Asian American (1.4 percent), Native American (0.6 percent), and others (Hawaiian/Pacific Islander, mixed race, and unknown race/ethnicity, 6.6 percent) rounded out the student body. Women represented 61 percent of the undergraduate student body, and men constituted 39 percent. Finally, about 84 percent of the campus undergraduate population was traditionally college-aged students (twenty-four years old or less), with almost 45 percent representing recent high school graduates (ages eighteen to twenty). As Table 3.1 illustrates, SHSU has a slightly less traditional and more female undergraduate student body than universities nationwide. Racially, the university's undergrad population has more African American and Latinx

Table 3.1 Demographic Characteristics of Study Participants Compared with University and National Populations of Undergraduate Students

	Sample	*University*	*Nation*
Sex			
Female	65.8%	61.2%	56.0%
Male	34.2%	38.8%	44.0%
Not reporting	2.9%	0.0%	0.0%
Race/Ethnicity			
White/Anglo	52.2%	52.6%	56.6%
Black/African American	19.4%	18.5%	16.6%
Hispanic/Latino	21.8%	20.5%	14.3%
Asian American	1.6%	1.6%	6.2%
Other	5.0%	5.1%	0.6%
Not reporting	6.5%	0.8%	0.0%
Age			
Traditional college age (18–24 years old)	94.3%	84%	90%
Nontraditional age (25 years and older)	5.7%	16%	10%

Notes: University data collected from the Sam Houston State University Office of Institutional Effectiveness. For race/ethnicity, the "Other" category includes individuals identifying as Native American and as two or more races.

and fewer Asian American students as well as having more students who report themselves as being multiracial and/or Native American.

In the spring semester of 2015, undergraduate students enrolled in introductory political science and history courses were asked to complete an online survey about college students' political attitudes. These courses serve as part of the university's core curriculum and are, therefore, required courses for all students. Thus, a sample pulled from these courses is likely to encompass students with varied majors. Students generally enroll in the required government and history courses early in their college careers, typically in the first or second year of study at the university, though about 15 percent wait until they are upper-class students to complete the courses. Consequently, the students participating in this study were a group of potential voters who had entered the electorate within about the previous three to four years. Because they were all pursuing a college education, they represented a group of young people more likely to be political informed, engaged, and involved in the electoral process. And, importantly, they were at a stage in the life cycle when their political attitudes were most likely to be susceptible to change (see chapter 2).

Faculty members teaching US government and US history courses solicited volunteers from among the students enrolled in their classes. Those teaching the courses had the option to decline the request, and I provided those who helped recruit study participants a summary of the study findings before the end of the academic term. I left to each faculty member's discretion the decision about how to incorporate both student participation and the summary report in their classes. Although some granted students class credit for participation, others chose not to do so but incorporated student participation and/or the study findings into class assignments and/or discussions. Still others chose only to inform their students of the opportunity to be involved in the study and provided them information about how to participate should they choose to do so.

Shortly after the start of the spring semester (February 23 through March 17, 2015), student participants completed an online survey that contained well-established survey measures of their interest in politics generally, their consumption of different types of media, their partisan identities, their ideological orientations, and their ratings of former president George W. Bush and then-president Barack Obama. Additionally, they were asked a number of newly developed measures aimed at tapping feelings about the major parties, their leaders, and rank-and-file party members.[2]

SAMPLE CHARACTERISTICS

In total, more than 1,400 students received a request to participate in the study, and 827 (59.1 percent) chose to complete the online survey. The sample of survey respondents ranged in age from eighteen to twenty-five years old, with an average age of about twenty-two, and, as shown in Table 3.1, reflects the diversity of the campus population. Mirroring the trend in university enrollment across the nation, female students outnumbered male students, though to a stronger degree in my sample (almost two to one).[3] White (Anglo) subjects constituted about half (52.2 percent) of the sample, whereas about 19 percent of the study participants were black (African American), nearly 22 percent were Hispanic (Latinx), less than 2 percent were Asian American, and almost 5 percent identified themselves as some other or mixed-race/ethnicity. Overall, then, the study participants were typically college aged, and as, if not more, racially and ethnically diverse than most college student samples. Thus, they offer a good picture of nascent likely voters from across the racial/ethnic spectrum.

Participants also reported political attitudes from across the spectrum. As shown in Table 3.2, and reflective of the US population in general, about one-third of the study participants claimed at first to be Independents. And just as with the general population, when pushed, they split fairly evenly between leaning more toward the Democratic Party, leaning more toward the Republican Party, and being truly independent of both parties. The remaining respondents split between the two major parties, with almost 42 percent reporting a Republican identity and fewer (about 28 percent) claiming an allegiance to the Democratic Party. Similarly, more than half (53.3 percent) reported ideological leanings in the middle of the spectrum, but only about half of those claimed to be completely moderate. The remainder said they are either slightly liberal (15.2 percent) or slightly conservative (15.4 percent). Although relatively small shares of the participants reported extremely liberal or conservative positions, a substantial proportion (about 39 percent) claimed moderate ideological outlooks, and slightly more reported conservative than liberal perspectives.

When it came to being interested in "information about what's going on in government and politics," as they were asked on the survey, the sample was fairly evenly distributed, though a slight positive skew is somewhat evident (see Figure 3.1). Almost three-quarters reported they were only "slightly" or "moderately" interested. Whereas more than 17 percent of the students expressed a stronger interest than the modal respondent, about 7.6 percent said they were "not at all" concerned with such information. On the whole, then, the group of young people under study here was likely to pay some attention to information about the political world but not be overly informed.

Table 3.2 Partisan and Ideological Characteristics of Study Participants

	Percent	*Valid Percent*
Partisanship		
Strong Democrat	7.3	7.3
Weak Democrat	20.4	20.4
Leaning Democrat	10.5	10.5
Independent	9.4	9.4
Leaning Republican	10.8	10.8
Weak Republican	19.5	19.5
Strong Republican	22.1	22.1
Missing	0.0	—
Ideology		
Extremely liberal	3.0	3.1
Moderately liberal	16.3	16.8
Slightly liberal	14.8	15.2
Neither liberal nor conservative	21.9	22.5
Slightly conservative	15.0	15.4
Moderately conservative	21.8	22.4
Extremely conservative	4.4	4.5
Missing	2.9	—

Note: "Missing" indicates respondents who chose not to disclose their sex or race/ethnicity.

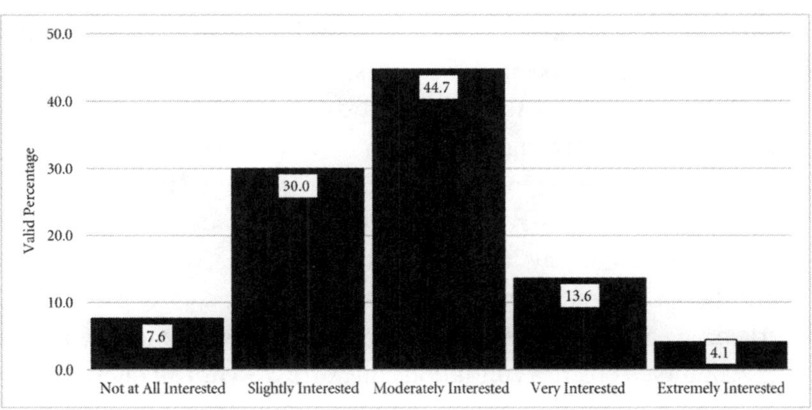

Figure 3.1 Political Interest of Study Participants

Notes: Only 0.7 percent of the respondents failed to choose one of these response options.

On the whole, then, my study participants reflected typical college-aged respondents fairly well, though perhaps they were a bit more racially/ethnically diverse and ideologically conservative. No matter how representative study respondents might have been of the college-aged electorate nationwide, it is still possible, even if improbable, that college-aged youth have not had enough experience with the workings of electoral politics to have developed a positive affect toward the party with which they identify and correspondingly negative sentiment toward the opposition party. There is, for instance, some evidence that young people might be souring on both parties (see, e.g., Longo and Meyer 2006). Because many of my arguments build on in-group devotion and out-group animosity, I took existing research on affective polarization in the US public as the launch point for my investigation into partisan attitudes among college students.

LOVE AND LOATHING ON CAMPUS

Like scholars before me, I asked study participants to express their feelings toward the two major parties and each party's most recent presidential officeholder using long-standing thermometer rating measures. Respondents rated then-president Obama and former president Bush Jr. as well as the Democratic and Republican Parties on a thermometer scale ranging from 0 to 100. Ratings between 51 and 100 "degrees" meant the respondent felt "favorable and warm toward that person/group," whereas ratings between 0 and 49 degrees meant he/she did not feel that way. Those who did not feel particularly warm or cold toward a person or party were asked to report a 50-degree rating. Intervening scale numbers can be interposed between these semantic anchor points to create a continuous measure. As with all questions on the survey, respondents also had the opportunity to skip the question. Thus, the thermometer ratings measure a range from 0 to 100, with lower scores indicating lower ratings of the officeholder or party.

Overall, the study participants rated both of the major parties and their presidential officeholders at about the center of the thermometer scale. Given the skew toward the Republican Party seen in self-identified partisanship, it is not surprising that both the GOP and former president Bush Jr. rated higher, on average, than the Democratic Party and then-president Obama. Whereas respondents rated the GOP above the midpoint, at almost fifty-nine, the Democratic organization averaged just below the center of the scale, at about forty-eight. This eleven-point rating gap also emerged with regard to the occupants of the White House. Obama averaged about a forty-four-degree rating, whereas the respondents were ten degrees warmer toward Bush, rating him at about fifty-four.[4]

Affective Polarization on Campus

These centrist tendencies did not persist across the partisan spectrum, though. Consistent with previous research, Figure 3.2 illustrates that those affiliating with a major party tended to rate their own party and officeholder much higher than those of the opposition. About 30 percent of the respondents who considered themselves either strongly, weakly, or leaning Republican rated Obama at the lowest possible point on the scale.[5] In contrast, less than 5 percent of those claiming Democratic affiliation of any strength rated him that low. Much the same holds for Bush, with 17 percent of those with Democratic attachments rating him a freezing zero degrees, and only about 2 percent of Republican adherents doing so. The pattern is much the same when it comes to the parties themselves. About one-tenth of partisans, Democrats and Republicans alike, rated the opposition party as low as possible. Conversely, slightly more rated their own party as high as possible—about 15 percent of self-identified Democrats and 12 percent of Republicans rated their own party at the century mark.

Similar patterns do not persist among the "pure" Independents in the sample, who expressed more ambivalent feelings. Among those who said they had no partisan attachments at all, 14 percent rated Bush at the lowest point, and 3.1 percent rated him at the highest. At the same time, 10.4 percent of pure independents rated Obama at the lowest point, and the same percentage rated him at the highest. Further, 17.6 percent of Independents rated the Republican Party and 11.8 percent rated the Democratic Party at 0, but none rated either party at

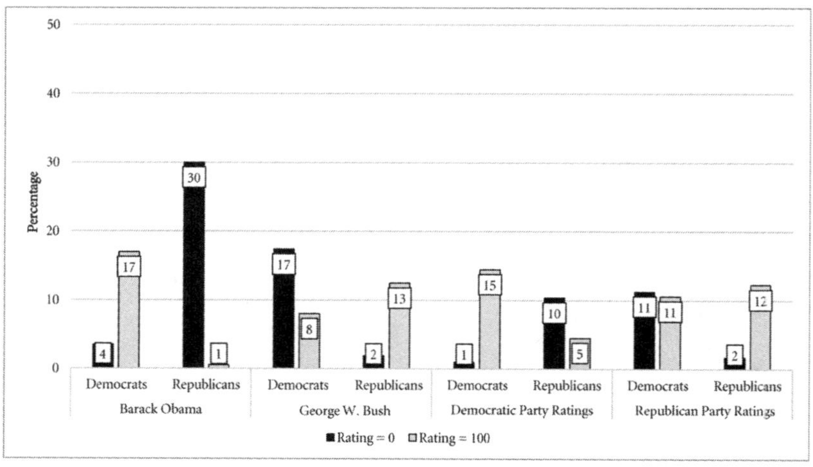

Figure 3.2 Extreme Thermometer Ratings of Parties and Officeholder—Partisans Only

100. As expected, Independents tended to harbor more neutral feelings about both parties and their most recent presidents (see Figure 3.3). Nearly half of Independents rated each party at the midpoint, nearly 30 percent did the same for former president Bush, and almost 38 percent did so for then-president Obama.

Far fewer partisans rated the officeholders and parties neutrally. Between about 14 and 19 percent of respondents with partisan attachments reported ratings of Bush and Obama at the fifty-degree mark. Partisans were also slightly more likely to report tepid feelings toward the opposition party's officeholder than their own, though this tendency was not as strong as might be expected. There was more variability when it came to ratings of the parties themselves, with about 12 and 24 percent of partisans rating the parties neutrally. A more striking in-party preference arises with regard to feelings about the party organizations themselves. Nearly a quarter of self-proclaimed Democrats rated the Republican Party in a lukewarm manner, and about one-fifth of Republicans returned the favor by rating the Democratic Party the same. The feeling thermometer ratings evidenced in this study's sample corroborate previous findings with regard to affective polarization in the US population more generally (see chapter 1). As telling as these

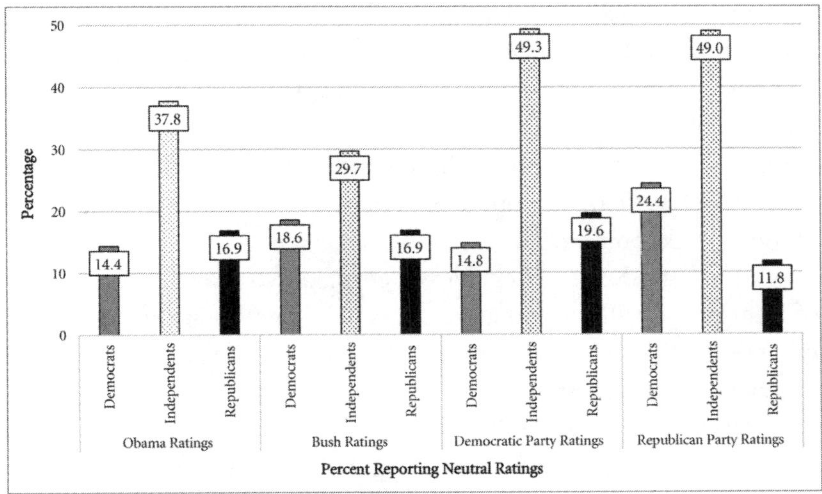

Figure 3.3 Neutral Thermometer Ratings of Parties and Officeholder—All Respondents

measures are, they remain generalized measures of partisan like or dislike (see Green 1988). Thus, although useful and informative, taking thermometer ratings as measures of partisan hatred itself can be problematic if we care to more precisely identify the sources of these more generalized feelings toward political entities.

MEASURING PARTISAN HATRED

Because partisan attachments theoretically operate similarly to those of ethnic identities, I turned to research in the area of ethnic hatred for measurement guidance. Scholars in that field of research have long argued that ethnic and racial identification with an in-group can give rise to prejudice and contempt and possibly even physical viciousness toward social out-groups (Haidt, Rosenberg, and Hom 2003; Mullen & Skitka 2006; Parker & Janoff-Bulman 2013; Skitka, Bauman, and Sargis 2005). In much the same way, I argue, partisan identification might lead to malignant attitudes and behavior toward partisan opponents. As some have pointed out, hatred can be especially powerful in the political arena (Cowan and Mettrick 2002; Halperin, Canetti, and Kimhi 2012). Politics often focuses on groups and group interests, and hatred often has a strong group basis. Further, political rhetoric often employs simple, symbolic messages that target group-relevant emotions. In fact, the use of (often hate-filled) in-group/out-group messages about partisan opponents have come to characterize much of modern US politics.

Ethnic hatred researchers have identified two separate dimensions of intergroup loathing: longer-term, stable emotional sentiment and more powerful, "burning" feelings (see Frijda et al. 1991; Halperin and Gross 2011). As illustrated in Table 3.3, the latter, termed *immediate hatred*, is an acute reaction to stimuli, whereas the former, designated *chronic hatred*, represents a more highly stable standing disposition (Ekman 1992; Halperin, Canetti, and Kimhi 2012).[6] Extreme and short term, immediate hatred usually arises in response to a particular incident, whereas chronic hatred is an ongoing emotional attitude that rejects all members of the out-group (Halperin, Canetti, and Kimhi 2012).

Taking a novel approach to measuring mass affective polarization, I used Halperin, Canetti, and Kimhi's (2012) ethnic hatred measure as my guide and constructed a survey measure of "partisan hatred" that targeted partisan out-groups instead of ethnic ones. Self-identified Republicans were asked a series of questions tapping their feelings about Democrats, those calling themselves Democrats were asked about their sentiments regarding Republicans, and self-professed Independents were asked about members of either of the two major US political parties.[7] Although some might object to using a term as connotatively loaded and provocative as *hatred* to describe partisan attitudes, I do so primarily because affective partisan polarization operates much as ethnic group dynamics do, and I am building on a measurement strategy developed by ethnic hatred researchers. Additionally, as the dehumanization and moral judgment literature reviewed in chapter 2 suggests, social identities can operate to create negative emotional (and sometimes behavioral) responses to counterpartisans that resemble hate-based reactions to other out-groups. This is especially the case when groups engage in intense conflict such as that in the current era of tight

Table 3.3 Ethnic Hatred Survey Measures

Chronic Ethnic Hatred:

To what degree do you feel that the actions of the Islamic Movement have offended you and/or members of your group over a long period of time?

To what degree do you estimate that some of the actions of members of the Islamic Movement and its leaders are a result of a "bad" internal character?

To what degree do you estimate that some of the actions of the members of the Islamic Movement and its leaders are a result of an intentional desire to harm you and members of your group?

To what degree does the thought of the Islamic Movement give rise to negative feelings in you?

To what degree do you estimate that the actions of the members and leaders of the Islamic Movement are just and legitimate? (reverse coded)

To what degree would you be glad to develop social relations with members of the Islamic Movement? (reverse coded)

To what degree would you be glad to know members of the Islamic Movement more closely? (reverse coded)

Immediate Ethnic Hatred: When you are in the presence of members of the Islamic Movement how often do you . . .

experience unpleasant physical feelings (e.g., increased blood flow or pulse rate, sweating, muscle tension, chest pains)

have extreme feelings toward members of the Islamic Movement

have thoughts of a desire to get rid of or destroy members of the Islamic Movement in any kind of manner

feel a desire to take action in order to take revenge on members of the Islamic Movement and its leaders

imagine a violent action against members of the Islamic Movement

feel negative and hard feelings toward members of the Islamic Movement

Source: Halperin, Canetti, and Kimhi (2012).

electoral competition. Further, some have argued that moral standards connected to social identities serve not only an identity function but also group dynamic and intergroup relation functions that shape regulation of behavior within groups and the manner such that members communicate with and behave toward out-group members in a hate-filled manner (e.g., Ellemers and van den Bos 2012). These functions operate in much the same way for political groups as for ethnic, religious, or cultural groups, leading to dehumanization and a desire to annihilate opposition groups. In addition, the past several years have borne witness to a number of acts of political violence in the United

States that resemble in many ways the ethnic violence examined by human rights scholars. From the campaign rally altercations of the 2016 election to the 2017 congressional softball game shooting to the 2018 mailing of pipe bombs to partisan opponents, headlines have repeatedly referred to contemporary political relations as hate-filled (see, e.g., Edsall 2019; French 2019). It would seem, then, that we might have entered an age of "modern hatred" in US politics that resembles that identified by Rudolph and Rudolph (1993) in the international setting. Although some might find the term distasteful or inflammatory, I contend that the many similarities between the theoretical motivations for and consequences of ethnic hatred justify the use of the term *partisan hatred* in the context of this project.

PARTISAN HATRED IN HIGHER EDUCATION

On their face, the chronic hatred measures reflect the sorts of partisan rhetoric so frequently heard on the US political scene. There might be some doubt, however, about the relevance of the immediate hatred measures in the US context. Although members of the public might be willing to admit they "have extreme feelings" or "feel negative and hard feelings" toward the other party, we might expect fewer to admit "a desire to get rid of or destroy" members of the other party. And the distribution of responses shown in Table 3.4 bears out this expectation to some degree.

Generally, respondents expressed more agreement with the chronic hatred items than with the immediate hatred statements. Whereas about half of the respondents agreed to some degree that the actions of the opposing party had offended them (54.6 percent) and that the thought of the opposing party had given rise to negative feelings (46.7 percent), nearly two-thirds (64.0 percent) ascribed the actions of the opposing party to the "bad" internal character of the opposition's leaders. At the same time, however, only about one-third (31.6 percent) expressed the sentiment that the opposing party intentionally desired to harm them.

Table 3.4 Partisan Hatred Survey Items

Chronic Hatred: How much do you agree with each of the following statements?	*Strongly Agree*	*Agree*	*Disagree*	*Strongly Disagree*
(1) "The actions of the [Democratic Party/Republican Party/Major Political Parties] have offended me and/or members of my party over a long period of time."	9.3% (75)	45.3% (365)	40.5% (326)	4.8% (39)
(2) "Some of the actions of the [Democratic Party/Republican Party/Major Political Parties] and [its/their] leaders are a result of a 'bad' internal character."	12.8% (103)	51.2% (412)	31.8% (256)	4.1% (33)
(3) "Some of the actions of the [Democratic Party/Republican Party/Major Political Parties] and [its/their] leaders are a result of an intentional desire to harm me and members of my party."	5.6% (45)	26.0% (223)	54.4% (438)	12.3% (99)
(4) "The thought of the [Democratic Party/Republican Party/Major Political Parties] gives rise to negative feelings in me."	8.1% (65)	38.6% (311)	44.0% (354)	9.3% (75)
(5) "The actions of [Democrats/Republicans/Democrats and Republicans] and the leaders of their [party/parties] are just and legitimate."	2.9% (23)	29.7% (238)	56.2% (450)	11.2% (90)
(6) "I would be glad to socialize with more members of the [Democratic/Republican/Democrat and Republican] Party."	3.3% (26)	40.1% (320)	48.0% (383)	8.6% (69)
(7) "I would be glad to know more [Democrats/Republicans/Democrats and Republicans]."	4.8% (38)	48.4% (386)	38.3% (306)	8.6% (69)
(8) "[Democrats/Republicans/Democrats and Republicans] are a threat to the nation's well-being."	7.1% (57)	34.5% (278)	46.5% (374)	11.9% (96)

Table 3.4 *(continued)*

Immediate Hatred: When you are in the presence of [Democrats/Republicans/Democrats and Republicans], how often do you:	*Almost Never*	*Sometimes*	*Frequently*	*Almost All of the Time*
(9) experience unpleasant physical feelings (e.g., increased blood flow or pulse rate, sweating, muscle tension, chest pains)?	64.5% (517)	29.5% (236)	4.4% (35)	1.6% (13)
(10) have extreme feelings toward [Democrats/Republicans/Democrats and Republicans]?	65.6% (524)	28.8% (230)	4.6% (37)	1.0% (8)
(11) have thoughts of a desire to get rid of or destroy [Democrats/Republicans/Democrats and Republicans] in any kind of manner?	84.5% (676)	12.5% (100)	2.3% (18)	0.8% (6)
(12) feel a desire to take action in order to take revenge on [Democrats/Republicans/Democrats and Republicans] and their leaders?	82.5% (661)	13.5% (108)	3.1% (25)	0.9% (7)
(13) imagine a violent action against [Democrats/Republicans/Democrats and Republicans]?	88.3% (705)	9.4% (75)	1.6% (13)	0.6% (5)
(14) feel negative and hard feelings toward [Democrats/Republicans/Democrats and Republicans]?	57.5% (460)	33.6% (269)	6.4% (51)	2.5% (20)

Notes: Cell entries are valid percentages and number of cases (in parentheses). Self-identified Republicans and Democrats were asked about the opposite party; pure Independents were asked about both major parties.

Though respondents admitted much less agreement with the statements meant to measure immediate hatred, relatively high levels of animosity still surfaced. A little more than one in three respondents (35.5 percent) claimed to at least sometimes experience an unpleasant physical response to the presence of opposition party members and to have had extreme feelings toward their partisan opponents (34.4

percent). Even the more extreme statements garnered substantial support. Nearly 18 percent of respondents admitted to feeling a desire to take revenge on their opponents, 16 percent said they had thoughts of a desire to get rid of or destroy opposition party members, and nearly 12 percent had imagined violent action against their political adversaries. So although expressions of immediate hatred seem to be less prevalent than those of chronic hatred, there appears to be a good deal of both sorts of hatred on the college political scene.

Dimensions of Partisan Hatred

In their study of ethnic hatred in Halperin, Canetti, and Kimhi (2012) isolate only two dimensions of hatred—chronic and immediate. The newly created partisan hatred measures reveal a different pattern, however. Findings from an exploratory factor analysis of the revised measures reveal four potential dimensions: one encompassing the six immediate hatred measures and three different dimensions of chronic hatred (see Table 3.5).

Mirroring the ethnic hatred findings (Halperin, Canetti, and Kimhi 2012), the immediate hatred items seem to constitute a single dimension of hate that exhibits strong factor loadings as well as high internal cohesion (Cronbach's alpha = 0.863) and interitem correlations (see Table 3.5). The items show statistically significant correlations ranging from 0.354 to 0.708 and averaging about 0.518. Because the six survey items referencing visceral, physical actions and reactions proved so interrelated, I combined them into an additive index by averaging responses to the items. This four-point index, which I designated *physical hatred,* thus ranges from one to four with lower scores indicating less physical hatred of opposing party members.

The remaining items, modeled after the chronic hatred dimension of ethnic hatred, displayed a different pattern. Diverging from Halperin, Canetti, and Kimhi's (2012) findings that all eight of these items formed one coherent dimension of hatred toward the ethnic outgroup, the factor analysis results suggest three possible dimensions of chronic partisan hatred. The first four items load strongly on the second factor in the present analysis (see Table 3.5). These four items focus

Table 3.5 Exploratory Factor Analysis

How much do you agree with each of the following statements?	*Factor 1* "PHYSICAL HATRED"	*Factor 2* "ORGANIZATIONAL HATRED"	*Factor 3* "INTERPERSONAL HATRED"	*Factor 4* "NATIONAL HATRED"
(1) "The actions of the [Democratic Party/Republican Party/Major Political Parties] have offended me and/or members of my party over a long period of time."	0.124	0.0807	0.041	0.043
(2) "Some of the actions of the [Democratic Party/Republican Party/Major Political Parties] and [its/their] leaders are a result of a 'bad' internal character."	0.021	0.737	0.113	0.025
(3) "Some of the actions of the [Democratic Party/Republican Party/Major Political Parties] and [its/their] leaders are a result of an intentional desire to harm me and members of my party."	0.184	0.733	−0.072	−0.024
(4) "The thought of the [Democratic Party/Republican Party/Major Political Parties] gives rise to negative feelings in me."	0.217	0.754	0.158	−0.001
(5) "The actions of [Democrats/Republicans/Democrats and Republicans] and the leaders of their [party/parties] are just and legitimate."	−0.91	−0.336	0.329	0.711
(6) "I would be glad to socialize with more members of the [Democratic/Republican/Democrat and Republican] Party."	0.027	0.072	0.797	0.138
(7) "I would be glad to know more [Democrats/Republicans/Democrats and Republicans]."	0.076	0.096	0.866	−0.129
(8) "[Democrats/Republicans/Democrats and Republicans] are a threat to the nation's well-being."	0.13	0.325	−0.22	0.798

Table 3.5 *(continued)*

When you are in the presence of [Democrats/Republicans/ Democrats and Republicans], how often do you:	*Factor 1* "PHYSICAL HATRED"	*Factor 2* "ORGANIZATIONAL HATRED"	*Factor 3* "INTERPERSONAL HATRED"	*Factor 4* "NATIONAL HATRED"
(9) experience unpleasant physical feelings?	0.644	0.236	0.295	0.066
(10) have extreme feelings toward [Democrats/Republicans/ Democrats and Republicans]?	0.757	0.188	0.161	0.045
(11) have thoughts of a desire to get rid of or destroy [Democrats/Republicans/ Democrats and Republicans] in any kind of manner?	0.857	0.041	−0.051	0.006
(12) feel a desire to take action in order to take revenge on [Democrats/Republicans/ Democrats and Republicans] and their leaders?	0.822	0.097	−0.058	−0.032
(13) imagine a violent action against [Democrats/ Republicans/Democrats and Republicans]?	0.833	0.019	−0.192	−0.03
(14) feel negative and hard feelings toward [Democrats/ Republicans/Democrats and Republicans]?	0.664	0.295	0.267	0.052

Note: Entries are loadings of the items derived from factor analysis (principal components analysis with varimax rotation).

on the ways in which the motivations for actions taken by the opposing party, as well as the actions themselves, offended the respondent (or the respondent's group). These items exhibit strong, statistically significant intercorrelations, ranging from 0.417 to 0.567 and averaging 0.476 (see Table 3.5) as well as strong internal cohesion (Cronbach's alpha = 0.784). Given the interconnectedness of these party organization–oriented items, I chose to combine them into a second additive index by averaging scores across the four items. Like the physical hatred index, comprised of the immediate hatred items, this chronic *organizational hatred* index, as I dubbed it, ranges from one to four, with lower scores representing less hatred of the opposition party.

The two items loading on the third factor emphasize reactions to socializing with members of the opposing party. These items also exhibit a statistically significant, strong correlation with each other (Pearson's r = 0.564) and good index cohesion (Cronbach's alpha = 0.720). Because these two items targeted the social aspect of interpartisan interaction, I describe the third factor as chronic *interpersonal hatred* of the opposing party's members and combined the two items into an index. I again took the average of responses to the two items, resulting in an index that once again ranges from one to four, with lower scores indicating less interpersonal hatred of opposition party members and thus more of a willingness to interact socially with them.

The items loading on the fourth factor proved more problematic. These items asked respondents to assess the legitimacy of the opposing party's actions and whether those actions were threatening to the nation as a whole. Though similar to the items loading on the second, chronic, organizational hatred factor, these last two items focused less on the party organization itself and more on the national impact the parties and their members had. Though showing strong factor loadings, these items exhibit a much lower correlation with each other (Pearson's $r = 0.161$, $p < 0.01$) and weak index cohesion (Cronbach's alpha = 0.275) than those loading on the other factors. Though skeptical of the validity or usefulness of an index built with these two items, I combined these two items into a four-point index for purposes of exploratory analysis and tentatively call this factor chronic *national hatred.*

A peak at the intercorrelations between the partisan hatred indices constructed from the individual items further confirmed my suspicions that the fourth, chronic, national hatred index was problematic (see Table 3.6). Although the other three indices correlate well with each other, the last does not show a good relationship to any of the others. Not surprisingly, immediate, physical hatred appears most strongly related to chronic, organizational hatred. After all, it makes sense that an individual who believes the opposing party has malicious motives would also feel physically repulsed in the presence of party members. Similarly, visceral feelings of physical hatred also show a significant,

Table 3.6 Correlations between Hatred Indices

	Factor 1 "Physical Hatred"	*Factor 2* "Organizational Hatred"	*Factor 3* "Interpersonal Hatred"
Factor 1: "Physical Hatred"	—	—	—
Factor 2: "Organizational Hatred"	0.375**	—	—
Factor 3: "Interpersonal Hatred"	0.158**	0.169**	—
Factor 4: "National Hatred"	0.063	0.054	0.070

Notes: Cell entries are Pearson's *r* bivariate correlation coefficients. **p < 0.01 (two-tailed).

positive relationship with chronic, interpersonal hatred. That is, those who harbored a gut-level disgust toward opposition party members disliked the idea of socializing with them. The chronic, national hatred measure, however, did not perform very well. Though positive, the correlations between that fourth index and the others are much smaller than those between the other indices. Further, all the national hatred correlations are statistically insignificant. These results further indicate that the measure tapping feelings about the opposition party's legitimacy performs poorly as an indicator of partisan hatred.

All four indices exhibit good variability, with observed values across the full four-point range (see Table 3.7). Overall, and as expected, respondents reported less intense feelings of immediate hatred than chronic hatred. Study participants registered a mean physical hatred level of just above the lowest point on the scale, with half of them registering below 1.67 on the four-point scale. In contrast, the students in the study sample averaged just above the middle of each of the chronic hatred scales, and fully half of the college students surveyed recorded chronic hatred levels of all three sorts above a score of 2.5. It thus appears that, at least on the largely typical public university campus examined here, young potential voters expressed repugnance for their perceived partisan opponents.

If these newly developed measures do indeed tap into feelings of partisan resentment, self-identified partisans should score higher on

Table 3.7 Partisan Hatred among College Students

	All	*Democrats*	*Independents*	*Republicans*
Physical hatred				
range	1–4	1–3.5	1–4	1–4
Mean (std. dev.)	1.32 (0.455)	1.31 (0.423)	1.23 (0.500)	1.35 (0.467)
Median	1.17	1.17	1.00	1.17
Organizational hatred				
range	1–4	1–4	1–4	1–4
Mean (std. dev.)	2.51 (0.580)	2.55 (0.595)	2.27 (0.689)	2.52 (0.538)
Median	2.50	2.50	2.25	2.50
Interpersonal hatred				
range	1–4	1–4	1–4	1–4
Mean (std. dev.)	2.56 (0.623)	2.60 (0.563)	2.45 (0.728)	2.55 (0.644)
Median	2.50	2.50	2.50	2.50
National hatred				
range	1–4	1–4	1–4	1–4
Mean (std. dev.)	2.56 (0.560)	2.62 (0.572)	2.38 (0.543)	2.55 (0.547)
Median	2.50	2.50	2.50	2.50

Note: Mean scores for the Independent subsample are significantly different than the partisan mean scores (at $p < 0.05$, two-tailed), except the difference in physical hatred means between Independents and Democrats and the difference in interpersonal hatred means between Independents and Republicans.

each hatred scale than those saying they have no affinity whatsoever for either of the two major parties. Looking at the descriptive statistics by subsample confirmed that the measures perform in the expected manner. The mean hatred levels for the nonpartisan study participants were lower than those for the partisans. Likewise, the median physical and organizational hatred levels were lower for Independents than for Democrats and Republicans. On the whole, then, students professing partisan leanings expressed higher levels of hatred than independent-minded students. Thus, the newly developed hatred measures appear to exhibit an acceptable level of face validity, distinguishing between partisans and nonpartisans as theoretically anticipated.

Partisan Hatred and Major Party Ratings

As an additional test of measurement validity, I correlated partisan hatred scores with the party thermometer ratings others have used as measures of partisan polarization. If the partisan hatred measures did indeed capture, to some degree, respondents' feelings of cross-partisan negative affect, I expected the measures to correlate in sensible ways with respondents' thermometer ratings of the major parties and their most recent presidential officeholders. Specifically, I expected to see positive correlations between feelings of out-party hatred and ratings of the in-party. That is, I thought that Democratic identifiers who expressed more hatred of Republicans would rate their own party and Obama higher (and the opposite would hold for Republican affiliates). Conversely, I believed there would be a negative correlation between stronger feelings of out-party animosity and out-party ratings. That is, I anticipated that self-professed Republican students who expressed higher degrees of partisan hatred would also rate the Democratic Party and Obama lower and that the opposite would be the case for the Democratic identifiers in my sample. Because nonpartisan study participants held no attachment to either party, and the hatred measure captured their dislike of both parties combined, I expected to see little association between their feelings of partisan hatred and ratings of both parties and their chief executives. And, importantly, if the partisan hatred measures and thermometer ratings did indeed capture different but related concepts, the correlation coefficients should not have been large.

The correlational results largely confirmed my expectations (see Table 3.8). Across all partisan groups, the coefficient sizes were small to moderate, suggesting that the measures of partisan hatred and thermometer ratings of the parties and their chief executives tap into different, though related, sentiments. Whereas the results for the partisan subsamples showed many statistically significant relationships, the nonpartisan results were largely null. Only Independents' feelings of national hatred showed a significant negative correlation with ratings of then-president Obama, suggesting that those who felt the two major parties were bad for the nation also tended to rate Obama higher. Though I am unable to investigate the possibility, this finding might reflect the perception that many had of Obama as a fresh face in the White House.

Looking at the partisan subsamples, the results differ somewhat for those on opposite sides of the aisle. Republican identifiers who

Table 3.8 Partisan Hatred and Feelings about Parties

	Physical Hatred			*Organizational Hatred*			*Interpersonal Hatred*			*National Hatred*		
	Dem.	*Ind.*	*Rep.*	*Dem.*	*Ind.*	*Rep.*	*Dem.*	*Ind.*	*Rep.*	*Dem.*	*Ind.*	*Rep.*
Republican Party rating	−0.168** (306)	−0.210 (49)	−0.086^ (411)	−0.433** (305)	−0.142 (49)	0.170** (417)	−0.160** (304)	−0.050 (45)	0.198** (413)	0.352** (305)	−0.273 (49)	0.166** (417)
Democratic Party rating	0.064 (306)	−0.052 (45)	−0.189** (410)	0.074 (305)	−0.097 (49)	−0.294** (416)	0.068 (304)	−0.052 (45)	−0.365** (412)	−0.071 (305)	0.867 (51)	−0.311** (416)
George W. Bush rating	−0.090 (306)	0.187 (62)	0.120* (412)	−0.329** (306)	0.035 (62)	0.197** (418)	−0.082 (304)	−0.013 (58)	0.209** (414)	0.263** (305)	0.075 (62)	0.140** (418)
Barack Obama rating	−0.003 (307)	0.208 (65)	−0.138** (401)	0.099 (306)	−0.057 (65)	−0.391** (407)	0.115* (305)	−0.074 (61)	−0.333** (403)	−0.132* (306)	−0.329** (64)	−0.353** (407)

Notes: Cell entries are Pearson *r* bivariate correlations and number of cases (in parentheses). $^{**}p < 0.01$; $^{*}p < 0.05$; ^$p < 0.10$ (all two-tailed tests).

expressed more hatred (of all sorts) for the Democrats and their party tended to rate their own party and ex-president Bush higher and expressed cooler feelings toward then-president Obama and his party. The results for the Democratic study participants, however, showed a far less consistent pattern. Feelings of physical, organizational, and interpersonal hatred exhibited the expected negative relationship with ratings of the Republican Party, as did ratings of ex-president Bush and organizational hatred for his party. And those who expressed dislike of the Republican Party organization also showed warmer feelings toward then-president Obama. At the same time, however, other relationships between Democratic students' expressed levels of physical, organizational, and interpersonal hatred fail to show significant relationships with their own party and officeholder ratings. This finding suggests that, as others have reported, out-party derogation might be a more motivating attitude than in-party loyalty (see chapter 2).

Perhaps most surprising, feelings that their partisan opponents were bad for the nation show unexpectedly positive correlations, with ratings of both the Republican Party and former president Bush and a negative relationship with ratings of their own presidential officeholder. The performance of the national hatred measure here further suggests that this measure does not operate as well as the other hatred measures. Consequently, in subsequent analyses, I exclude that measure and focus on the connections physical, organizational, and interpersonal hatred might have with other politically relevant factors.[8]

PARTIES AND POLARIZATION AND HATRED, OH MY!

Frightening noises certainly seem to be resonating from the political forest these days. Even within the relatively safe confines of a university campus, potentially divisive partisan emotions appear prevalent. If such negative sentiments have spread broadly among the nation's college students, and my analyses of the 2017 Pew Research Center data in chapters 1 and 2 suggests they do, it could bode ill for the future of political leadership in this nation. But, even if such animus toward political opponents exists across racial, ethnic, gender, and engagement levels, if such negative sentiment does not translate into behavioral patterns, especially ones that might hinder the democratic processes in the nation, they could be argued to stand as little more than interesting blips on the public opinion radar. In chapter 4 I turn to the question of just who expressed the most partisan animosity.

4. Who Hates? Correlates of Partisan Hatred

My analyses in chapter 4 offered a glimpse of the negative partisan sentiments prevalent on a fairly typical university campus. Although the college students I studied certainly were not afraid to express a substantial degree of bitterness toward those they perceived as their partisan opponents, there was also a good degree of variation in such attitudes across the student body. Taking my lead from existing research into the partisan sentiments of the general US population, I investigate the sociodemographic, attitudinal, and contextual correlates of partisan hatred in this chapter.

Looking for theoretical guidance, I first turn to the well-established literature in the fields of political behavior, public opinion, and political participation. Researchers have long established the connection between age, education, income, race/ethnicity, and gender and a range of attitudes and behaviors (e.g., Berelson, Lazarsfeld, and McPhee 1954; Campbell et al. 1960; Rosenstone and Hansen 1993). Because a number of these factors has also been shown to relate to expressions of negative interparty affect, I focus on these tried-and-true demographic correlates of things political in my investigation of possible correlates of partisan hatred.

THE DEMOGRAPHY OF PARTISAN HATRED

Although little direct work has been done with regard to the expression of partisan hatred as I operationalize it here, existing research with regard to similar measures does suggest that we might expect certain sociodemographic groups to exhibit higher levels of out-party animosity than others do. In particular, several researchers have recently documented significant differences in reported feelings of cross-party negativity along racial and gender lines. Examinations of net partisan affect have shown that men tend to exhibit larger differences between in- and out-party ratings than women do. There is also some reason to believe racial minorities might be more likely to express significantly more positive affect toward their own parties (see, e.g., Abramowitz and Saunders 2005; Iyengar, Sood, and Lelkes 2012). Similar effects have been documented when it comes to candidate trait ratings across party lines, with Hetherington, Long, and Rudolph (2016) reporting a connection between such ratings and respondents of different races and sexes. Additionally, some have also shown that older individuals as well as those with higher levels of education tend to express less out-party tolerance (Iyengar, Sood, and Lelkes 2012).

Because I focus on currently enrolled, college-age students in this book, the variability in age and education level is too constrained to allow me to fully analyze the connection between partisan animosity and these characteristics. Still, existing research leads me to believe younger individuals as well as those with at least some college education should express lower levels of negative affect toward their partisan opponents. The youthfulness of the participants here suggests they are more likely to express lower levels of partisan hatred than do individuals who have left their college days well behind them. Though my data do not offer much analytical leverage on this question, the comparisons across age and educational attainment I presented in chapter 2 suggest that, in general, younger adult Republican identifiers with at least some college education tend to report lower levels of out-party negative affect than their elders do. Younger Democratic adults, in contrast, sometimes report higher levels of dislike for the Republican Party than older Democrats do. Thus, I remained agnostic about whether my sample of respondents would report higher, lower, or similar levels of partisan negativity than existing research suggests for older adults.

Turning specifically to the students who answered the survey, more than one-third of those expressed the opinion that the opposition party and its members are bad for the nation as a whole and expressed no desire to socialize with their partisan enemies. About 35 percent of respondents rated three or above on the four-point national partisan hatred index, and slightly more than 41 percent did the same when it came to the (similarly scaled) interpersonal hatred index. These dismal sentiments extended to the party organizations themselves, with more than one-quarter (25.5 percent) of respondents scoring in the upper ranges of the organizational hatred index. If there is any good news in the current data, it is that far fewer respondents reported harboring feelings of physical repulsion or retaliation. Only 1.3 percent of those participating in this study scored three or above on the physical hatred index. Overall, these findings paint a picture of a youthful electorate with robust disgust for counterpartisans but not such extreme hatred that a large proportion of them feel driven to physical retaliation.

Fortunately, I can examine differences between the sexes and racial/ethnic groups more directly, and given the truncated age and constancy of education level in my sample, any differences observed along these demographic lines can be viewed as already controlled for these two factors. Turning first to questions of men and women, a number of existing studies has observed that women tend to express less negative partisan affect of different kinds than men. Men tend to show more commitment to their own party (Abramowitz and Saunders 2005), rate their own party higher (Iyengar, Sood, and Lelkes 2012), and report more negative views of presidential trait characteristics (Hetherington and Rudolph 2016). Taking the existing knowledge about the proclivities of men and women when it comes to dealing with opponents of different sorts, I expected women to express lower levels of partisan hatred than men, especially when it came to physical hatred.

I find mixed support for my hypothesis in the results from a series of comparison-of-means test reported in Table 4.1. Women reported lower levels of overall physical and organizational hatred as anticipated, but out-paced men in their interpersonal hatred. The latter difference, however, reached a statistically significant level with regard to only one of index items. Women and men in this study appeared to be about equally willing to socialize with more people from the opposing party, but women were less likely to report a desire to know more opposition party members personally. In contrast, women reported lower levels of thoughts about physical actions toward and reactions to partisan opponents than did men on five of the six physical hatred index items. When it came to the party organizations themselves, the men eclipsed women on only one point: they were significantly more likely to believe that the out-party and its leaders intentionally aspired to harm them and their party.

Because men, in general, tended to affiliate with the Republican Party more than women did, I thought this difference might be

Table 4.1 Partisan Hatred by Sex and Race

	Respondent Sex		*Respondent Race/Ethnicity*		
	Female	*Male*	*White/ Anglo*	*Black/ African American*	*Hispanic/ Latino*
"Organizational Hatred"	2.49	2.55	2.55	2.57	2.37[b, c]
	(0.57)	(0.60)	(0.56)	(0.59)	(0.60)
(1) "The actions of the [opposing party] have offended me and/or members of my party over a long period of time."	2.60	2.59	2.63	2.66	2.44[b, c]
	(0.72)	(0.75)	(0.70)	(0.76)	(0.73)
(2) "Some of the actions of the [opposing party] and [its/their] leaders are a result of a 'bad' internal character."	2.72	2.76	2.76	2.78	2.56[b, (c)]
	(0.73)	(0.74)	(0.71)	(0.76)	(0.75)
(3) "Some of the actions of the [opposing party] and [its/their] leaders are a result of an intentional desire to harm me and members of my party."	2.22	2.36	2.24	2.42	2.18[a, (c)]
	(0.73)	(0.77)	(0.74)	(0.75)	(0.74)
(4) "The thought of the [opposing party] gives rise to negative feelings in me."	2.42	2.51	2.55	2.42	2.28[a, b]
	(0.77)	(0.78)	(0.76)	(0.75)	(0.77)
"Interpersonal Hatred"	2.59	2.52	2.60	2.51	2.48
	(0.62)	(0.64)	(0.63)	(0.61)	(0.60)
(6) "I would be glad to socialize with more members of the [opposition] Party."^	2.63	2.61	2.63	2.58	2.58
	(0.69)	(0.70)	(0.68)	(0.71)	(0.69)
(7) "I would be glad to know more [members of the opposing party]."^	2.55	2.43	2.57	2.46	2.38[b]
	(0.71)	(0.73)	(0.71)	(0.75)	(0.71)

"Physical Hatred"	1.29 (0.41)	1.40 (1.17)	1.34 (0.46)	1.28 (0.41)	1.25 (0.41)
When you are in the presence of [members of the opposing party], how often do you:					
(9) experience unpleasant physical feelings?	1.43 (0.67)	1.44 (0.63)	1.47 (0.68)	1.40 (0.64)	1.31 (0.54)
(10) have extreme feelings toward [members of the opposing party]?	1.38 (0.61)	1.48 (0.65)	1.44 (0.63)	1.32 (0.57)	1.33 (0.57)
(11) have thoughts of a desire to get rid of or destroy [members of the opposing part] in any kind of manner?	1.14 (0.43)	1.30 (0.59)	1.19 (0.49)	1.14 (0.36)	1.16[c] (0.47)
(12) feel a desire to take action in order to take revenge on [members of the opposing party] and their leaders?	1.17 (0.47)	1.32 (0.64)	1.22 (0.54)	1.21 (0.50)	1.17 (0.48)
(13) imagine a violent action against [members of the opposing party]?	1.10 (0.78)	1.23 (0.54)	1.12 (0.40)	1.14 (0.38)	1.16[(a), b] (0.51)
(14) feel negative and hard feelings toward [members of the opposing party]?	1.50 (0.70)	1.62 (0.77)	1.62 (0.77)	1.46 (0.70)	1.39[(a), b] (0.59)

Notes: Cell entries are mean and standard deviation (in parentheses). ^item reverse coded. Significance reported for two-tailed independent samples comparison-of-means tests. $^{**}p < 0.01$; $^{*}p < 0.05$ (two-tailed); a = white/black subsamples significantly different; b = white/Hispanic subsamples significantly different; c = black/Hispanic subsamples significantly different (double letter indicates $p < 0.01$, single letter indicates $p < 0.05$, letter in parentheses indicates $p < 0.01$).

associated more closely with partisanship than with sex, but the women in my sample were only slightly less likely to report Republican affiliation than were the men. About 56 percent of male participants and nearly 50 percent of women reported a strong, weak, or leaning identification with the GOP. Additionally, and as I report below, the difference between partisans on this item fail to reach statistical significance. Thus, at least with regard to the current sample, men said they felt more threatened by partisan opponents than did women. It is, of course, possible that this sentiment might have been attached to particular policy stances or recent election rhetoric, both of which, unfortunately, I am unable to explore with the available data.

Turning to questions of race and ethnicity, only the organizational hatred index shows significant differences overall, with Hispanic participants reporting significantly lower levels of organizational dislike than either white or black respondents (who reported similar levels of organizational hatred). This finding suggests that much of the venom spewed about the parties themselves might be related to the age-old division between black and white culture and the threat perceptions generated by that conflict. At the same time, Hispanic respondents in the current study were more likely to say they thought about getting rid of members of or destroying the opposition party than did black respondents and were more likely than white participants to say they imagined violent action against such out-party members. Hispanics were also more likely to report not wanting to know more opposition party members than whites reported. Recalling the electoral context within which this study was conducted might help put this finding in perspective. Conducted in spring 2015, this study took place in the shadow of two presidential election contests that highlighted issues relevant to the Hispanic community in a way that might trigger feelings of in-group threat. More immediately, in the wake of President Obama's November 2012 announcement of a plan to expand his 2012 Deferred Action for Childhood Arrivals (DACA) executive order to include more illegal immigrants, partisan rancor over the issue of immigration once more arose. The tendency of Hispanic study participants to admit having thoughts of physical retaliation against partisan opponents might be indicative of a feeling of in-group threat and defensive posturing against the out-group.

PUTTING THE PARTISAN IN PARTISAN HATRED

Though it seems almost too obvious to state, the strength and direction of an individual's partisan attachments should show a strong association to their feelings about both their own party and that of the opposition. One of the most consistent findings with regard to negative partisan affect and partisan polarization is that stronger partisans were more likely to report negative feelings about the out-party, positive sentiment about the in-party, and larger differences between the two than those for weaker partisans and Independents (see chapter 1). Though some recent studies have also suggested that these effects might not be bilateral (e.g., Iyengar, Sood, and Lelkes 2012), the general consensus has been that those on opposite sides of the partisan aisle tend to harbor similar, though opposing, attitudes and that only the true Independents differ. Thus, I approached my investigation of partisan differences in partisan hatred levels with the expectation that the strongest partisans would be more likely to express hatred of all types than did weak or leaning partisans and that Independents would report less hatred than partisans of any degree would.

My findings offer strong support for my expectations (see Table 4.2). Republican and Democratic alike, study participants who purported stronger attachments to their parties reported significantly higher levels of organizational, interpersonal, and physical hatred. This holds for both the overall index scores and each of the index items. As would be expected, feelings of organizational hatred showed the largest difference. On average, strong partisans scored a little more than 9 percent (or 0.37 points on the four-point scale) higher than weaker partisans did when it came to saying they hated the opposing party itself. Strong partisans and weaker partisans showed weaker differences when it came to feelings of interpersonal and physical hatred. Those feeling the strongest ties to their parties reported interpersonal hatred of opposition party members on average about 6.5 percent (or 0.25 points on the four-point scale) higher than did those with weaker partisan ties. And those same strong party adherents also exhibited about 5.5 percent (or 0.22 points) higher feelings of overall physical hatred than respondents with weaker partisan ties did.

As with previous studies of college and noncollege students alike,

Table 4.2 Partisan Hatred by Partisanship

	Partisan Strength		*Partisanship*		
	Not Strong	*Strong*	*Dem.*	*Ind.*	*Rep.*
"Organizational Hatred"	2.40	2.77**	2.55	2.27	2.52[b, c]
	(0.56)	(0.55)	(0.60)	(0.69)	(0.54)
(1) "The actions of the [opposing party] have offended me and/or members of my party over a long period of time."	2.48	2.87**	2.67	2.24	2.60[b, c]
	(0.71)	(0.70)	(0.74)	(0.90)	(0.66)
(2) "Some of the actions of the [opposing party] and [its/their] leaders are a result of a 'bad' internal character."	2.63	2.96**	2.76	2.55	2.73[b, c]
	(0.73)	(0.68)	(0.76)	(0.78)	(0.71)
(3) "Some of the actions of the [opposing party] and [its/their] leaders are a result of an intentional desire to harm me and members of my party."	2.19	2.46**	2.33	2.14	2.24[(c)]
	(0.72)	(0.76)	(0.78)	(0.83)	(0.70)
(4) "The thought of the [opposing party] gives rise to negative feelings in me."	2.32	2.79**	2.45	2.16	2.51[b, c]
	(0.73)	(0.77)	(0.78)	(0.86)	(0.74)
"Interpersonal Hatred"	2.49	2.74**	2.60	2.45	2.55[(c)]
	(0.59)	(0.66)	(0.56)	(0.73)	(0.64)
(6) "I would be glad to socialize with more members of the [opposition] Party."^	2.56	2.76**	2.72	2.53	2.56[a, c]
	(0.67)	(0.72)	(0.68)	(0.79)	(0.67)
(7) "I would be glad to know more [members of the opposing party]."^	2.42	2.71**	2.49	2.38	2.54
	(0.69)	(0.74)	(0.72)	(0.85)	(0.69)

"Physical Hatred"	1.26	1.48**	1.31	1.23	1.35[b, c]
	(0.42)	(0.51)	(0.42)	(0.50)	(0.47)
When you are in the presence of [members of the opposing party], how often do you:					
(9) experience unpleasant physical feelings?	1.35	1.64**	1.45	1.19	1.46[b]
	(0.60)	(0.60)	(0.68)	(0.49)	(0.66)
(10) have extreme feelings toward [members of the opposing party]?	1.13	1.60**	1.40	1.31	1.43
	(0.59)	(0.69)	(0.64)	(0.60)	(0.63)
(11) have thoughts of a desire to get rid of or destroy [members of the opposing part] in any kind of manner?	1.16	1.28**	1.17	1.18	1.22
	(0.46)	(0.56)	(0.44)	(0.58)	(0.52)
(12) feel a desire to take action in order to take revenge on [members of the opposing party] and their leaders?	1.16	1.37**	1.19	1.20	1.25
	(0.49)	(0.62)	(0.45)	(0.68)	(0.57)
(13) imagine a violent action against [members of the opposing party]?	1.12	1.20*	1.13	1.15	1.15
	(0.42)	(0.48)	(0.37)	(0.59)	(0.46)
(14) feel negative and hard feelings toward [members of the opposing party]?	1.43	1.79**	1.53	1.37	1.58[b, (c)]
	(0.64)	(0.85)	(0.70)	(0.69)	(0.74)

Notes: Cell entries are mean and standard deviation (in parentheses). ^item reverse coded. Significance reported for two-tailed independent samples comparison-of-means tests. $^{**}p < 0.01$; $^{*}p < 0.05$ (two-tailed); a = Democrat/Republican subsamples significantly different; b = Independent/Republican subsamples significantly different; c = Independent/Democrat subsamples significantly different (double letter indicates $p < 0.01$, single letter indicates $p < 0.05$, letter in parentheses indicates $p < 0.01$).

I find that my sample of self-reported leaning, weakly, or strongly partisan college students expressed more highly negative sentiments about their partisan opponents than their purely independent counterparts did about the two major parties and their members. Turning to the righthand side of Table 4.2, the findings reveal a larger difference vis-à-vis organizational hatred than interpersonal or physical hatred. Participants expressing no partisan attachments whatsoever reported hating the Democratic and Republican Party organizations and their leaders about 7 percent (0.25 points) less than did those with an affinity for the Democratic Party and about 6.25 percent (0.28 points) less than did those expressing an attraction to the Republican Party. Those same nonpartisans reported about 2.5–3.75 percent less interpersonal hatred and 2–3 percent less physical hatred than did Democrats and Republicans, respectively. Altogether then, my sample of college students displayed negative partisan affect in much the same pattern as other previously studied samples of different sorts.

PARTISAN HATRED ACROSS THE IDEOLOGICAL DIVIDE

Hand in hand with partisanship, ideological differences often portend political acrimony. Some have shown that ideological differences accompany negative affect toward the opposing party, and partisan sorting along ideological lines over the past four decades has exacerbated this association (see chapter 1). As the party ranks became more ideologically homogenous, the tendency of those holding more liberal views to hurl insults at Republicans and those holding conservative views to cast aspersions on Democrats increased (see chapter 2). And with few moderate officeholders remaining, conciliatory relationships between those in opposing partisan camps dwindled. Both political elites and rank-and-file partisans increasingly found little common ground on which to engage their political foes. Policy debates increasingly pitted one side of the partisan/ideological spectrum against the other. Winner-take-all contests became the norm, and the rhetoric surrounding these decisions took on more personal and heated tones. It is little surprise, then, that empirical research has revealed a tendency for policy stances and negative partisan affect to correlate (see, e.g., Hetherington and Rudolph 2016; Kimball, Summary, and Vorst 2013). My sample of college students grew up with the echo of such divisive and acrimonious political fights in their ears. I thus expected that those professing either liberal or conservative ideological leanings would be more likely to express out-party hatred and that those with the strongest ideological commitments would be the most likely to do so.

Comparisons of participants who reported the strongest ideological outlooks (those who indicated they were strong liberals or conservatives) with less staunch ideologues (those claiming to be moderately or slightly liberal/conservative or moderate) confirm my expectations (see Table 4.3). On each of the three partisan hatred measures, and on each of the items making up these indices, strong ideologues expressed more bitterness toward the opposing party. Given the ideological consistency of the contemporary parties, it is little surprise that the largest differences emerge for the organizational hatred measure. Strong ideologues scored more than 14 percent (0.57 points on the four-point scale) higher than did those with weaker ideological commitments on the organizational hatred index. Feelings of interpersonal physical hatred show less difference across the two groups of respondents. Participants professing the strongest ideological commitments rate about 8.5 percent higher on the physical hatred scale and about 7.5 percent higher on the interpersonal hatred scale (0.34 and 0.30 points, respectively). Taken together, these results suggest that stronger ideological beliefs and out-party hatred tend to coalesce. This finding might help explain the connection between policy stances and negative partisan affect that others have reported (see, e.g., Asch 1951; Berelson, Lazarsfeld, and McPhee 1954; Sherif 1966; Turner 1991).

Asking ideologues who is most to blame for the virulence that pervades the political world is like asking two children who broke the living room lamp. Each passionately argues that the other is solely to blame. For their part, moderates, like the inquiring parent, typically assume they both bear some responsibility. The results regarding partisan hatred across the ideological spectrum, summarized on the right side of Table 4.3, reveal that those admitting an ideological outlook,

Table 4.3 Partisan Hatred by Ideological Orientation

	Ideological Strength		*Ideology*		
	Not Strong	*Strong*	*Lib.*	*Mod.*	*Cons.*
"Organizational Hatred"	2.47	3.04**	2.55	2.35	2.57[b, c]
	(0.55)	(0.72)	(0.56)	(0.63)	(0.56)
(1) "The actions of the [opposing party] have offended me and/or members of my party over a long period of time."	2.54	3.25**	2.64	2.38	2.67[b, c]
	(0.70)	(0.77)	(0.71)	(0.77)	(0.70)
(2) "Some of the actions of the [opposing party] and [its/their] leaders are a result of a 'bad' internal character."	2.70	3.12**	2.74	2.59	2.80[b, c]
	(0.72)	(0.83)	(0.72)	(0.77)	(0.72)
(3) "Some of the actions of the [opposing party] and [its/their] leaders are a result of an intentional desire to harm me and members of my party."	2.23	2.66**	2.34	2.21	2.23[a, c]
	(0.72)	(0.91)	(0.74)	(0.75)	(0.75)
(4) "The thought of the [opposing party] gives rise to negative feelings in me."	2.40	3.05**	2.44	2.21	2.59[a, b, c]
	(0.74)	(0.92)	(0.78)	(0.75)	(0.75)
"Interpersonal Hatred"	2.54	2.84**	2.58	2.41	2.63[b, c]
	(0.59)	(0.90)	(0.58)	(0.64)	(0.64)
(6) "I would be glad to socialize with more members of the [opposition] Party."^	2.60	2.92**	2.67	2.49	2.65[b, c]
	(0.65)	(1.00)	(0.68)	(0.72)	(0.68)
(7) "I would be glad to know more [members of the opposing party]."^	2.48	2.75**	2.49	2.34	2.61[a, b, c]
	(0.69)	(0.98)	(0.72)	(0.71)	(0.70)

"Physical Hatred"	1.30 (0.41)	1.64** (0.730)	1.36 (0.48)	1.22 (0.38)	1.35[b, c] (0.46)
When you are in the presence of [members of the opposing party], how often do you:					
(9) experience unpleasant physical feelings?	1.40 (0.62)	1.80** (0.91)	1.46 (0.70)	1.27 (0.51)	1.50[b, c] (0.68)
(10) have extreme feelings toward [members of the opposing party]?	1.38 (0.59)	1.79** (0.88)	1.48 (0.68)	1.23 (0.49)	1.45[b, c] (0.64)
(11) have thoughts of a desire to get rid of or destroy [members of the opposing part] in any kind of manner?	1.17 (0.46)	1.46** (0.79)	1.21 (0.52)	1.17 (0.48)	1.19 (0.48)
(12) feel a desire to take action in order to take revenge on [members of the opposing party] and their leaders?	1.21 (0.51)	1.46** (0.79)	1.25 (0.54)	1.20 (0.54)	1.22 (0.53)
(13) imagine a violent action against [members of the opposing party]?	1.13 (0.41)	1.34** (0.70)	1.16 (0.47)	1.13 (0.43)	1.14 (0.43)
(14) feel negative and hard feelings toward [members of the opposing party]?	1.50 (0.68)	1.98** (1.04)	1.60 (0.73)	1.32 (0.57)	1.61[b, c] (0.78)

Notes: Cell entries are mean and standard deviation (in parentheses). ^item reverse coded. Significance reported for two-tailed independent samples comparison-of-means tests. **$p < 0.01$; *$p < 0.05$ (two-tailed); a = liberal/conservative subsamples significantly different; b = moderate/conservative subsamples significantly different; c = moderate/liberal subsamples significantly different (double letter indicates $p < 0.01$, single letter indicates $p < 0.05$, letter in parentheses indicates $p < 0.01$).

whether slight, moderate, or strong, tended to report higher levels of out-party hatred than did those who said they were completely moderate. The differences between moderates and those to the left or right range from about 3 percent to 5.5 percent, with the largest differences, not surprisingly, arising with regard to organizational hatred. As the two major parties fill with more consistently liberal or conservative rank-and-file members, those holding divergent ideological outlooks become more committed to defending their partisan turf. Moderates, meanwhile, feel more and more alienated from both sides (and the party system more generally) and are consequently less likely to take offense when one side attacks the other.

Although differences between liberals and conservatives were few in my analyses, conservative respondents were significantly more likely to say that the thought of the other party gave rise to negative feelings and they would not be glad to know more out-party members. For their part, liberals were marginally more likely to say that members and leaders of the out-party harbored an intentional desire to harm them and their in-party brethren. Altogether, though, my findings suggest that levels of partisan hatred differ more between stronger and weaker ideologues than between liberals and conservatives. Extremity, it appears, rather than valence of ideological commitment, seems to matter more.

INTEREST AND IRE

Thus far, I have shown that ideologically moderate and nonpartisan college students tend to assert less partisan enmity than do their ideological or partisan peers. In part, I have argued that this is a result of the fact that those in the middle feel somewhat alienated by both parties and thus do not feel loyalty to one party or threat from the other. Instead, they simply feel that the interparty feuds hold no interest for them. This fits well with the tendency many have reported for those moderates and, especially, partisan independents to show less of an interest in politics (see, e.g., Huckfeldt, Johnson, and Sprague 2004; Zaller and Feldman 1992). Consequently, when it came to my college student sample, I suspected that those who expressed more interest in politics would also divulge more partisan hatred.

Study participants were asked how interested they were in information about "what's going on in government and politics" and requested to respond on a five-point scale ranging from "(1) not at all interested" to "(5) extremely interested." Confirming the well-established tendency of younger people to pay less attention to news about current events, almost 38 percent of the students indicated they were not at all or only slightly interested. The modal response, garnering nearly 45 percent of the responses, was to report being moderately interested. Meanwhile, slightly less than 18 percent reported being very or extremely interested (see chapter 3, Figure 3.1).

As I expected, those who reported more interest were also more likely to have reported higher levels of partisan hatred. The analyses summarized in Table 4.4 reveal a monotonic increase in reported hatred levels across levels of expressed interest. Once again, organizational hatred showed the strongest relationship with interest level. Those who said they were not at all interested in politics rated about 13 percent (0.67 points) higher on their hatred of party organizations than did those who said they were extremely interested in such things. This degree of difference is the largest observed so far. In fact, it is about 50 percent larger than that observed between strong partisans and weaker partisans earlier in this chapter. This finding fits well with research showing that partisan cues can act to drive down support for policies that help an out-group (e.g., Pearson-Merkowitz, Filindra, and Dyck 2016).

The other types of partisan hatred exhibit different relationships with political interest, with physical hatred showing a stronger connection than animosity of the interpersonal sort. Those who showed the most interest in politics scored about 6 percent (0.31 points) higher when it came to being physically repulsed by partisan opponents. If there is any good news in these findings, it is that the three index items that show significant connections to political interest involve expressions of unpleasant, extreme, and negative and hard feelings about the out-party. Being more interested in political goings-on does not, however seem to relate as strongly to thoughts about getting rid of

Table 4.4 Partisan Hatred by Level of Political Interest

	Not at All Interested	*Slightly Interested*	*Moderately Interested*	*Very Interested*	*Extremely Interested*
"Organizational Hatred"	2.32	2.40	2.54	2.60	2.99**
	(0.64)	(0.57)	(0.54)	(0.60)	(0.58)
(1) "The actions of the [opposing party] have offended me and/or members of my party over a long period of time."	2.34	2.46	2.63	2.72	3.12**
	(0.77)	(0.72)	(0.67)	(0.77)	(0.74)
(2) "Some of the actions of the [opposing party] and [its/their] leaders are a result of a 'bad' internal character."	2.52	2.61	2.76	2.85	3.18**
	(0.76)	(0.73)	(0.69)	(0.78)	(0.77)
(3) "Some of the actions of the [opposing party] and [its/their] leaders are a result of an intentional desire to harm me and members of my party."	2.15	2.22	2.27	2.32	2.55*
	(0.81)	(0.72)	(0.71)	(0.80)	(0.91)
(4) "The thought of the [opposing party] gives rise to negative feelings in me."	2.26	2.32	2.50	2.51	3.09**
	(0.83)	(0.72)	(0.74)	(0.81)	(0.84)
"Interpersonal Hatred"	2.44	2.58	2.57	2.57	2.59
	(0.75)	(0.58)	(0.58)	(0.70)	(0.81)
(6) "I would be glad to socialize with more members of the [opposition] Party."^	2.44	2.63	2.64	2.65	2.64
	(0.79)	(0.64)	(0.66)	(0.77)	(0.86)
(7) "I would be glad to know more [members of the opposing party]."^	2.47	2.52	2.51	2.50	2.55
	(.88)	(0.69)	(0.67)	(0.75)	(0.91)

"Physical Hatred"	1.37 (0.56)	1.25 (0.39)	1.32 (0.43)	1.37 (0.42)	1.68* (0.76)
"When you are in the presence of [members of the opposing party], how often do you:					
(9) experience unpleasant physical feelings?	1.41 (0.67)	1.37 (0.60)	1.43 (0.66)	1.46 (0.65)	1.79* (0.93)
(10) have extreme feelings toward [members of the opposing party]?	1.46 (0.70)	1.30 (0.54)	1.44 (0.63)	1.40 (0.56)	1.82* (0.98)
(11) have thoughts of a desire to get rid of or destroy [members of the opposing part] in any kind of manner?	1.36 (0.71)	1.14 (0.42)	1.78 (0.47)	1.16 (0.37)	1.49 (0.87)
(12) feel a desire to take action in order to take revenge on [members of the opposing party] and their leaders?	1.36 (0.73)	1.15 (0.43)	1.20 (0.48)	1.31 (0.60)	1.52 (0.91)
(13) imagine a violent action against [members of the opposing party]?	1.28 (0.66)	1.11 (0.35)	1.12 (0.38)	1.16 (0.47)	1.36 (0.82)
(14) feel negative and hard feelings toward [members of the opposing party]?	1.36 (0.66)	1.41 (0.63)	1.55 (0.72)	1.71 (0.81)	2.12** (0.89)

Notes: Cell entries are mean and standard deviation (in parentheses). ^item reverse coded. Significance reported for two-tailed independent samples comparison-of-means tests between those "not at all interested" and those "extremely interested). $^{**}p < 0.01$; $^{*}p < 0.05$ (two-tailed).

or destroying political enemies or imagining violent action against them.

The relationship between political interest and interpersonal hatred took a somewhat different character than the other forms of hatred. Whereas the reported levels of both organizational and physical hatred show large differences for those at the end points of the interest scale, levels of interpersonal hatred show the largest difference between those who reported being completely uninterested and those showing any level of interest. The group of students who said they were not at all interested in politics showed an interpersonal hatred level only 3 percent (0.14) lower than that of those expressing more interest. Though somewhat disconcerting for those tasked with the job of getting young people more engaged in the political process, the results suggest that even a slight interest in politics is associated with about the same amount of interpersonal dislike of partisan opponents as a moderate or extreme interest.

Because interested students, like other potential voters generally, rely heavily on the media for information about political goings-on, it makes sense that political curiosity and partisan antagonism might move in tandem. These findings point to an important contextual factor that likely plays a role in shaping feelings of partisan resentment. Much of the electoral vitriol being flung in modern US politics comes to the electorate through a variety of media outlets, and the media have frequently been accused of creating, or at least egging on, venomous partisan rhetoric. I next address the media consumption habits of the college students in my sample.

MEDIA AND MALEVOLENCE

The media entanglement with politics has a long history in the United States. From the partisan presses of the founding era to Franklin D. Roosevelt's Fireside Chats to today's twenty-four-hour news cycle, media outlets of different sorts have connected the people to politics. The fourth estate has long been recognized as having a major influence on the public's perceptions of a variety of political phenomenon. When it comes to questions of affective polarization, recent research suggests that media not only feed existing cross-partisan disgust but also can occasionally dampen it as well. Cross-partisan differences in policy views and negative emotional reactions to questions about whether the nation is headed in the "right" direction have been shown to relate to media exposure (Kimball, Summary, and Vorst 2013). At the same time, Levendusky (2017) provides some evidence that affective polarization can be reduced when the media prime consumers with cues about a social identity as an American rather than as a partisan. To give some perspective on how such media dynamics might play out among a college population, I asked my study participants to indicate, on a six-point scale, how often they got information about politics from six different types of media—print newspapers, magazines, television, radio, internet news sites, and blogs.

Because I studied college students, I expected, and found, a much lower incidence of print media consumption than either broadcast or internet media (see Table 4.5). More than half (58.2 percent) of respondents reported getting political information from television, and a little more than one-third (34.5 percent) said they used the radio to gather political information almost every week or more frequently.[1] At the same time, less than one in ten (9.8 percent) reported turning to print newspapers, and only about 7 percent claimed to read magazines to get political information with the same frequency. Perhaps reflecting the relative youth of the college students in this sample, nearly two-thirds (64.8 percent) reported using internet news sites, and 36 percent said they used blogs to gather political information just about every week or more often.[2]

As an initial foray into the connection between media habits and partisan sentiment, I examined the bivariate correlations between overall reported media consumption (measured by summing up responses to the six separate media consumption questions) and the different partisan hatred measures. Based on the state of the contemporary media landscape, I hypothesized that, in general, more media consumption would be associated with higher levels of partisan hatred, particularly for the least partisan students, who would be most open to the media's influence. Looking first at the entire sample of participants,

Table 4.5 Media Consumption by Source

	News-paper	*Magazine*	*Television*	*Radio*	*Internet News*	*Blogs*
Never	44.5	46.6	3.7	20.2	6.4	32.2
	(361)	(373)	(30)	(162)	(52)	(263)
Less than once a month	29.7	31.2	13.2	21.3	10.3	17.3
	(241)	(250)	(107)	(171)	(84)	(141)
One to three times a month	15.9	15.2	24.9	23.9	18.6	14.5
	(129)	(122)	(202)	(192)	(152)	(118)
Almost every week	6.2	5.6	28.4	20.6	24.7	15.4
	(50)	(45)	(231)	(165)	(202)	(126)
Three times a week or more	1.8	1.1	15.5	7.7	18.8	9.9
	(15)	(9)	(126)	(62)	(154)	(81)
Every day	1.8	0.2	14.3	6.2	21.3	10.7
	(15)	(2)	(116)	(50)	(174)	(87)

Note: Cell entries are valid percentages and number of cases (in parentheses).

the left-hand column of Table 4.6 reveals that although overall media consumption is positively and significantly related to higher levels of physical and interpersonal hatred, it shows a negative and insignificant relationship with organizational hatred. Honing the analyses by splitting the sample into partisan groups begins to illustrate the varied impact the media might be exerting on feelings of partisan hatred across the electorate. Whereas reported media consumption habits and expressed interpersonal hatred toward partisan opponents show a significantly positive relationship for Democrats, Independents, and Republicans alike, harsh feelings about members of the two major parties appear to be especially connected to media consumption among the Independent students. The correlations between media use and hatred of the major parties are more than five times as large when it comes to physical disgust, and almost four times as large for interpersonal disregard, for the Independent subsample than for Republicans. Similarly, the association between media intake and shunning social interaction with partisan rivals is more than three times as high for nonpartisans than for Democrats.

The results for physical and organizational hatred offer a more mixed message. For both Republicans and Independents, more media consumption is associated with higher levels of physical partisan

Table 4.6 Media Consumption and Partisan Hatred

	All	*Democrats*	*Independents*	*Republicans*	*Strong Partisan*	*Not Strong Partisan*
"Organizational Hatred"	–0.034 (743)	–0.126* (293)	–0.049 (64)	–0.019 (385)	0.057 (531)	0.197** (214)
"Interpersonal Hatred"	0.177** (750)	0.135* (293)	0.441** (67)	0.119 (390)	0.018 (534)	–0.083 (216)
"Physical Hatred"	0.159** (745)	0.069 (293)	0.619** (67)	0.119 (385)	0.136* (527)	0.147** (216)

Notes: Cell entries are Pearson *r* bivariate correlations and number of cases (in parentheses). **$p < 0.01$; *$p < 0.05$ (two-tailed tests).

hatred but not significantly related to organizational hatred. And, in both cases, the correlations again exhibited a larger magnitude among the Independents than among the Republicans in the sample. This finding supports the contention of some who argue that the partisan bickering made so prevalent by the media might be driving the middle of the electorate away from contemporary party politics. In contrast, the media consumption habits of the Democratic subsample showed a significant, but surprisingly negative, relationship with organizational hatred. Though the magnitude of the coefficient is rather low, the finding still suggests that the Democratic students in my sample who reported more media usage expressed lower levels of hate for the Republican Party.

This unexpected finding might have arisen from the media use measurement I employed. Researchers have argued that broadcast and internet media more readily than print media create partisan "echo chambers," within which news consumers may selectively expose themselves to reinforcing, rather than conflicting, partisan messages (see chapter 5). Because I combined media intake across all forms of media, my analyses could have masked variation in the association that print, broadcast, and internet media have with negative partisan affect. To explore this possibility, I created three new media-use measures—one for print media (newspapers and magazines), a second for broadcast media (radio and television), and a third for internet media (news websites and blogs).[3] The correlation results for these new measures

Table 4.7 Media Consumption and Partisan Hatred, by Media Format

	Print Media	*Broadcast Media*	*Internet Media*
"Organizational Hatred"	0.077*	0.130**	0.195**
	(775)	(767)	(787)
"Interpersonal Hatred"	−0.099**	0.006	−0.017
	(768)	(760)	(780)
"Physical Hatred"	0.145**	0.113**	0.136**
	(769)	(762)	(781)

Notes: Cell entries are Pearson *r* bivariate correlations and number of cases (in parentheses).
**$p < 0.01$ (two-tailed tests).

(shown in Table 4.7) somewhat confirm my suspicion, showing positive (and significant) correlations between higher levels of expressed organizational and physical hatred and for those who reported more media use across all three media formats. Print media, however, shows a much weaker bivariate relationship with organizational hatred and a significantly negative relationship with interpersonal hatred (see chapter 5 for further discussion).

The results in the two columns on the far-right side of Table 4.6 also lend some support to my hypothesis that the media consumption habits and partisan sentiments of the weakest partisans would show the closest connection. All three of the coefficients are larger for those with weaker partisan attachments than for the strongest partisans. And the levels of both physical and organizational hatred reported by weaker partisans show a positive relationship with their frequency of media use. For those who held only leaning or weak attachments to a major political party, reading, hearing, and seeing media coverage of politics tended to accompany a contempt of the party organizations themselves and a sense of physical repulsion for members of the major parties. For those who said they were strong partisans, this relationship held only in the case of physical hatred.

Taken as a whole, these preliminary findings with regard to media effects suggest that the media might indeed have had something to do with the level of partisan hostility among my college student sample. The results also suggest that not all forms of media relate to partisan sentiments in the same manner and that the media show a different relationship with partisan rage for some members of the electorate than others. These are concerns for chapter 5, in which I further explore those possibilities and others.

Altogether, my findings thus far suggest that issues of race and ethnicity might play a substantial role in stoking the embers of partisan resentment. Because issues of this sort show no sign of resolution, it is likely that fuel will continue to be added to the fire. It also seems likely that political elites and the media might be fanning the flames. Partisan candidates and officeholders frequently rely on such issues to carve out their electoral support. For their part, the media bring their feuds to the public, often in the most dichotomous and dramatic terms. Although I cannot investigate the possible influences of the candidates and officeholders in this study, I turn to media effects and devote chapter 5 entirely to that task.

5. Media Messages and Partisan Hatred

Whoever controls the media, controls the mind.

—Jim Morrison

Strong social identities can lead to intolerance (and even abuse) of out-groups, and some conditions appear to make intergroup intolerance more likely than others. Brewer (2001, 19) argues that four key conditions, when met, typically lead to intergroup intolerance and violence. The US political context readily meets the first two conditions in that individuals organize themselves into discrete in-group and out-group categories and see their own group more positively than they do opposing groups. Americans readily sort themselves into the Democrat, Republican, or Independent groups, and differences in feeling thermometer ratings for those identifying with different partisan groups suggest that Americans rate their own partisan group higher than they do the opposing party and that Independents rate both parties more negatively (Greene 1999).

The last two conditions—that people judge their in-group as superior to out-groups and that the relationship between competing groups is viewed as inhospitable—are somewhat dependent on the context within which individuals find themselves, and media messages are likely to play an important role in fostering these conditions. Exposure to political discussion encourages individuals to make the sorts of intergroup judgments on which hostility is based. Hearing about politics and the various partisan groups' positions on the issues of the day likely allow individuals to make explicit comparisons between their partisan in-group and the opposing partisan out-group. Studies show, for instance, that individuals exposed to clear messages about the candidate preferences of fellow group members are more likely to provide concrete reasons for liking or disliking different candidates (Huckfeldt, Johnson, and Sprague 2004, 189). Further, the social rewards received from in-group interaction likely reinforce positivity toward their own group and breed negativity toward other groups.

SELECTIVE MEDIA EXPOSURE

Although the idea that the media can be used to manipulate public opinion dates back to Lasswell's (1927) argument that "propaganda is one of the most powerful instrumentalities in the modern world" (220), empirical research suggests a more limited influence. As those in the minimal effects camp argue, "Instead of pushing citizens around, exposure to mass communication merely reinforces preexisting attitudes" (McDonald and Lenz 2009, 394; see also Ansolabehere and Iyengar 1995; Berelson, Lazarsfeld, and McPhee 1954; Finkel 1993; Klapper 1960; Lazarsfeld, Berelson, and Gaudet 1944; Markus 1988; McGuire 1986). Many have argued that this reinforcement effect materializes in part because media consumers seek out media messages based on their preexisting political beliefs and actively "avoid exposure to information which is not congenial" to those beliefs (Hyman and Sheatsley 1947, 417).[1] Those with Republican leanings gravitate toward Republican-friendly media outlets and Democrat-friendly media outlets attract viewers with already existing Democratic sympathies.

Empirical studies investigating the prevalence of such selectivity have offered mixed results. Some find evidence that people do indeed seek out confirming media messages (e.g., Jonas, Schulz-Hardt, and Frey 2005; Klapper 1960), while others argue that very few people engage in such behavior (e.g., Kinder 2003; Zaller 1992). And, importantly, some point out that the nature of the media universe can affect such behavior. "As the number of potential news sources multiplies, consumers must choose among them, and that exercise of choice may lead to less diversity of political exposure" (Mutz and Martin 2001, 111). Compared to traditional print and broadcast media, newer internet-based media offer consumers a much larger market in which to shop for their political news. Consequently, we might expect consumers of online media to be able to more selectively expose themselves to messages that reinforce, rather than contradict, their preexisting beliefs.

Traditional Media

The traditional print and broadcast media outlets on which the public mostly relied in the past presented a challenge to consumers attempting to selectively expose themselves to reinforcing messages. Before the rise of cable television in the 1980s, viewers relied largely on national evening news broadcasts, which, like radio and print outlets, tended to cover similar stories from a common, mainstream perspective (Lau et al. 2016; Prior 2007). Consequently, the traditional media universe, on the whole, tended to present viewers largely unbiased news coverage (D'Alessio 2012; D'Alessio and Allen 2000). Even though some studies showed that journalists tended to self-identify as left-leaning (see, e.g., Weaver et al. 2007), others showed that newspaper publishers tended to lean in the opposite direction (see, e.g., Mitchell 2000) and that reporters' personal partisan beliefs were "clearly secondary to a professional orientation" of neutrality (Patterson and Donsbach 1996, 466). Further, the economic imperative facing news organizations such as the Associated Press, upon which many outlets at the time relied, required the production of news that served a range of ideological perspectives (Chancellor and Mears 1995; Schwartz 2002). Empirical studies have repeatedly found little, if any, bias in aggregate newspaper, newsmagazine, television, and radio news coverage of politics (Bennett and Entman 2000; Domke et al. 1997; Entman 1989; Eveland and Shah 2003; Graber 1980; Iyengar 1991; Iyengar and Kinder 1987; Robinson and Clancey 1985; Robinson and Sheehan 1983; Shah et al. 1999; Waldman and Devitt 1998; Weaver 1972). At the same time, it is important to note that although the overall traditional media universe as well as mainstream outlets might be less biased, particular media outlets have been documented to espouse a clearly ideological or partisan positions (D'Alessio and Allen 2000). Still, on the whole, broadcast and print media outlets tended to present consumers fairly centrist content, which some have argued led to moderate and homogenous attitudes among members of the public (Prior 2007). The relative neutrality of traditional media outlets of the time suggests that consumers of such media, at least those consuming a variety of such media, would have difficulty avoiding contrary viewpoints. As some have pointed out, "in the middle of the twentieth century, selectively exposing oneself to just one side of every issue was difficult because the mainstream media attempted to provide balanced, contrapuntal news" (Valentino et al. 2009, 594).

The Online Media Universe

The rise of cable television and internet-based media sources, however, made "passive exposure [to contradictory viewpoints] more difficult, and selective information seeking easier" (Valentino et al. 2009, 591). Whereas the traditional media market presented consumers coverage of a variety of viewpoints, cable and online offerings come from smaller outlets with greater specialization (Chan and Stone 2013; Stroud 2011). Thus, cable and online media allow "consumers to fit their news exposure to their own political preferences" (Bennett and Iyengar 2008; Dilliplane 2011; Jerit and Barabas 2012; Mutz and Mondak 2006; Nie et al. 2010, 429; Stroud 2008, 2010; Warner 2010) in a way traditional media did not (Gentzkow and Shapiro 2011; Mullainathan and Shleifer 2005).[2]

The ease with which online media allow selective media exposure has many concerned that internet media use will "usher in an era of information isolation, of islands of opinion, permanently separated by the motivation to avoid other points of view" (Valentino et al. 2009, 607; see also Bimber and Davis 2003; Negroponte 1995; Selnow 1998; Sunstein 2001, 2007). In fact, Chan and Suen (2008) show that a proliferation of media sources can lead voters to more selectively consume news congruent with their existing political stances, and others have shown that the likelihood of encountering dissimilar viewpoints is lower among consumers of internet-based news than among those consuming traditional print and broadcast news (Gentzkow and Shapiro 2011; Mutz and Martin 2001). Online, it seems, people can isolate themselves in "bubbles of ideological consistency" (Warner 2010, 432; see also Gergen 2003, 2008) that reinforce rather than challenge their existing beliefs (Bimber and Davis 2003; Campbell and Kwak 2010; Tewksbury 2006; Warner 2010).

SELECTIVE EXPOSURE AND PARTISAN ATTITUDES

Concern about the isolating capacity of online media has led some to argue that its use will "breed extremism and even hatred and violence" (Sunstein 2007, 44). Exposure to homogenous messages allows individuals to remain "insulated from the influence of contrasting viewpoints, which may elicit a higher degree of group conformity" (Campus, Pasquino, and Vaccari 2008, 432). Such repeated reinforcement of preexisting viewpoints can lead to attitude extremity and polarization (Rhodes 2012). Research shows that those exposed to congruent messages (rather than contradictory ones) tend to express more extreme attitudes (Abelson 1995; Binder et al. 2009; Moscovici and Zavalloni 1969; Warner 2010), and attitude polarization increases when messages become more homogenous (Huckfeldt, Johnson, and Sprague 2004, 196; see also Sunstein 2009). Additionally, recent evidence suggests that in an ideologically diverse media environment that easily allows selective exposure, partisans tend to seek information that reinforces their standing opinions, especially when political elites provided polarizing messages (Lau et al. 2016). In essence, individuals exposed to likeminded messages lack an appreciation for those holding contrasting political positions (Sunstein 2001). So it appears that those who get their political news on the internet might be particularly exposed to reinforcing and homogenous messages, which are, in turn, likely to lead to higher levels of dislike for the opposing party.

Conversely, "higher levels of tolerance can be caused by greater levels of exposure to different people and divergent viewpoints" (Rhodes 2012, 164; see also Borhek 1965). Exposure to contradictory points of view has been shown to be important in establishing the perception of a legitimate opposition (Benhabib 1996) and tolerance of oppositional political positions (Mutz and Mondak 2006). This effect has been largely attributed to the greater awareness of the rationale behind opposing viewpoints that comes from more conflict-filled interactions (Mutz 2002; Mutz and Mondak 2006; Price, Cappella, and Nir 2002). When exposed to contradictory arguments, individuals are often forced to reevaluate their own viewpoint, and moderation results (Knight and Johnson 1994; Scheufele, et al. 2004). In fact, some have argued that such contemplation results in increased cognitive activity (Levine and Russo 1995), drives individuals to seek out more information (Scheufele et al. 2004), and "[enhances] political knowledge and understanding" (Scheufele et al. 2004, 321; see also McPhee, Smith, and Ferguson 1963). Thus, I expected that consumers of traditional media, which likely present viewers more diverse viewpoints, would be more likely to express tolerance of their partisan opponents.

MEDIA HABITS OF COLLEGE STUDENTS

Because some media formats are much more amenable to selective exposure than others, I wanted to include a number of different media sources in my study. Thus, I asked my study participants to rate how often they got information about politics from six different media sources—print newspapers, magazines, television, radio, news websites, and blogs—on a six-point scale ranging from never to every day, with higher values indicating more frequent use. I expected participants' use of similar types of media to be highly correlated. That is, I expected respondents who said they read print newspapers frequently to report more regular print magazine use as well. Similarly, I thought those consuming one type of broadcast media (television or radio) would also be likely to report higher reliance on the other, and those who turned to one internet source to also rely more heavily on the other. Bivariate correlations confirmed this expectation, with use of the two print media sources showing a strong association, as did consumption of the two broadcast media sources and the two internet media sources. At the same time, however, respondents' reported television news consumption and internet news use correlated highly as well.[3] The latter might reflect the tendency of younger generations to rely much more heavily on cable news than that of the major networks (see, e.g., Pew Research Center 2004; Shearer 2018). In fact, almost any profile of today's college students includes a discussion of their tendency to shun the forms of media upon which previous generations relied for news of the day concerning politics and government. Researchers have cited rates of print media consumption among younger cohorts that lag the most senior segments of the electorate by as much as 43 percent (Mitchell et al. 2016; Pew Research Center 2004; Wattenberg 2015).

The college students in my sample differ little from those of previous studies (see Table 5.1). The frequency with which study participants consulted print media sources lagged well behind their reported consumption of broadcast and internet media, especially television broadcasts and blogs. Study respondents showed the heaviest reliance on internet news and rarely flipped the pages of newspapers or magazines. About 40 percent of study participants reported going to the internet for news at least three days a week, but less than 4 percent said they read a newspaper (and less than 2 percent said they read magazines) that often (see Table 5.1). In fact, nearly 45 percent reported that they never looked at newspapers to keep up with political goings on, even though a campus readership program provided them ready daily access to the local town paper, the most proximate urban media market's major newspaper, and *USA Today* as well as the student newspaper, which also contained political updates, all of which were also incorporated into classes across campus.

Students reported a much higher reliance on broadcast media outlets, especially, and unsurprisingly, television. Nearly 60 percent said they turned to television for news about political happenings at least weekly, though, as some have observed, they were less likely to tune in to the national nightly news from the major networks in favor of cable news or entertainment programs (e.g., Pew Research Center 2004) for such information than older people do. Although study respondents reported far less reliance on radio as a news source, they still said they listened to radio programming much more frequently than they read newspapers. Echoing a recent Pew Research report, almost 14 percent of my sample respondents reported listening to the radio for political news several times a week, and a little more than 20 percent said they did so almost every week (Mitchell et al. 2016).

Table 5.1 Frequency of Media Use

	Print Media		*Broadcast Media*		*Internet Media*	
	Newspapers	*Magazines*	*Television*	*Radio*	*Internet News*	*Blogs*
Mean (std. dev.)	1.97	1.84	3.81	2.93	4.03	2.86
	(1.15)	(0.980)	(1.34)	(1.45)	(1.49)	(1.72)
Never	44.5	46.6	3.7	20.2	6.4	32.2
	(361)	(373)	(30)	(162)	(52)	(263)
Less than once a month	29.7	31.2	13.2	21.3	10.3	17.3
	(241)	(250)	(107)	(171)	(84)	(141)
One to three times a month	15.9	15.2	24.9	23.9	18.6	14.5
	(129)	(122)	(202)	(192)	(152)	(118)
Almost every week	6.2	5.6	28.4	20.6	24.7	15.4
	(50)	(45)	(231)	(165)	(202)	(126)
Three times a week or more	1.8	1.1	15.5	7.7	18.8	9.9
	(15)	(9)	(126)	(62)	(154)	(81)
Every day	1.8	0.2	14.3	6.2	21.3	10.7
	(15)	(2)	(116)	(50)	(174)	(87)

Note: Cell entries are valid percentages and number of cases (in parentheses).

By far, however, internet news outlets drew more interest from study participants than did the other media formats studied here. About 40 percent of the students in this study said they turned to internet news sites at least three times a week, including more than 20 percent who claimed to do so every day. In addition, nearly a quarter said they looked to the web for news weekly. And behind the internet and television, blogs captured the attention of almost 21 percent of the respondents, though, at the same time, nearly one-third said they never read blogs for information about political matters. So unlike the other media formats, blog use, arguably the most likely to offer opportunities for opinion isolation, tended to bifurcate the sample.

MEDIA USE ACROSS PARTISANSHIP

Researchers have long argued that political Independents exhibit lower levels of political interest and knowledge than do their partisan counterparts (Berelson, Lazarsfeld, and McPhee 1954; Campbell et al. 1960).

Being less interested in politics generally, self-avowed Independents also tend to report consuming political media at lower rates (e.g., Pew Research Center 2009). The information presented in Table 5.2 offers the first comparison of the media habits of partisans and Independents in my study. Across all three types of media, those disavowing partisan attachment of any sort reported less frequently gathering political news than did the partisan adherents in the sample, though the differences in print media across the partisan spectrum did not rise to traditional levels of statistical significance. Partisan differences also emerged from this analysis. The Republican identifiers in the sample reported more frequent broadcast media use than the Democratic identifiers did. At the same time, study participants on the left showed a tendency to rely more heavily on internet media sources than did those on the right.

Taking a more detailed look at media consumption habits revealed even greater interparty differences. As previous studies have suggested, partisan students in this sample reported consuming more broadcast and internet media messages about politics than Independents did, but a different pattern of reported behavior arose with print media. Although print newspaper and magazine consumption was generally low across the partisan spectrum, self-professed Democratic students reported more frequently reading these news formats than did others in the sample. Interestingly, though, self-claimed Independents said they turn to print media more than their Republican-identifying peers did. Nearly 5 percent of the Democratic students said they read newspapers at least several times a week, and they were joined by nearly 4 percent of the Independents in the study. Meanwhile, about 3 percent of Republican identifiers did the same. The same pattern emerged with regard to magazine readership. However, in both cases the differences across the partisan spectrum were rather small, so not too much should be made of them because the findings with regard to print media serve primarily to emphasize the low level of print media use among this college-aged sample.

When it came to broadcast and internet news sources, however, Independents, as expected, lagged behind their partisan counterparts in news consumption. Whereas about one-third of partisans, Democrat and Republican alike, reported relying on television for news about

Table 5.2 Frequency of Media Use by Party

	Democrats (N=316)	*Independents (N=78)*	*Republicans (N=433)*
Newspaper (mean/std. dev.)	(1.93/1.22)	(1.86/1.11)	(2.01/1.10)
Never	49.0	46.8	40.7
Less than once a month	26.8	33.8	31.2
One to three times a month	13.7	13.0	18.1
Almost every week	5.7	2.6	7.1
Three times a week or more	1.9	1.3	1.9
Every day	2.9	2.6	1.0
Magazine	(1.86/1.04)	(1.65/0.89)	(1.86/0.95)
Never	48.1	52.0	44.5
Less than once a month	28.4	37.3	32.2
One to three times a month	15.5	6.7	16.6
Almost every week	5.8	2.7	6.0
Three times a week or more	1.9	0.0	0.7
Every day	0.3	1.3	0.0
Television	(3.78/1.39)	(3.07/1.47)	(3.98/1.24)
Never	3.2	15.6	1.9
Less than once a month	16.7	18.2	9.7
One to three times a month	25.6	35.1	22.5
Almost every week	24.0	14.3	34.3
Three times a week or more	15.1	6.5	17.5
Every day	15.4	10.4	14.2
Radio	(2.83/1.42)	(2.39/1.44)	(3.10/1.44)
Never	21.0	34.7	17.0
Less than once a month	24.6	26.7	17.9
One to three times a month	23.0	18.7	25.6
Almost every week	18.4	12.0	23.7
Three times a week or more	7.8	1.3	8.9
Every day	5.2	6.7	6.9
Internet News	(4.06/1.51)	(3.65/1.52)	(4.08/1.46)
Never	5.8	10.5	6.1
Less than once a month	11.8	11.8	8.9
One to three times a month	17.3	23.7	18.6
Almost every week	24.3	26.3	24.7
Three times a week or more	17.6	11.8	21.0
Every day	23.3	15.8	20.7
Blogs	(3.10/1.76)	(2.50/1.64)	(2.74/1.68)
Never	27.6	39.5	34.3
Less than once a month	14.7	18.4	18.9
One to three times a month	17.6	17.1	11.7
Almost every week	14.1	13.2	16.8
Three times a week or more	12.5	1.3	9.6
Every day	13.5	10.5	8.6

Notes: Cell entries are valid percentages.

politics, only about 17 percent of Independents did so. Radio news use followed the same pattern, with only 8 percent of Independents tuning their radio dials in to political news updates, compared with 13 percent of Democratic followers and nearly 16 percent of those expressing a loyalty to the GOP. This tendency emerged again when it came to the internet-based forms of media. Whereas slightly more than 40 percent of partisan identifiers reported turning to internet news for political information at least three times a week, less than 30 percent of Independents did the same. When it came to blogs, only about 12 percent of study participants disavowing a partisan allegiance said they visited blogs more than weekly to gather political updates. Though partisans on both sides of the aisle reported similarly frequent consumption of internet, radio, and television news, those on the left showed a slightly stronger tendency to read blogs than their rightwing counterparts did—about 18 percent of Republican and 26 percent of Democratic adherents said they did so.

On the whole, the cross-partisan results confirmed much of what previous studies based on larger samples had to say. Partisans in my sample tended to consume more media than nonpartisans when it came to broadcast and internet media, and all respondents reported low levels of print media use. With added confidence about the representativeness of my sample of college students, I next turn to questions of the ways in which media use and feelings of partisan animosity relate to each other.

MEDIA USE AND PARTISAN HATRED

Although partisans on both sides of the aisle expressed similar levels of broadcast and internet news media consumption, it is important to remember that those on the left and right likely tuned their televisions and radios to different channels and pointed their browsers to different web pages. Data constraints prevent me from examining the particular television and radio networks or programs upon which respondents relied, but a good deal of existing research has shown that partisans of different stripes as well as Independents selectively expose themselves to different media environments. And this contextual variation might help to explain some of the differences in partisan hatred across the electorate. Because broadcast and, especially, internet media outlets more readily lend themselves to selective exposure on the part of users, I expected those reporting higher levels of broadcast and, especially, internet media exposure, to express higher levels of partisan hatred. When it came to print media, I expected little association with partisan hatred or perhaps negative associations such that those reporting more frequent use of print media would express less partisan animosity. I also suspected that any relationship between media use and partisan hatred might vary across the political spectrum, affecting partisans and nonpartisans differently.

The bivariate correlations I present in Table 5.3 offer a first peek at the associations between media use and feelings of partisan bitterness. As the first column of results reveals, when considering all respondents together, increased consumption of all media types shows a positive and statistically significant relationship with visceral feelings of physical hatred. Those who consumed more media of any type were more likely to report feeling more physical revulsion and harboring more thoughts of taking violent actions against their partisan opponents. All three types of media exhibit the same relationship with feelings of organizational hatred as well. Those who said they turned to print media, particularly magazines, broadcast media of both sorts, and internet news or blogs more also reported more hostility toward the party organizations.

The dampening effect I expected print media consumption to have arises only with regard to feelings of interpersonal hatred. Respondents who reported more frequently reading about politics in newspapers were also less likely to say they did not want to socialize with out-party members. Though the same relationship holds for magazine readers, the association rises to only marginal statistical significance. At the same time, broadcast and internet media use fails to show an association with feelings of interpersonal hatred.

As expected, however, the ways in which media use and interparty resentment related varied across partisanship. Among those professing a preference for the Democratic Party, broadcast media as well as print

Table 5.3 Bivariate Correlations between Partisan Hatred and Media Use by Party

	Physical Hatred				*Organizational Hatred*				*Interpersonal Hatred*			
	All	*Dem.*	*Ind.*	*Rep.*	*All*	*Dem.*	*Ind.*	*Rep.*	*All*	*Dem.*	*Ind.*	*Rep.*
Print Media												
Newspapers	0.109**	–0.012	0.438**	0.130**	0.077*	–0.007	0.232*	0.030	–0.101**	–0.182**	–0.125	–0.042
	(769)	(306)	(73)	(401)	(775)	(306)	(73)	(407)	(777)	(305)	(69)	(403)
Magazines	0.132**	0.134*	0.611**	0.044	0.039	0.099 ^	0.299*	0.014	–0.063^	–0.125*	–0.056	–0.028
	(770)	(302)	(71)	(397)	(786)	(302)	(71)	(403)	(769)	(302)	(68)	(399)
Broadcast Media												
Television	0.078*	–0.036	0.394**	0.071	0.130**	–0.027	0.332**	0.119*	0.032	–0.097 ^	–0.062	0.132**
	(783)	(304)	(73)	(406)	(767)	(304)	(73)	(411)	(779)	(303)	(69)	(400)
Radio	0.120**	0.045	0.342**	0.110*	0.100**	0.068	0.277*	0.123*	-0.011	-0.125*	-0.063	0.066
	(772)	(301)	(71)	(400)	(788)	(301)	(71)	(406)	(771)	(301)	(68)	(406)
Internet Media												
Internet News	0.089*	0.037	0.364**	0.062	0.171**	0.179**	0.364**	0.091	0.008	0.022	0.008	–0.008
	(787)	(305)	(72)	(410)	(793)	(305)	(72)	(416)	(785)	(304)	(69)	(411)
Blogs	0.146**	0.151**	0.445**	0.090	0.177**	0.200**	0.445**	0.097*	-0.044	-0.012	0.002	–0.088
	(785)	(304)	(72)	(409)	(791)	(304)	(72)	(415)	(784)	(304)	(69)	(411)

Notes: Cell entries are Pearson's *r* bivariate correlations and number of cases (in parentheses). **$p < 0.01$; *$p < 0.05$; ^$p < 0.10$ (two-tailed).

media consumption is associated with lower levels of interpersonal hatred, but Republican identifiers exhibited the opposite with regard to their television habits. GOP supporters who reported viewing television news more frequently also tended to report higher levels of interpersonal animosity toward Democrats. Finally, Independents' feelings about socializing with partisans showed no relationship to their media use habits at all.

In contrast, nonpartisans' hatred of the party organizations showed positive relationships with all forms of media consumption. Independents who reported more frequently gathering news about politics also tended to offer more negative views of the Democratic and Republican Parties, with online news and blog consumption showing the strongest associations, closely followed by television use. Online media also proved most closely associated with Democratic students' hatred of the GOP, but broadcast media showed the strongest relationships with Republican respondents' loathing of the Democratic Party. Similarly, nonpartisan's feelings of physical revulsion showed associations with all forms of media usage. Independent students who gathered political news from any source, but particularly from blogs and print newspapers, more frequently also expressed higher levels of physical disgust at and/or thoughts of physical retaliation against partisans. Partisans, however, showed fewer associations. Whereas Democratic students' levels of physical hatred of Republicans showed a positive association with blog use, print newspaper and radio consumption did the same for GOP supporters' feelings about Democrats.

Taken together, these results and previous studies suggest that the potential relationships between media use and partisan hatred might be nuanced. Different media sources might relate to feelings of partisan ill will in dissimilar ways, depending on the type of hatred involved. Further, media use might affect some segments of the electorate more than it does others. Those with the weakest preexisting political sentiments should be most open to media influence. Thus, Independents might be affected differently than partisans are. It is possible that feelings of partisan acrimony might actually drive an individual's choice of media. Perhaps those with existing partisan leanings intentionally choose media outlets that serve to reinforce their beliefs.

To better model the many possible dynamics that might be at play between media and partisan hatred, I performed a series of multivariate analyses in which I took the three different types of partisan hatred as dependent variables and the different media sources as independent variables.[4] Because a number of attitudinal and demographic correlates of hatred emerged from the analyses in chapter 4, I controlled for partisan strength, ideological direction and strength, political interest, and respondents' sex and race/ethnicity in all the models that follow. I further performed separate analyses for self-identified Democrats, Republicans, and Independents.

I summarize the results of multivariate models predicting feelings of immediate, physical hatred of partisan opponents for the different media types in Table 5.4.[5] Bringing no preexisting partisan leanings with them, Independent members of the electorate have long been argued to be most susceptible to media influence (see, e.g., Zaller 1992). And both the adjusted R-squared and F-values suggest a better model fit for the self-proclaimed Independents than for those who professed a partisan affiliation. In fact, the R-squared value for the Independent subsample suggests that media consumption, along with the attitudinal and demographic control variables in the model, explained nearly half (an estimated 47.9 percent) of the variance in that subsample's feelings of physical revulsion for partisans and their parties. In comparison, the same model accounted for only a projected 6 percent of Democratic and about 13.6 percent of Republican sentiments of this type. Further, and as expected, standing partisan and ideological commitments played larger explanatory roles for partisans than for nonpartisans.

Turning to the performance of the different types of media, model coefficients suggest that Democratic and Independent study participants who reported frequently reading blogs also expressed higher levels of physical disgust with their partisan opponents. Among the Democratic subsample, blog consumption showed an impact of about the same magnitude as that of partisan strength (standardized betas were 0.172 and 0.193, respectively), suggesting that blog content and partisan attachment played about an equal role in driving up feelings of immediate partisan hatred.[6] The magnitude of effect exerted by media among the Independents proved to be about twice as strong. Blog

Table 5.4 Media Use's Relationship to Physical Partisan Hatred

	Democrats	*Independents*	*Republicans*
Print Media			
Newspapers	–0.021	0.077	0.032
	(0.022)	(0.057)	(0.024)
Magazines	0.037	0.187**	–0.004
	(0.028)	(0.067)	(0.029)
Broadcast Media			
Television	–0.011	0.030	–0.011
	(0.022)	(0.047)	(0.023)
Radio	0.009	0.029	0.025
	(0.020)	(0.041)	(0.019)
Internet Media			
Internet news	–0.022	–0.076^	–0.024
	(0.023)	0.043	0.021
Blogs	0.040	0.108**	0.022
	(0.017)	(0.035)	(0.016)
Strong Partisan	0.203	—	**
	(0.063)		(0.051)
Liberal	0.073	0.020	0.143
	(0.059)	(0.113)	(0.080)
Conservative	0.023	0.159	0.015
	(0.081)	(0.125)	(0.065)
Strong ideologue	0.132	0.208	0.363
	(0.094)	(0.215)	(0.089)
Political interest	–0.028	0.028	0.011
	(0.030)	(0.055)	(0.028)
Male	0.077	0.146	0.160
	(0.053)	(0.095)	(0.049)
Hispanic/Latino	–0.066	–0.086	–0.092
	(0.062)	(0.107)	(0.064)
Black/African American	–0.035	–0.317**	–0.188
	(0.057)	(0.128)	(0.131)
Constant	1.245	0.521**	1.093
	(0.113)	(0.149)	(0.101)
Adjusted R-squared	0.060	0.479	0.136
F (significance)	2.321	5.667	5.284
	(0.005)	(0.000)	(0.000)
Number of cases	289	67	383

Notes: Cell entries are OLS regression coefficients and standard errors (in parentheses).
^p < 0.10; *p < 0.05; **p < 0.01, (two-tailed).

consumption among nonpartisans exhibited a standardized beta of 0.388. In comparison, race, the only other significant variable in the Independent model, showed a standardized beta of 0.266. In fact, the predicted impact of blog consumption on Independent respondents' feelings of immediate hatred was the highest of any variable included in any of the models presented in this table. Comparably, the standardized beta for the frequency of magazine use was nearly as high (0.358).

To better convey the impact of blog use, I predicted levels of physical hatred using the results of these regression models and present a comparison of those estimated values for both Democratic and Independent study participants in Figure 5.1.[7] Notably, the predicted values showed limited variation, ranging from just over 1 (the lowest level on the physical hatred measure) to about 1.6 (on a four-point scale). All the same, the relative amount of predicted increase in feelings of the most immediate form of partisan animosity across the blog consumption scale displayed somewhat impressive substantive importance. Whereas self-identified Independent students who said they never perused blogs registered an estimated 1.06 on the physical hatred scale, their peers who said they did so every day were predicted to express about 14 percent higher levels of negative physical reaction to partisans[8]

In comparison, the calculated substantive impact for self-proclaimed Democratic students was much smaller. Because this group of respondents expressed an attachment to the Democratic Party, they likely brought into this study preexisting sentiments about the Republican Party and its members—as evidenced in chapter 4 by the significantly higher observed level of reported physical hatred among Democratic participants. Likewise, the estimated level of physical hatred held by Democratic students who never turned to blogs is slightly higher than that of Independent students. The opposite holds at every other level on the blog usage scale, however. And across the range of blog consumption the Democratic subsample is only predicted to show about 5 percent higher levels of physical hatred, an amount about one-third that of their Independent counterparts. Still, whether respondents were Democratic supporters or free of partisan attachment altogether, blog reading was associated with increased levels of physical repulsion toward partisan opponents. Although the same cannot be said of

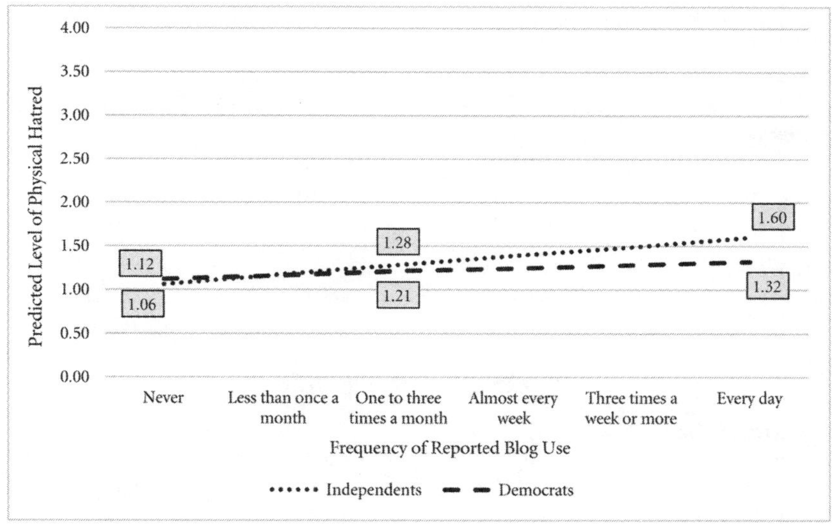

Figure 5.1 Predicted Impact of Blog Use on Feelings of Physical Hatred

Notes: Predicted using OLS regression coefficients reported in Table 5.4. All control variables were held at their modal values, the media measure of interest was manipulated over the range of valid values, and all other media usage measures were held at their means.

those who reported support for the Republican Party, their use of blogs showed a similar association with their expressed feelings about the Democratic Party organization itself (see Table 5.5).

Among those who reported an emotional attachment to the GOP, frequent blog readers expressed, on average, higher levels of organizational hatred. Those saying they never surfed over to politically related blogs expressed a mean organizational hatred of the Democratic Party of about 2.21 (see Figure 5.2). In comparison, those who said pointing their web browsers to political blogs was a daily occurrence showed a slightly higher level of interparty organizational hatred. The difference between every-day Republicans blog readers and those who abstained from such media amounted to about 5 percent on the four-point organizational hatred scale. Although blog use failed to reveal a significant relationship with organizational hatred for Democrats, the web still provided some content that showed a positive association with hatred of the Republican Party. Democratic respondents who said they often went to online news sites to catch up on the political events of the day

Table 5.5 Media Use's Relationship to Organizational Partisan Hatred

	Democrats	*Independents*	*Republicans*
Print Media			
Newspapers	−0.026	−0.013	−0.029
	(0.031)	(0.109)	(0.026)
Magazines	0.028	0.041	−0.004
	(0.039)	(0.129)	(0.031)
Broadcast Media			
Television	−0.069*	−0.043	0.000
	(0.021)	(0.087)	(0.026)
Radio	0.021	0.086	0.016
	(0.028)	(0.076)	(0.020)
Internet Media			
Internet news	0.074*	0.07	−0.037^
	(0.031)	0.081	0.022
Blogs	0.034	0.077	0.041*
	(0.023)	(0.067)	(0.017)
Strong partisan	0.488**	—	**
	(0.087)		(0.055)
Liberal	−0.016	0.101	0.127
	(0.081)	(0.211)	(0.088)
Conservative	−0.113	0.346	0.151*
	(0.111)	(0.236)	(0.072)
Strong ideologue	0.130	0.119	0.492**
	(0.133)	(0.402)	(0.097)
Political interest	0.009	0.117	0.082**
	(0.041)	(0.103)	(0.031)
Male	−0.006	−0.027	0.118*
	(0.073)	(0.179)	(0.053)
Hispanic/Latino	−0.110	−0.168	−0.176*
	(0.085)	(0.201)	(0.068)
Black/African American	0.073	−0.321	−0.347*
	(0.079)	(0.249)	(0.143)
Constant	2.260**	1.447	2.092**
	(0.156)	(0.278)	(0.110)
Adjusted R-squared	0.167	0.144	0.206
F (significance)	5.112	1.839	1.827
	(0.000)	(0.061)	(0.000)
Number of cases	288	66	384

Notes: Cell entries are OLS regression coefficients and standard errors (in parentheses).
^p < 0.10; *p < 0.05; **p < 0.01 (two-tailed).

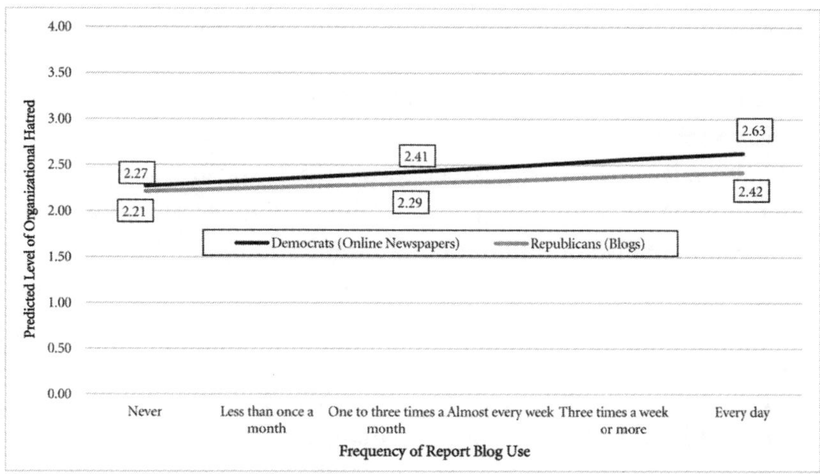

Figure 5.2 Predicted Impact of Media Use on Feelings of Organizational Hatred

Notes: Predicted using OLS regression coefficients reported in Table 5.5. All control variables were held at their modal values, the media measure of interest was manipulated over the range of valid values, and all other media usage measures were held at their means.

reported about 9 percent higher levels of disdain for the GOP than did their copartisans who bypassed them entirely. At the same time, the findings for television use among Democrats contradicted my expectations. As the regression results in Table 5.5 indicate, those Democrats who tuned in to their televisions to catch up on political goings on tended to express slightly lower levels of organizational hatred for the Republican Party. Those who said they fired up their televisions every day were estimated to report about 8 percent lower levels of interorganizational hatred than did those who avoided the talking heads on the tube.

Theoretically, I argued, television use would result in higher levels of interparty animosity as a result of the tendency of partisan individuals to tune in to programming that reinforced their preexisting opinions. It appears, however, that viewing habits among my sample of students did not conform to my theoretical expectation. Perhaps this is because of a lesser reliance on television as a source of news for younger generations (see, e.g., Edgerly et al. 2018). Further, it might be possible that the life stage in which my subjects found themselves was precisely the period long shown to be associated with partisan (and ideological) fluctuations. It might have been that subjects in my sample who came to college proclaiming Democratic allegiances were exposed to television content that influenced their existing opinions about the Republican Party. Because SHSU is located in a rural Texas county consistently about two-thirds Republican in its voting tendencies and in a town populated by an even more strongly Republican electorate, it is possible students encountered television coverage of politics more supportive of the GOP, and perhaps more critical of the Democratic Party, than that to which they had been accustomed. Anecdotally, many of the local retail establishments in this university town regularly tune their televisions to the Fox News channel. So it would not be an unusual experience for students in my sample to encounter television broadcasts of this sort when they had their hair cut or their cars serviced, grabbed a bite to eat or a cup of coffee, or engaged in countless other daily activities.

Reinforcing this argument, the relationship between television viewership and Republican students' feelings of interpersonal hatred of counterpartisans was positive (see Table 5.6). Republican participants who reported more frequently tuning their televisions to political news also said they were about 8.5 percent less happy to know more Democrats and socialize with them than were their copartisans who said they did not fire up the tube to catch up on political happenings at all. Whether students who professed a GOP allegiance intentionally sought out reinforcing television messages or encountered them in their daily forays around town, their preexisting negative sentiments about hanging around with Democrats appear to have been stronger with increased exposure. Further, it is possible that the Republican identifiers in my sample had many opportunities to interact on a personal level with counterpartisans in the glow of the Republican-leaning television broadcasts around town with potential conversations about television news content. In this context, cross-partisan interpersonal exchanges might have exacerbated Republican-affiliated students' aversion to socializing with counterpartisans.

The same cannot be said about frequent print newspaper reading, however. As expected, partisans on both sides of the aisle who said they

Table 5.6 Media Use's Relationship to Interpersonal Partisan Hatred

	Democrats	*Independents*	*Republicans*
Print Media			
Newspapers	−0.081**	−0.040	−0.077*
	(0.030)	(0.117)	(0.033)
Magazines	−0.019	0.054	0.006
	(0.038)	(0.142)	(0.039)
Broadcast Media			
Television	−0.015	−0.044	0.067*
	(0.029)	(0.094)	(0.032)
Radio	−0.030	−0.082	0.018
	(0.027)	(0.084)	(0.025)
Internet Media			
Internet news	0.026	0.178*	−0.04
	(0.030)	0.088	0.028
Blogs	−0.012	−0.078	−0.007
	(0.023)	(0.072)	(0.022)
Strong partisan	0.144^	—	**
	(0.085)		(0.069)
Liberal	0.109	0.038	0.074
	(0.079)	(0.225)	(0.110)
Conservative	0.045	−0.274	0.248**
	(0.109)	(0.277)	(0.090)
Strong ideologue	0.135	0.157	0.363**
	(0.127)	(0.436)	(0.121)
Political interest	0.047	−0.130	−0.018
	(0.040)	(0.112)	(0.038)
Male	−0.164*	−0.631**	0.059
	(0.071)	(0.194)	(0.066)
Hispanic/Latino	−0.065	−0.371^	−0.153^
	(0.083)	(0.219)	(0.086)
Black/African American	−0.135^	0.285	0.087
	(0.077)	(0.275)	(0.178)
Constant	2.739**	2.943**	2.319**
	(0.152)	(0.304)	(0.138)
Adjusted R-squared	0.075	0.133	0.126
F (significance)	2.661	1.733	4.900
	(0.001)	(0.083)	(0.000)
Number of cases	288	63	380

Notes: Cell entries are OLS regression coefficients and standard errors (in parentheses).
^p < 0.10; *p < 0.05; **p < 0.01 (two-tailed).

got newsprint on their fingers every day reported (an average of about 10 percent) less interpersonal hatred of their political opponents (see Figure 5.3). For the Republican study participants, the magnitude of this association was equivalent to the countervailing relationship between television news consumption and interpersonal hatred for that group of students (both coefficients show a standardized beta with an absolute value of 0.133). Though some valid arguments suggest that those who rely on television tend to neglect print newspapers, especially among younger generations (e.g., Wattenberg 2015), newspaper reading and television viewing among my sample students exhibited a significantly positive correlation for the Republican students (Pearson's $r = 0.304$, $p < 0.000$).

When it came to Independents, however, not print newspapers but online news sites showed a relationship with feelings about socializing with partisans. More frequent visits to online news sites showed a strongly positive association with feelings of interpersonal hatred among the Independent students in my sample. Study participants who did not feel at home in either party reported about 22 percent more hatred of Democrats and Republicans on a personal level when they clicked on internet news links daily rather than never doing so. As with Independents' use of blogs and their feelings of physical hatred discussed earlier in this chapter, the magnitude of this effect is the strongest of all the coefficients in Table 5.6 for all partisan groups—even partisan and ideological intensity among partisans.

Taken altogether, the results with regard to the relationships between print, broadcast, and online media use and feelings of partisan hatred presented a nuanced story, particularly with regard to print media. Traditional newspaper reading showed a negative association with feelings of interpersonal hatred for partisans, whereas magazine use was positively related to feelings of immediate, physical hatred among Independents. Television exposure operated in opposite ways for Democrats and Republicans, but radio showed no relationship for partisans and nonpartisans alike. Both types of online media were positively associated with partisan hatred, though internet news site use showed no relationship to Republican students' feelings of partisan hatred of any kind. For their part, though, blogs variously correlated

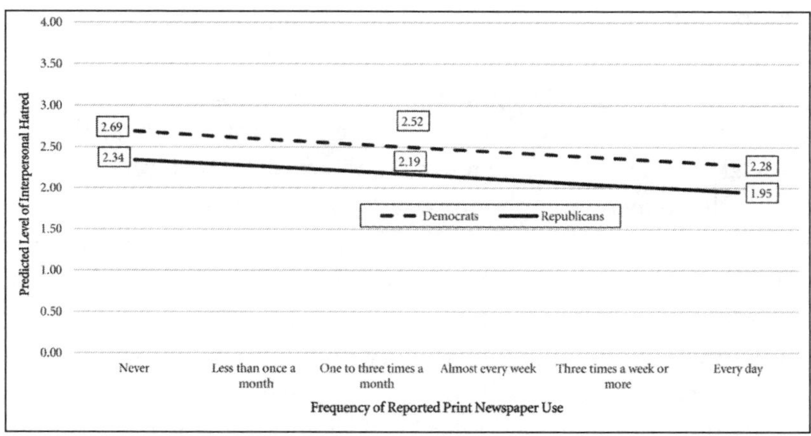

Figure 5.3 Predicted Impact of Media Use on Feelings of Interpersonal Hatred
Notes: Predicted using OLS regression coefficients reported in Table 5.6. All control variables were held at their modal values, the media measure of interest was manipulated over the range of valid values, and all other media usage measures were held at their means.

with feelings of physical and organizational hatred across the partisan spectrum.

The findings thus far have offered some optimistic news. The negative association between traditional newspaper readership and feelings of interpersonal hatred among partisans from both camps suggests that the arguments of many about that media format's ability to alleviate some of the rampant partisan animosity in the nation might have some merit. The concerns of some about the low levels of traditional paper reading among young people might be well placed. Should future research replicate the findings here, boosting newspaper readership among younger members of the electorate might serve to tamp down some of the voluntary social segregation between Democrats and Republicans. Further, the finding that Democratic students in this study who reported more frequent exposure to political news broadcasts expressed less animosity toward the Republican Party itself might reinforce the idea that universities can be a place where the diversity of ideas and opinions can lead previously isolated young people to a more openminded approach to political matters.

At the same time, the findings with regard to internet news site consumption and interpersonal hatred among Independents suggest that reports of the partisan bickering and name-calling found frequently online might be leading young people in the middle to sour on interacting socially with partisans of either stripe. Perhaps the rise of social media use could be related to this finding, with nonpartisans finding themselves caught in the middle of social media wars between partisans. As partisans on both sides post links to and discuss internet news reports disparaging their partisan enemies, young people in the middle become disgusted with both sides. Though beyond the scope of this study, if such an effect were at play, it might account in part for the increasing number of young citizens who shy away from electoral politics altogether and instead seek opportunities for nonpartisan community engagement (see, e.g., Zukin et al. 2006).

Taken together, these findings suggest that the nature of the media environment to which individuals are exposed can affect their partisan attitudes. The online media market, especially blogs, which more easily accommodates selective exposure to reinforcing political messages, tended to be associated with higher levels of partisan hatred. In contrast, exposure to messages seen in traditional print newspapers were related to higher interpersonal tolerance across party lines. At the same time, traditional broadcast television media messages exhibited contrasting effects on partisan hatred. Higher reported television news consumption showed a negative relationship with Democratic students' feelings of hatred toward the Republican Party organization but a positive one with Republican respondents' interpersonal animosities toward Democrats. For those caught between the partisans, increased consumption of online media as well as news from print magazines tended be variously related to higher levels of all types of bitterness toward the two major parties and their supporters.

These findings speak to the important effects the media can have in shaping political attitudes and the ways in which the diversity of media sources can affect political attitudes (Chan and Stone 2013; Nie et al. 2010; Warner 2010). The relatively smaller number of available traditional print media news sources offering consumers more neutral and unbiased coverage of politics can expose consumers to viewpoints that contradict their preexisting partisan attitudes, and this exposure might breed some forms of tolerance for opposing partisans. At the same time, however, it appears that printed news can also tap into more deeply seated hatred on the part of some young voters. In contrast, the numerous, specialized online media sources for political news might provide consumers more messages that reinforce their preexisting partisan stances and elevate their hostility toward the opposing party. For their part, broadcast media tended to occupy the middle ground—showing smaller effects only among partisans and even then, in contrasting ways.

The findings presented here, though, must be taken with a bit of caution. First, it is important to remember that the sample here was comprised of undergraduate students typically in their first or second year of study. Thus, the sample is not likely to be truly representative of the general public. Although media use does appear related to feelings of partisan animosity among the college students in my sample, it is important to keep in mind that the relationships seen here might be different for other segments of the electorate. With a longer history of partisanship as well as media use, older potential voters might exhibit different tendencies. Further, if media consumption does indeed influence feelings of hostility toward members of the out-party, and such attitudinal negativity in turn affects media consumption habits, it is possible that those college students already showing signs of partisan animosity might continue to reinforce such feelings as they mature.

On the whole, though, these results suggest that where college students read and hear about politics might indeed matter, even if negativity toward partisan opponents might be, in part, influencing what college students choose to read and hear. Whatever its source, counterpartisan negativity has been increasingly viewed as going hand in hand with unwillingness to compromise across party lines on Capitol Hill and across the nation. Reluctance to give in to the out-party even to a minor degree might not seem surprising among those with long histories of conflict-filled engagement in the partisan electoral process, but the youngest members of the electorate have not had as many opportunities to personally engage in conflictual policy battles or even follow them as they played out on the larger stage. Consequently, college students might be expected to bring fewer interpartisan battle scars with them when making policy decisions and thus view and treat the opposing party less harshly. At the same time, however, the impact media seem to have on young voters might influence their behavior so that it mimics that of their elders. I turn in chapter 6 to the question of how the college student respondents to my survey viewed and treated their political opponents.

6. The Political Consequences of Partisan Hatred

In any compromise between good and evil, it is only evil that can profit.
—Ayn Rand, *Atlas Shrugged*

With slim partisan majorities in Congress, contemporary policy debates frequently take on tones of intense intergroup battles rather than bipartisan negotiations to arrive at a policy to address the nation's interests. As some have argued, a sort of teamsmanship emerges under conditions of tight interparty competition akin to those we have seen in recent years. Social identity theory predicts that when threatened, in-group members will view out-group members as inferior, seek to distinguish themselves from the out-group, model archetypal in-group behavior, and strongly enforce in-group norms. Thus, closely balanced party representation in Congress would be predicted to result in each party's members assessing the opposite party's members more negatively and seeking to gain in-group credibility by displaying behavior targeted at the out-group that meets with strong in-group approval. Those who expressed opinions or showed behavior that aligned with in-group norms would suffer less in-group shunning. Such conditions represent well the institution that led Senator Evan Bayh to assert, upon his retirement from the chamber, that for some time he "had a growing conviction that Congress [was] not operating as it should. There [was] too much partisanship and not enough progress" (Theriault 2015, 11).

Scholars, too, have noted such tendencies, which they often refer to as political teamsmanship. Some argue, for instance, that polarization trends reflect not only ideologically based policy decisions but "Congress members' increasing efforts to favorably differentiate their own party from the opposition" (Barber and McCarty 2015, 37; see also Lee 2009). When this happens, partisans can become driven by a growing team spirit that is disconnected from policy considerations (Mason 2018, 55). Some contend that such conditions represent well the idea of strategic disagreement (Gilmour 1995; Groseclose and McCarty 2001). As Barber and McCarty (2015) suggest, actors refuse to compromise (even when compromise is feasible or even desirable) in order to transfer blame for a stalemate to the other side and gain electoral advantage. The result, the scholars argue, is to create battles over issues for which little ideological difference exists. Retiring Senator Arlen Specter saw this mind-set as a leading cause in the polarization of the political parties and the resulting gridlock in the policy-making process. As he put it, "Politics is no longer the art of the possible when senators are intransigent in their positions" (Specter 2010).

Unwillingness to compromise in order to come to policy decisions also appears among academic observers' top concerns (e.g., Halperin 2011; Halperin et al. 2011; Maoz and McCauley 2005). In the US setting, some point to the polarization of the mass public as the source of governmental gridlock, which destroys the cooperation needed to find solutions to today's most pressing problems (e.g., Hetherington and Rudolph 2014), and recent studies reveal a polarized electorate that appears less willing to seek an equitable compromise on the important political issues of the day (Pew Research Center 2014).

HOT OR COLD? PARTISAN HATRED AND THERMOMETER RATINGS

Recent research documents growing animosity across party lines, with more and more people offering negative opinions of the opposite party (Doherty 2014). The students in my sample are no different. The distribution of thermometer ratings of the two major parties for study participants holding different partisan allegiances reflects the national trend (see Table 6.1). Democratic identifiers rate the Republican Party substantially lower than those claiming a Republican affiliation, and vice versa. Students in my study showed a tendency to rate their own party about thirty points higher than they rated the opposition. Further, about 10 percent more of the partisan students reported a score of zero for the opposition party than for their own party.

Table 6.1 Party Thermometer Ratings

	Republican Party Ratings			*Democratic Party Ratings*		
	Democrats	*Independents*	*Republicans*	*Democrats*	*Independents*	*Republicans*
Mean (std. dev.)	41.7 (26.9)	36.6 (21.9)	70.3 (20.2)	68.1 (20.4)	40.5 (21.2)	34.7 (23.6)
Percent reporting 0	11.30	17.60	1.70	1.00	11.80	10.40
Percent reporting 50	24.40	49.00	11.80	14.80	49.30	19.60
Percent reporting 100	10.60	0.00	12.30	14.50	0.00	4.50

Notes: Ratings range from 0 to 100. See Appendix for question wording.

Much the same is true of officeholder ratings (see Table 6.2). Democratic students rated ex-president Bush about twenty-eight points lower, on average, than their Republican peers did, and the ratings of then-president Obama were even more striking. GOP supporters rated him about forty-three points lower, on average, than the Democratic students did. Similarly, almost 16 percent more of the Democratic identifiers scored Bush at the lowest possible point than did their Republican counterparts. And Republican identifiers reciprocated—almost 27 percent more of them scored Obama a zero than their Democratic peers did.

At the same time, nonpartisans were much more likely to report middling scores for the parties and their officeholders. About half of those claiming no partisan allegiance scored the parties at the midpoint of the thermometer, and Independents' ratings of both Bush and Obama hovered near the midpoint. On the whole, the students participating in this study reported attitudes about the two major parties and their most recent presidents in much the same way as national samples of the US public have. There appears to have been a good deal of affective partisan polarization among the students taking part in this study.

In this chapter, I turn to the question of whether feelings of partisan animosity might be tied to such cross-partisan coldness. As the bivariate analyses in chapter 3 revealed, feelings of physical, organizational,

Table 6.2 Presidential Thermometer Ratings

	Bush Ratings			*Obama Ratings*		
	Demo-crats	*Indepen dents*	*Repub-licans*	*Demo-crats*	*Indepen dents*	*Repub-licans*
Mean	38.6	43.4	67.0	66.4	52.8	25.4
(std. dev.)	(28.1)	(24.1)	(21.9)	(24.9)	(27.5)	(23.4)
Percent reporting 0	17.40	14.10	1.90	3.50	10.40	30.00
Percent reporting 50	18.60	29.70	16.90	14.40	37.80	16.90
Percent reporting 100	8.00	3.10	12.50	17.00	10.40	0.50

Notes: Ratings range from 0 to 100. See Appendix for question wording.

and interpersonal hatred among those with partisan ties corresponded in expected ways with ratings of the parties and their officeholders, whereas Independents' attitudes proved largely unrelated. Though telling, those results failed to account for other possible correlates of party and presidential ratings. I thus begin my investigation into the possible political consequences of partisan animosities by returning to an examination of the connections between partisan animosity and the thermometer ratings of the major parties and their most recent presidential officeholders in a multivariate setting.[1]

Turning first to ratings of the two major parties, I find that the multivariate results somewhat support my expectation that feelings of partisan hatred would be significantly related to thermometer scores for partisan respondents but not for the nonpartisans in the sample (see Table 6.3). Independent students' feelings of partisan hatred were not significantly related to their ratings of either party. In fact, few of the variables in the nonpartisan models showed a relationship with party ratings, and the model fit statistics for these models were quite poor as well. Taken together, these results suggest that Independent ratings of the two major parties might have their source in factors other than those considered here.

Table 6.3 Partisan Hatred and Party Thermometer Ratings

	Republican Party Thermometer Ratings			*Democratic Party Thermometer Ratings*		
	Demo-crats	*Indepen-dents*	*Repub-licans*	*Demo-crats*	*Indepen-dents*	*Repub-licans*
Physical hatred	−1.502 (3.553)	−9.377 (7.044)	−1.733 (2.321)	−3.354 (2.831)	−9.186 (6.468)	0.821 (2.464)
Organizational hatred	−16.978** (2.643)	0.305 (6.041)	2.872 (2.099)	2.531 (2.106)	−0.423 (5.547)	−3.896^ (2.224)
Interpersonal hatred	−4.326 (2.620)	−2.060 (5.305)	3.553* (1.628)	2.722 (2.088)	−1.001 (4.871)	−8.850** (1.729)
Strong partisan	−5.979 (4.000)	— —	9.650** (2.232)	8.491** (3.188)	— —	−9.003** (2.367)
Liberal	−0.126 (3.511)	6.535 (8.143)	2.102 (3.466)	−4.353 (2.798)	10.283 (7.477)	4.422 (3.672)
Conservative	4.596 (4.832)	0.284 (9.912)	0.677 (2.899)	4.339 (3.851)	2.798 9.101	−3.203 (3.061)
Strong ideologue	−2.847 (6.071)	−22.513^ (12.168)	−0.854 (3.737)	−11.817* (4.838)	−12.566 (11.173)	−6.983^ (3.962)
Political interest	−3.507* (1.686)	2.567 (4.213)	0.798 (1.080)	3.170* (1.343)	4.050 (3.869)	−1.475 (1.145)
Male	5.435^ (3.167)	2.049 (7.155)	−2.613 (2.073)	−1.461 (2.524)	4.074 (6.570)	−6.633** (2.199)
Hispanic/ Latino	1.192 (3.707)	0.661 (8.991)	−3.045 (2.718)	7.735 (2.954)	1.682 (8.256)	3.645 (2.880)
Black/African American	2.149 (3.437)	3.230 (10.084)	−5.363 (5.367)	10.414** (2.739)	9.662 (9.259)	14.679 (5.686)
Constant	105.808** (10.592)	46.988^ (25.048)	51.090 (6.355)	45.647** (8.441)	41.407^ (22.999)	77.311** (6.733)
Adjusted R-squared	0.211	0.003	0.089	0.126	−0.009	0.273
F (signifi-ance)	8.158 (0.000)	1.011 (0.455)	4.550 (0.000)	4.859 (0.000)	0.962 (0.493)	14.561 (0.000)
Number of cases	294	44	400	295	44	399

Notes: Cell entries are OLS regression coefficients and standard errors (in parentheses).
^p < 0.10; *p < 0.05; **p < 0.01 (all two-tailed tests of significance).

Rating the Opposition

When it came to rating the opposition party, Democratic students' feelings of organizational hatred proved to be strongly associated with their ratings of the Republican Party, whereas Republican students' feelings of interpersonal hatred proved to be more strongly related to their ratings of the Democratic Party. In fact, feelings of organizational hatred among Democrats showed a standardized beta coefficient more than three times as strong as that of political interest and about ten times as strong as that of race. The effect of interpersonal hatred in the Republican subsample was stronger than that exerted by partisan strength. Thus, out-party affective ratings did indeed show strong associations with some forms of partisan hatred, though the effects differed across party lines.

To put the magnitude of these estimated effects into some perspective, I calculated the predicted thermometer ratings of the opposition party for partisans holding differing levels of associated partisan hatred. Because the organizational hatred measure was meant to capture sentiments about the opposition party organization itself, it is somewhat unsurprising that, as shown in Figure 6.1, the estimated impact of organizational hatred dwarfed that of the other significant forms of hatred. Democratic identifiers who registered the weakest organizational hatred of the Republican Party were estimated to rate the party above the midpoint of the 100-point thermometer scale (at about 65). In contrast, their copartisans expressing the strongest organizational dislike of the GOP had a predicted Republican Party rating about 51 points lower.

The estimated effects for interpersonal hatred among the Republican adherents were nearly as impressive. Those expressing the strongest opposition to interacting with Democrats in social settings were predicted to rate the Democratic Party almost twenty-seven thermometer points lower. In contrast to the findings for the Democratic subsample, organizational hatred was more weakly associated with opposition party ratings for the Republican segment of study participants ($p < 0.10$). Still, the predicted effect was substantial. Those GOP supporters holding the weakest organizational hatred were estimated to rate

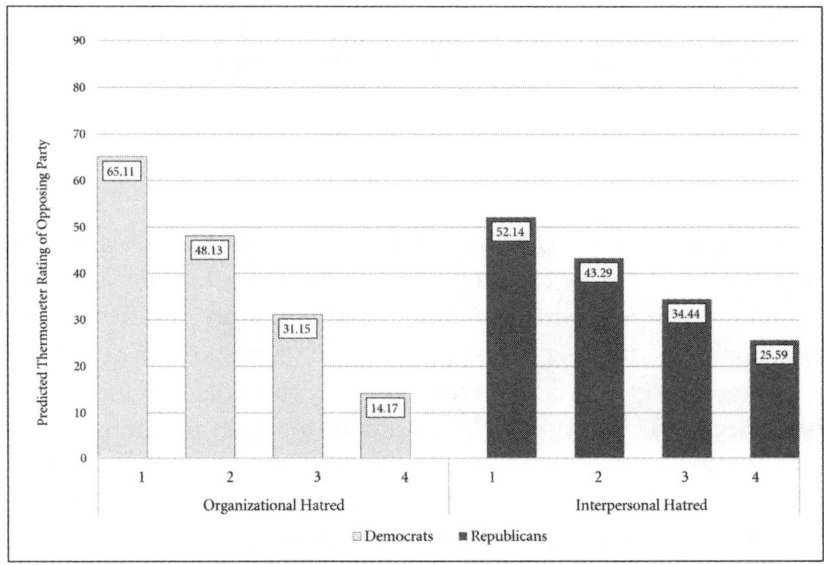

Figure 6.1 Predicted Thermometer Ratings of the Opposing Party

Notes: Predicted probabilities were calculated using ordered logit regression coefficients shown in Table 6.3. All control variables were held at their modal values, the hatred measure of interest was manipulated over the range of valid values, and all other hatred measures were held at their means.

the Democratic Party just below the thermometer midpoint (at about forty-four), but those expressing the strongest organizational dislike were predicted to assign a score about twelve points lower.

Rating the Home Team

When it came to rating the in-party, Democratic participants' feelings of partisan hatred showed no significant association with their ratings of their own party. In contrast, there is some evidence of out-party negativity accompanying in-party loyalty among the Republican subsample. Feelings of interpersonal hatred toward Democrats were related to Republicans' ratings of their own party, and the magnitude of the effect was estimated to be about half as strong as that of partisan strength. Republican identifiers who expressed the strongest repulsion at the thought of interpersonal interactions with Democrats were estimated to assign thermometer ratings about ten points lower than were their copartisans, who were more accepting of socializing with out-party members.

Rating the Deciders in Chief

Presidential officeholder ratings further corroborate the connections between feelings of organizational hatred and negative affect toward the out-party (see Table 6.4). Among both Democratic and Republican study participants, those expressing more organizational hated of the opposition party were likely to rate that party's presidential officeholder more negatively. The effects, the magnitude of which are stronger than partisan strength in both models, are roughly equivalent across parties. Further, interpersonal hatred levels also showed relationships with presidential ratings. As with their out-party ratings, Republican study participants' feelings of interpersonal hatred showed a negative relationship to their ratings of the opposition, this time with regard to Obama. Similarly, in-party presidential ratings showed an association with feelings of interpersonal hatred across partisan lines, though more strongly for Democrats than for Republicans. Partisans who expressed more dislike for the thought of socializing with opposition party members tended to rate their own party's presidential officeholder higher. Again, the magnitude of these effects was among the strongest in the model, typically outperforming that of partisan strength.

To put these relationships in perspective, I once again used the regression coefficients to predict presidential thermometer ratings across levels of the relevant forms of partisan hatred. As shown in Figure 6.2, ex-president Bush's ratings were estimated to be almost thirty-two points lower among Democrats expressing the highest levels of hatred for his party's organization than among Democrats reporting the lowest levels of organizational hatred for the GOP. In contrast, he was predicted to get about a ten-point boost among his party's supporters who held the most interpersonal hatred for their partisan opponents.

In comparison, then-president Obama's ratings were most strongly associated with Republicans' feelings of organizational hatred for his party. Among Republicans, those expressing the highest levels of

Table 6.4 Partisan Hatred and Presidential Thermometer Ratings

	Bush Thermometer Ratings			*Obama Thermometer Ratings*		
	Democrats	*Indepen-dents*	*Republicans*	*Democrats*	*Indepen-dents*	*Republicans*
Physical hatred	2.328	9.561	0.133	–2.506	14.312*	3.720
	(3.663)	(6.302)	(2.447)	(3.385)	(7.123)	(2.336)
Organizational hatred	–10.555**	–2.655	3.142	2.145	–8.582	–11.968**
	(2.754)	(5.363)	(2.209)	(2.545)	(6.533)	(2.143)
Interpersonal hatred	–3.353	2.199	3.362^	7.740**	–3.007	–7.401**
	(2.714)	(4.587)	(1.715)	(2.508)	(5.618)	(1.660)
Strong partisan	–15.789**	—	9.046**	6.474^	—	–8.531**
	(3.656)	—	(2.346)	(3.850)	—	(2.247)
Liberal	–4.393	–8.967	–2.520	2.045	15.251*	13.708**
	(3.656)	(6.872)	(3.640)	(3.379)	(7.391)	(3.541)
Conservative	5.910	12.579	1.834	–0.391	–9.543	4.062
	(5.000)	(8.434)	(3.046)	(4.621)	(9.262)	(2.948)
Strong ideologue	2.716	–15.210	–0.710	–12.979*	11.456	–5.388
	(6.190)	(11.635)	(3.940)	(5.720)	(13.879)	(3.863)
Political interest	0.513	4.587	0.657	–0.499	2.653	0.788
	(1.748)	(3.166)	(1.138)	(1.616)	(3.355)	(1.099)
Male	–1.349	–7.304	–4.391*	5.665^	–2.356	4.505*
	(3.295)	(5.942)	(2.186)	(3.045)	(6.435)	(2.093)
Hispanic/ Latino	–5.571	–23.068**	–8.864**	6.000^	8.747	7.867**
	(3.865)	(7.562)	(2.864)	(3.572)	(8.380)	(2.789)
Black/African American	–13.662**	–13.079(^)	–15.470**	20.686**	35.359	23.823**
	(3.581)	(7.834)	(5.659)	(3.310)	(8.333)	(5.800)
Constant	81.377**	31.609	47.803**	32.191**	45.245(^)	62.080**
	(11.026)	(21.562)	(6.698)	(10.189)	(25.795)	(6.399)
Adjusted R-squared	0.185	0.236	0.144	0.157	0.223	0.330
F (significance)	7.091	2.730	7.123	5.996	2.693	18.429
	(0.000)	(0.010)	(0.000)	(0.000)	(0.010)	(0.000)
Number of cases	296	57	401	296	60	390

Notes: Cell entries are OLS regression coefficients and standard errors (in parentheses). **$p < 0.01$; *$p < 0.05$; ^$p < 0.10$ (all two-tailed tests of significance).

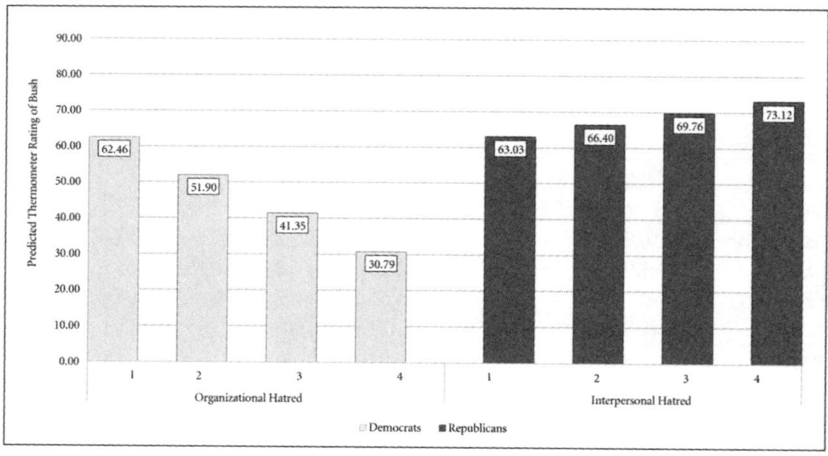

Figure 6.2 Predicted Thermometer Ratings of Bush

Notes: Predicted probabilities were calculated using ordered logit regression coefficients shown in Table 6.4. All control variables were held at their modal values, the hatred measure of interest was manipulated over the range of valid values, and all other hatred measures were held at their means.

hatred for the Democratic Party were estimated to rate Obama almost thirty-six points lower than did their copartisans who expressed the lowest levels of organizational hatred (see Figure 6.3). At the same time, feelings of interpersonal hatred had countervailing predicted effects for Democratic and Republican study participants. Whereas Obama was estimated to get about a twenty-three-point boost with his party supporters who reported the highest level of interpersonal hatred toward Republicans, his ratings were predicted to drop by about the same amount with GOP supporters who reported the most dread at the thought of socializing with Democrats.

Partisan hatred and thermometer ratings again showed little association among the nonpartisan segment of study participants. Only their feelings of physical hatred toward partisans showed a rather weak positive relationship with Obama's ratings. Self-professed Independents who reported the highest levels of physical animosity toward partisans were estimated to rate him about four points higher than their nonpartisan peers holding the lowest level of such hatred did. The magnitude of this effect is swamped by that of race. Black Independents were

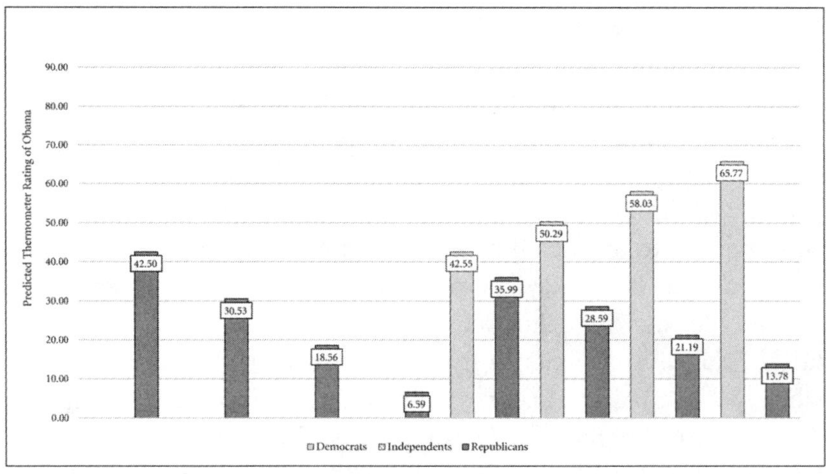

Figure 6.3 Predicted Thermometer Ratings of Obama

Notes: Predicted probabilities were calculated using ordered logit regression coefficients shown in Table 6.4. All control variables were held at their modal values, the hatred measure of interest was manipulated over the range of valid values, and all other hatred measures were held at their means.

estimated to rate Obama about thirty-five points higher than did their nonblack counterparts; not a surprising finding in light of the modern history of African American loyalty to the Democratic Party and the persistent strength of racial identity in the United States.

Taken on the whole, the findings with regard to affective thermometer ratings of both the parties and their presidential officeholders show stronger relationships with expressed levels of partisan hatred for the partisan members of my sample than with those who had no partisan ties whatsoever. As expected, partisans who recorded higher levels of organizational and interpersonal partisan hatred were more likely to rate the opposition party and/or its presidential officeholder lower. There was also some evidence among the partisan subsample in support of social identity arguments connecting feelings of in-group warmth with out-group coldness. Interpersonal hatred was shown to positively relate to evaluations of presidential officeholders for partisans on both sides of the aisle, and among Republicans, so were ratings of their own party.

PARTISAN HATRED AND EXTREMIST ATTITUDES

Although these findings raise concerns about the state of contemporary partisan politics in the United States, some could argue that expressing support for one's own party and dislike of the other simply reflects the state of properly functioning parties. After all, such a commitment to one's own party and contrariness to the other party represents one of the key components espoused by supporters of the responsible party model of democratic representation (American Political Science Association 1950; see also chapter 8). Still, even those who espouse partisan loyalty have expressed concerns that not only do devoted party members hold low opinions of their political opponents but that these negative sentiments have become so severe that they motivate those holding such feelings to target their opponents with extreme statements and actions akin to those taken by an Illinois resident who had posted "strident anti-Republican views on social media and directed particular ire at Trump after he became president" before arming himself and opening fire on twenty-four Republican Congress members practicing for a congressional baseball game in Virginia (Allen and Shapiro 2017).

To explore possible connections between extreme feelings toward the parties and their most visible officeholders, I created a measure of relative attitude extremity by coding all respondents who reported thermometer ratings of the either party or its presidential officeholder in the upper or lower ranges of the ratings proffered. Respondents were assigned a score of zero if their thermometer rating of a party or president was within one standard deviation of the mean rating for that target or one if their scores were more outside that range (in either direction). Thus, about 67 percent of all respondents were coded as "nonextremist," whereas the remainder were considered to have expressed "more extremist" attitudes, either supportive or unsupportive of the party or president. Unsurprisingly, partisans were much more likely to record thermometer ratings in the upper or lower 16 percent of the distribution (see Table 6.5). About 40 percent of both Democratic and Republican identifiers expressed extremely negative opinions about their partisan opponents and their most recent presidential

Table 6.5 Extreme Thermometer Ratings of Officeholders and Parties

	Democrats	*Independents*	*Republicans*
Bush Thermometer			
Percent extreme	39.6	19.2	27.7
Percent missing	1.6	17.9	1.8
Obama Thermometer			
Percent extreme	40.8	26.9	41.6
Percent missing	1.3	14.1	4.4
Republican Party Thermometer			
Percent extreme	37.0	19.2	29.1
Percent missing	1.6	34.6	2.1
Democratic Party Thermometer			
Percent extreme	32.6	14.1	36.7
Percent missing	1.6	34.6	2.3

Notes: Extremity measured dichotomously: 0 = respondent's rating within one standard deviation of the mean thermometer rating; 1 = respondent's rating greater than 1 standard deviation above or below the mean thermometer rating.

officeholder. About an equal proportion reported overly positive scores for their own party and president. In contrast, less than 20 percent of nonpartisan partisans showed such tendencies.

I then repeated the earlier multivariate analyses to test for possible connections between partisan hatred levels and extreme thermometer ratings, controlling for other attitudinal and demographic factors. The resulting model fit statistics and regression coefficients suggest that my models did little to help explain Independent respondents' tendency to express extreme opinions about the parties and their most recent chief executives.[2] In contrast, the findings for partisans showed that higher levels of some forms of partisan hatred were associated with a tendency to report extreme (negative) ratings of the opposition party and its most recent president as well as more extreme (positive) ratings of their own party (see Table 6.6).

Among both Democrats and Republicans, stronger expressions of organizational and interpersonal hatred showed a positive (and significant) relationship with more extremely negative ratings of the opposite party. For both forms of partisan hatred, the predicted probability of a respondent reporting an extreme rating moved from about 10 percent

Table 6.6 Partisan Hatred and Extreme Party Thermometer Ratings

	Republican Party Thermometer Ratings			*Democratic Party Thermometer Ratings*		
	Democrats	*Indepen-dents*	*Republicans*	*Democrats*	*Indepen-dents*	*Republicans*
Physical hatred	−0.398	1.434	0.047	−0.531	10.564	0.041
	(0.349)	(1.045)	(0.267)	(0.367)	(6.806)	(0.288)
Organizational hatred	1.197**	0.733	0.693**	0.534*	−0.172	0.799**
	(0.275)	(0.792)	(0.256)	(0.254)	(1.393)	(0.256)
Interpersonal hatred	1.014**	0.420	−0.018	0.288	3.697	0.695**
	(0.266)	(0.696)	(0.193)	(0.253)	(2.361)	(0.196)
Strong partisan	0.537	—	0.994**	0.960**	—	0.621**
	(0.361)	—	(0.266)	(0.363)	—	(0.252)
Liberal	0.011	−1.141	0.212	−0.764*	−5.527	−0.475
	(0.339)	(1.155)	(0.413)	(0.333)	(4.270)	(0.419)
Conservative	0.476	−0.283	−0.258	0.207	1.211	−0.426
	(0.461)	(1.248)	(0.355)	(0.436)	1.67187	(0.343)
Strong ideologue	0.020	1.291	0.174	0.159	5.489	0.974*
	(0.596)	(1.472)	(0.408)	(0.581)	(4.319)	(0.470)
Political interest	0.005	−0.460	−0.177	0.306^	−0.385	0.056
	(0.166)	(0.526)	(0.128)	(0.167)	(1.057)	(0.130)
Male	−0.100	0.136	−0.449^	−0.031	−3.686	0.330
	(0.309)	(0.904)	(0.254)	(0.303)	(2.633)	(0.242)
Hispanic/Latino	0.448	−0.604	−0.100	0.781*	−8.459	−0.079
	(0.364)	(1.254)	(0.342)	(0.378)	(5.693)	(0.331)
Black/African American	0.598^	−0.943	0.560	1.072**	—	−0.048
	(0.333)	(1.354)	(0.669)	(0.347)	—	(0.641)
Constant	−6.315**	−4.255	−2.351**	−3.437**	−21.765	−4.639**
	(1.150)	(3.231)	(0.765)	(0.077)	(13.304)	(0.808)
Pseudo R-squared	0.145	0.206	0.074	0.122	0.466	0.143
Likelihood ratio (sig.)	56.30	10.20	36.02	45.51	16.52	75.91
	(0.000)	(0.423)	(0.000)	(0.000)	(0.057)	(0.000)
Number of cases	295	44	399	295	36	399

Notes: Cell entries are logistic regression coefficients and standard errors (in parentheses).
**p < 0.01; *p < 0.05; ^p < 0.10 (two-tailed).

or less to about 50 percent or more (see Figure 6.4). Though the magnitude of the association between organizational hatred and out-party party ratings was a bit stronger than that between interpersonal hatred and such ratings, both were quite impressive. Self-admitted Republican study participants who reported the highest levels of animosity against the opposing party organization were estimated to be about 42 percent more likely to offer extremely low ratings of the Democratic Party, whereas the chances of those on the other side of the aisle reciprocating by assigning extremely low ratings to the GOP were about 58 percent higher. When it came to the relationship between interpersonal loathing and extreme ratings, partisans behaved similarly. Those in both camps who reported the least desire to socialize with out-party members were predicted to be more than 40 percent more likely to report extremely low ratings of the opposing party.

In comparison, only feelings of organizational hatred showed an association with more extremely positive ratings of respondents' own party. For both Republican and Democratic identifiers, those expressing the most distaste for the competing party organization also had a higher estimated probability of reporting extremely negative thermometer ratings of that party. Interestingly, the magnitude of the relationship between organizational hatred and expressing extremely warmer feelings about one's own party was weaker than that reported above for the connection between voicing organizational and interpersonal hatred and reporting extremely cold feelings toward the opposition (see Figure 6.5). Taken together, these results suggest that partisan hatred tends to more strongly accompany less support for the opposing party than it does increased support for the home party.

Turning to evaluations of the opposing party's officeholder, partisans met expectations with those who expressed out-party hatred also evaluating the opposition's officeholder in a more negatively extreme fashion (see Table 6.7). For both the Democratic and Republican participants taking part in my study, feelings of organizational and interpersonal hatred showed significant relationships with extremely negative thermometer ratings of the opposition party's most recent White House occupant (see Figure 6.6). The strength of the associations for the different types of partisan hatred was roughly equivalent,

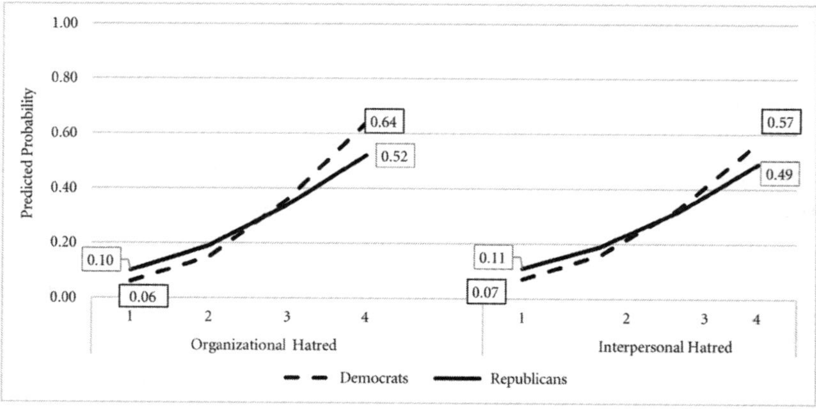

Figure 6.4 Predicted Probability of Extreme Ratings of Opposing Party

Notes: Predicted probabilities were calculated using ordered logit regression coefficients shown in Table 6.6. All control variables were held at their modal values, the hatred measure of interest was manipulated over the range of valid values, and all other hatred measures were held at their means.

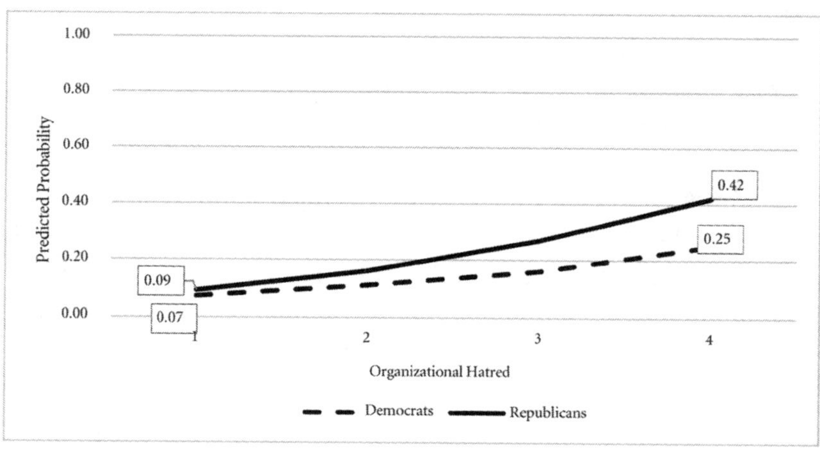

Figure 6.5 Predicted Probability of Extreme Ratings of Own Party

Notes: Predicted probabilities were calculated using ordered logit regression coefficients shown in Table 6.6. All control variables were held at their modal values, the hatred measure of interest was manipulated over the range of valid values, and all other hatred measures were held at their means.

Table 6.7 Partisan Hatred and Extreme Officeholder Thermometer Ratings

	Extreme Bush Thermometer Rating			*Extreme Obama Thermometer Rating*		
	Democrats	*Indepen-dents*	*Republicans*	*Democrats*	*Indepen-dents*	*Republicans*
Physical hatred	−0.032	1.699^	−0.149	−0.175	−0.494	0.637*
	(0.324)	(0.870)	(0.274)	(0.319)	(0.810)	(0.286)
Organizational hatred	0.679**	−1.098	0.325	0.229	0.883	0.858**
	(0.253)	(0.756)	(0.246)	(0.241)	(0.749)	(0.265)
Interpersonal hatred	0.804**	−0.036	0.205	0.039	1.222	0.870**
	(0.249)	(0.603)	(0.188)	(0.236)	(0.761)	(0.205)
Strong partisan	0.813*	—	0.206	0.357	—	0.507*
	(0.362)	—	(0.261)	(0.358)	—	(0.255)
Liberal	0.043	0.022	0.140	0.135	0.824	−0.713^
	(0.331)	(0.982)	(0.400)	(0.320)	(0.790)	(0.416)
Conservative	0.035	−15.654	−0.214	0.068	0.384	0.673^
	(0.452)	(1709.163)	(0.342)	(0.436)	(1.001)	(0.345)
Strong ideologue	−0.378	17.606	0.887*	−0.545	1.392	0.980^
	(0.561)	(1709.164)	(0.401)	(0.553)	(1.536)	(0.534)
Political interest	0.075	−0.950^	−0.022	0.222^	0.379	0.039
	(0.160)	(0.513)	(0.126)	(0.152)	(0.388)	(0.133)
Male	−0.118	−0.021	−0.275	0.049	−1.439^	−0.202
	(0.297)	(0.976)	(0.248)	(0.286)	(0.778)	(0.249)
Hispanic/ Latino	0.816*	2.233*	−0.346	−0.392	−1.163	−0.047
	(0.362)	(1.063)	(0.339)	(0.351)	(1.192)	(0.332)
Black/African American	1.326**	0.665	0.156	1.277**	1.568^	−0.897
	(0.337)	(1.118)	(0.632)	(0.307)	(0.913)	(0.818)
Constant	−5.353**	0.650	−1.918**	−1.981*	−6.543^	−5.175**
	(1.084)	(3.057)	(0.747)	(0.968)	(3.382)	(0.843)
Pseudo R-squared	0.132	0.383	0.035	0.101	0.209	0.174
Likelihood ratio (sig.)	52.39	23.42	16.87	40.51	15.30	93.30
	(0.000)	(0.093)	(0.112)	(0.000)	(0.1215)	(0.000)
Number of cases	297	57	401	297	60	390

Notes: Cell entries are logistic regression coefficients and standard errors (in parentheses). **$p < 0.01$; *$p < 0.05$; ^$p < 0.10$ (two-tailed).

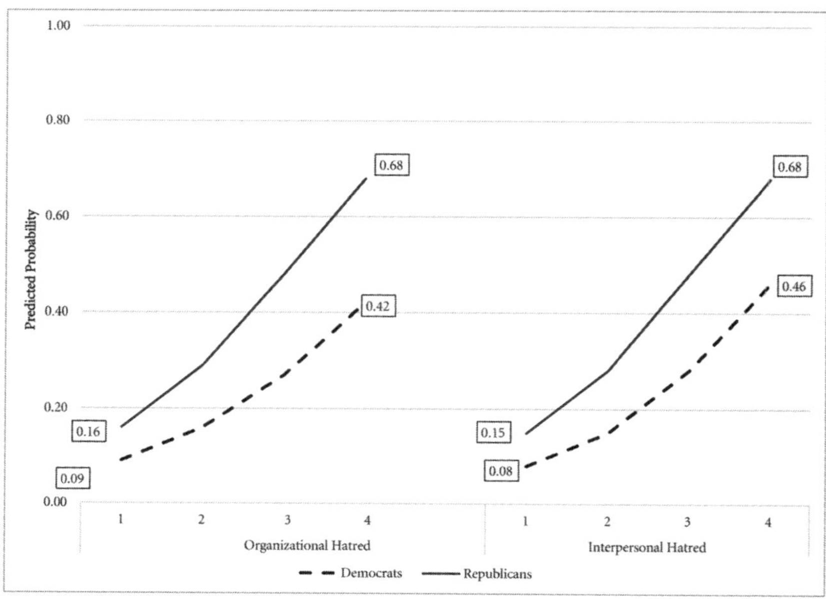

Figure 6.6 Predicted Probability of Extreme Ratings of Opposite Party's Officeholder

Notes: Predicted probabilities were calculated using ordered logit regression coefficients shown in Table 6.7. All control variables were held at their modal values, the hatred measure of interest was manipulated over the range of valid values, and all other hatred measures were held at their means.

though the Republican subsample exhibited a slightly stronger connection between reporting extremely negative ratings of Obama and their feelings of hatred for Democrats and their party.

I did not have ability to test the possibility with the data at hand, but perhaps the relationships were somewhat attenuated among the Democratic subsample because their own party occupied the White House. Whether that was the case, affiliates of either party who registered more animosity toward their partisan opponents and the organization they supported also were predicted to have a much higher probability of rating the out-party's president more extremely negatively. Interestingly, in-party candidate ratings showed no similar associations with levels of partisan hatred. The respondents in my study showed a tendency to connect their disfavor of the opposite party to their negative impressions of that party's commander in chief more than they did to their positive impressions of their own party's chief executive.[3]

The results I present in this chapter thus far have been largely unsurprising. After all, uncovering evidence that feelings about political officeholders and party organizations show an association with expressions of disfavor toward the opposite party will likely not be breaking news to many. Still, the findings do further validate the partisan hatred measures and suggest that the degree of animosity felt toward political opponents among college students is akin to that expressed by the larger electorate and that such sentiments might be playing a role in worsening the public's feelings about the major parties and their chief executives as well as other citizens. Even so, if citizens' derision for those who support contrary political stances does not have any real consequences beyond creating further bad feelings, it might not be worth concern. I next turn to the possible consequences partisan hatred might have for policy making.

PARTISAN HATRED AND POLITICAL COMPROMISE

Many bemoan the lack of political compromise evident among those in Congress as well as those with whom they have everyday conversations. Increasingly, politics at both the elite and mass level have become the battleground for a zero-sum game in which neither side feels conceding any ground to its opponent could be considered acceptable. As reviewed earlier, academic researchers, too, have argued that a context of hatred might have a deleterious effect on political compromise. After all, the perception of a group's humanity brings with it a moral obligation to treat out-group members as equals (Cassese 2019), but when out-group derogation erodes perceptions of the oppositions' morality and humanness, the chances of equitable compromises decrease. Even when groups are in moral agreement, group members might still believe that the in-group is better at acting on those moral values and resist compromise with the out-group (Ellemers and van den Bos 2012).

To test this proposition, I took the partisan hatred indices as independent predictors of political compromise points and controlled for the same set of control variables contained in the models thus far. I assessed respondents' compromise points by asking them to identify the point (on a 0-to-100-point scale) at which Democrats and Republicans should meet when attempting to address the most important issues facing the country. A score of 0 on the compromise scale indicated that Democrats would get everything they wanted, whereas a score of 100 meant that Republicans would get everything they desired. In addition to reporting the raw numeric compromise points, I also created a measure of the extremity of the proposed compromise point by "folding" the 100-point compromise scale.[4] This measure thus ranges from 0 to 50, with higher values indicating more extreme compromise positions.

On the whole, my study participants reported a mean raw compromise point of nearly an even split, though, as expected, the mean compromise points reported by partisan identifiers benefitted their own side (see Figure 6.7). For their part, nonpartisan respondents reported an almost neutral ideal compromise point, averaging only about a single-point Democratic advantage. Partisan identifiers, in contrast, recorded compromise points more favorable to their own party, with Republicans showing a slightly stronger overall tendency to do so than Democrats did. Whereas Democrats, on average, felt that slightly advantageous compromises favoring their side (at about a fifty-five to forty-five split) were ideal, Republicans preferred, on average, compromising closer to fifteen points from even, with their side getting about 65 percent of what it wanted compared with only 35 percent for the Democrats. Interestingly, the partisan compromise points somewhat mirrored the partisan split in the chambers of the US Congress at the time—Senate seats were evenly split along partisan lines, and the Republicans held about a 14 percent advantage in House seats.

I then assessed the relationships between feelings of partisan hatred and willingness to make political compromises, using the same multivariate regression approach I presented previously. The results suggest an association between all three types of partisan hatred and compromise points, though the results again vary across the partisan spectrum (see Table 6.8). Among those disavowing attachments to either major party, feelings of interpersonal hatred showed a strong

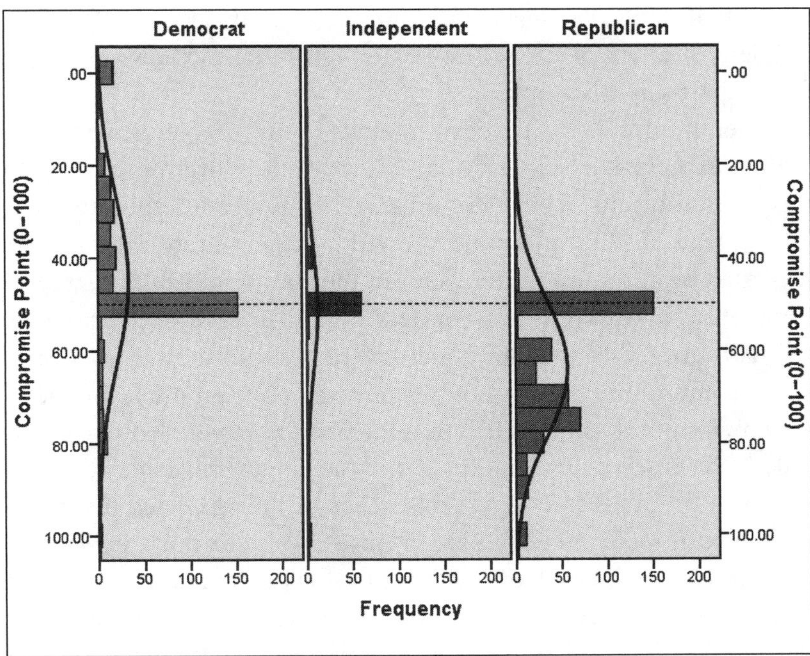

Figure 6.7 Willingness to Compromise

relationship with suggested compromise positions. Looking first at the raw compromise point offered, I find that those Independent respondents who said partisans made them feel physically unwell—and therefore harbored thoughts of physical retaliation toward them—were predicted to offer compromise points almost fifteen points more favorable to the Democratic Party than did the nonpartisans who reported less visceral physical reactions to partisans. The second set of results further reveals that Independent participants admitting more physical hatred of partisans offered, on average, compromises almost ten and a half points farther from an even partisan split. Taken together, these findings predict that Independents saying they felt the least animosity toward partisans offered an almost even ideal compromise point that gave slight favor to the Democratic side, but nonpartisans expressing the highest levels of physical hatred toward partisans were likely to offer an ideal compromise point that offered the Democratic side about a thirty-two-point advantage. Thus, it would seem that the GOP was the recipient of much of the vitriol-related retribution expressed among the nonpartisan subsample.

When it came to the partisan students in my sample, however, the results predictably showed in-party favoritism. However, unlike the nonpartisan results, feelings of organizational and interpersonal hatred instead of physical hatred showed significant associations with suggested compromise points. Further, the effects were relatively symmetrical across party lines. For Democrats and Republicans alike, stronger feelings of organizational hatred were associated with suggested compromise points about six to seven points more favorable to their own party. It is important to remember, however, that these estimated effects serve to compound the baseline difference between two groups of partisans (see Figure 6.8). Though the estimated five-point gap between recommended compromise points for those expressing the lowest level of hatred toward the opposing party organization could require some deft political negotiation, that gap seems miniscule when compared with the thirty-seven-point gulf predicted for partisans who reported the highest levels of interpersonal antipathy. Interestingly, the models predict bipartisan agreement near, but not at, the lowest end of the interpersonal hatred scale, suggesting that harboring a little outgroup animosity might not be impossible to surmount.

On the whole, the relationship between feelings of interpersonal hatred and recommended compromise positions, though significant, was seemingly less divisive. In fact, though it did show an association with reporting compromise points further from an even split, Democrats' feelings of interpersonal repulsion toward Republicans failed to show a significant relationship with the raw suggested compromise points. In comparison with the predicted impact of organizational hatred, interpersonal antagonism was associated with a much smaller interparty separation in the compromise points offered (see Figure 6.9). Among partisans, Democratic and Republican alike, those expressing dislike for socializing with their partisan opponents were predicted to offer compromise points about three points more favorable to their own side. The compromise points of partisans who reported the lowest level of bitterness about their partisan opponents were predicted to be

Table 6.8 Partisan Hatred and Political Compromise

	Proposed Compromise Point (0–100)			*Extremity of Proposed Compromise Point (0–50)*		
	Democrats	*Independents*	*Republicans*	*Democrats*	*Independents*	*Republicans*
Physical hatred	-2.780	-14.877**	-0.152	2.219	10.366**	0.627
	(2.777)	(3.171)	(1.621)	(2.269)	(3.432)	(1.498)
Organizational hatred	-7.843**	4.512^	6.188**	7.574**	-2.035	6.792**
	(1.975)	(2.347)	(1.497)	(1.614)	(2.540)	(1.382)
Interpersonal hatred	-2.962	-0.594	2.932*	3.787*	1.103	3.158**
	(1.959)	(2.053)	(1.160)	(1.601)	(2.222)	(1.071)
Strong partisan	0.599	—	6.076**	0.799	—	5.714**
	(2.995)	—	(1.560)	(2.447)	—	(1.444)
Liberal	1.556	11.573**	-0.040	-0.354	0.566	0.861
	(2.629)	(3.437)	(2.457)	(2.000)	(3.720)	(2.269)
Conservative	5.802	2.045	0.453	3.346	1.486	2.000
	(3.617)	(4.236)	(2.045)	(2.955)	(4.584)	(1.889)
Strong ideologue	0.598	-3.718	2.647	-1.485	2.971	1.866
	(4.582)	(5.981)	(2.674)	(3.744)	(6.473)	(2.470)
Political interest	-1.132	2.621^	0.327	0.168	-2.249	-0.196
	(1.255)	(1.452)	(0.768)	(1.026)	(1.571)	(0.709)
Male	1.389	4.868^	2.151	-1.112	-5.536^	0.558
	(2.364)	(2.877)	(1.457)	(1.931)	(3.114)	(1.346)
Hispanic/Latino	1.119	8.590*	0.237	1.054	-4.709*	-0.021
	(2.765)	(3.270)	(1.920)	(2.259)	(3.538)	(1.774)
Black/African American	-1.628	6.020	-7.386^	3.955	-5.851^	-0.318
	(2.559)	(3.820)	(3.891)	(2.091)	(4.134)	(3.594)
Constant	77.455**	43.281**	36.548**	-23.149**	3.567	-14.772**
	(7.913)	(8.747)	(4.505)	(6.466)	(9.466)	(4.161)
Adjusted R-squared	0.081	0.330	0.198	0.122	0.115	0.223
F (significance)	3.281	4.296	9.718	4.575	1.875	11.128
	(0.000)	(0.000)	(0.000)	(0.000)	(0.068)	(0.000)
Number of cases	284	68	389	284	68	389

Notes: Cell entries are OLS regression coefficients and standard errors (in parentheses). **p < 0.01; *p < 0.05; ^p < 0.10 (two-tailed).

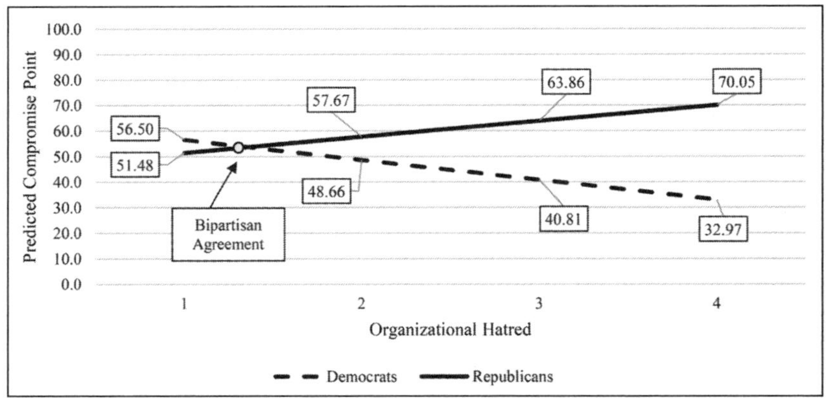

Figure 6.8 Organizational Hatred and Predicted Political Compromise Points

Notes: Predicted probabilities were calculated using OLS regression coefficients shown in Table 6.8. All control variables were held at their modal values, the hatred measure of interest was manipulated over the range of valid values, and all other hatred measures were held at their means.

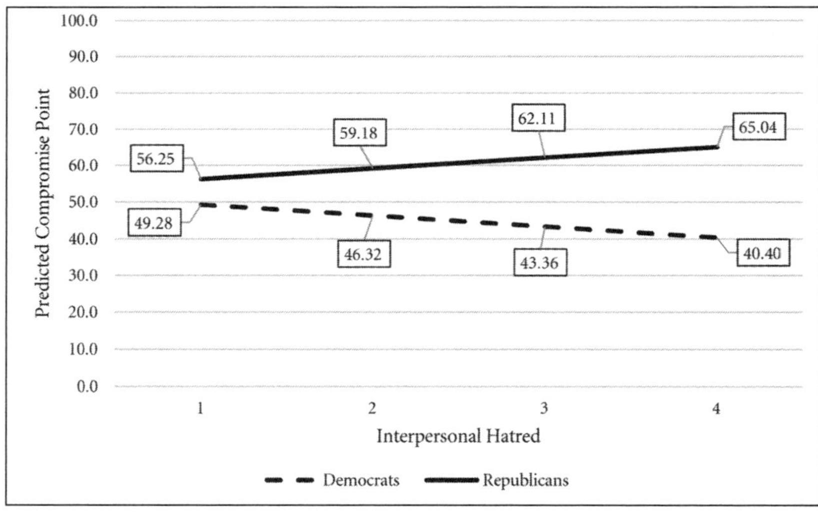

Figure 6.9 Interpersonal Hatred and Predicted Political Compromise Points

Notes: Predicted probabilities were calculated using OLS regression coefficients shown in Table 6.8. All control variables were held at their modal values, the hatred measure of interest was manipulated over the range of valid values, and all other hatred measures were held at their means.

only about seven points apart. Though significant, a gap in negotiation starting points of this amount is much more feasibly surmountable than the twenty-five-point rift estimated for partisans who expressed the strongest rancor toward the opposing party's organizational body. And, unlike feelings of organizational hatred, no level of interpersonal hatred is predicted to result in bipartisan agreement on a compromise point.

On the whole the results I present in this chapter suggest that feelings of hatred toward partisan opponents might indeed be connected to college students' distaste for counterpartisans as well as their willingness to compromise with partisan enemies. Should these relationships extend to the young population more generally, voters in their early adult years might be cementing their feelings of partisan acrimony, and these feelings could affect their political behavior in the future. The bad news might not end there. In addition to connections between partisan polarization and attitudes toward political negotiation, scholars have increasingly noted the social polarization of the US public. Should college students exhibit the same tendencies as the general public when it comes to socially interacting with counterpartisans, the tendencies evidenced in this chapter might only continue to strengthen. Conversely, should members of the younger generation be more ecumenical in their social relations, we might have reason to hope for a less polarized political future. In the following chapter, I examine my study participants' attitudes about engaging in social relations across party lines.

7. The Social Consequences of Partisan Hatred

It is impossible to live in peace with those one believes to be damned.

—Jean-Jacques Rousseau

Although many lament the rise in political polarization for the effects it might have on effective and efficient governance, some have argued that political identities take root more quickly in the social sphere than in the political one (Mason 2015a). Recent research bears out this possibility. By about 2014 "ideological silos" were common on both sides of the aisle, with nearly two-thirds of consistent conservatives and almost half of consistent liberals reporting that their close friends shared their political views. In comparison, only about one-third of the rest of the public reported the same (Doherty 2014). It is perhaps not too surprising that by 2017, nearly half of all those expressing a partisan identity admitted that learning a friend had voted for the out-party candidate would negatively affect the friendship (see chapter 1, Figure 1.3).

Similarly, an increasing number of citizens express a preference for living in a place where most people share their political views (Pew Research Center 2014). The idea that geographical location might relate to political attitudes is certainly not a new one. After all, Elazar (1966) long ago pointed to interstate differences with regard to perceptions about the purposes and practices of government as well as expectations about public involvement in politics. These differences, he argued, resulted in partisan and ideological variation across the nation. Although contemporary scholars also highlight the different partisan and ideological loyalties of the states, recent arguments often focus less on states' histories and more on the way in which Americans are increasingly relocating to surround themselves with those who share their political views. That is, they argue that Americans are "steadily sorting into Democratic (liberal) and Republican (conservative) strongholds" (Schier and Eblery 2016, 51), creating a sort of "geographic polarization" along partisan lines in the nation (Bishop 2008). Looking at election returns since the 1970s, Bishop (2009) notes that in 1976 about a quarter of Americans lived in counties that witnessed what would be considered a landslide win (by at least 20 percentage points) by one presidential candidate, but by 2004 fully half of the US population resided in such counties. A quick review of the 2016 election returns reveals that 60 percent of the nation's residents were living in such electorally lopsided counties. Through processes both subtle and obvious, the US population is sorting itself into neighborhoods that are reliably Democratic or Republican.

Our sorting does not appear to stop at the community level. The effects of partisan polarization seem to extend even into our most intimate relationships. Commonality on political attitudes has been shown to relate to dating and marital decisions. Spousal commonality on political views appears to be stronger than physical or personality characteristics, and the similarity between marriage partners seems to be less about persuasion and accommodation over time than from initial mate choice (Alford et al. 2011). Along the same lines, parents have become increasingly likely to express dismay at the prospect of a child taking a counterpartisan spouse. Estimates suggest that about one-third of Democrats and one-half of Republicans report that they would be upset or very upset if one of their children were to marry a person from the other party (Iyengar, Sood, and Lelkes 2012). Just as mate selection seemed more driven by political attitudes than by other social and biometric traits (Alford et al. 2011), distress about welcoming an out-partisan into the immediate family increased. Interestingly, over the same period, negative attitudes about intermarriage across race and religious lines decreased (Iyengar, Sood, and Lelkes 2012), perhaps because partisanship displaced race and religion but more likely because of increased alignment of partisanship, racial, and religious divides resulting from mass partisan shifts over the period.

The behavioral effects of partisan family structure were made strikingly clear when Chen and Rohla (2018), investigated the time people spent over Thanksgiving dinner following the 2016 presidential election. Using anonymized smartphone-location data and precinct-level voting, these researchers found that dinnertimes were thirty to fifty minutes shorter when attended by residents from precincts that supported opposing parties in the 2016 election (even accounting for an extensive set of controls). Tellingly, the decline in time spent over dinner tripled for residents of media markets that had received heavy political advertising. In total, the researchers estimated that about 34 million hours of cross-partisan discourse was lost in 2016. "Turkey and tribalism" do indeed seem "an uncomfortable combination" (Jacobs 2018).

Even the economic sector is not immune from the effects of partisan polarization. Recent experimental research suggests that partisanship can shape individual-level economic decisions regarding where people work and shop. McConnell and colleagues (2018) found that subjects acting as consumers are nearly twice as likely to transact business with a seller when the two share partisanship. Even weak or leaning partisans exhibit such tendencies, though to a lesser degree. When it comes to salary demands, their experiments revealed that subjects were willing to accept wages about 6.5 percent lower from employers who shared their partisan views (an amount equivalent to the wage demand differential between the least- and most-educated segments of the subject workforce). Looking at a nationally representative sample, these same researchers discovered that people were willing to pass up economic gains when the opposing party would also benefit. About three-quarters of their respondents preferred not to double their bonus payment when the out-party would receive a concomitant small donation (a much higher rate of rejection than being asked to allow a small donation to a religious organization that differed from the that of respondents).

On the whole it seems we have a society balkanized (Cassese 2019) in a number of ways. No matter where it occurs—in the community, in the workplace, or in the household—Americans simply do not want to engage in face-to-face social interactions with their partisan opponents. To investigate the possibility that the social isolation others have identified in the population more generally also pervades the youngest segment of the electorate, I asked students in this study how important it was to them to live in a place where most people shared their political views and whether they would be upset if an immediate member of their families were to marry a member of the opposite party (or, for Independent identifiers, a member of either major party).

COLLEGE STUDENTS' VIEWS ON PARTISAN NEIGHBORS AND IN-LAWS

Although students were very likely to say they preferred to live near people with similar political views, they were less likely to express dread about ending up with counterpartisan in-laws. More than six in ten of the respondents said they favored having like-minded neighbors (see Figure 7.1). Conversely, less than 5 percent strongly objected to living around others sharing their political views. These results echo those shown by others for the population more generally. The preference for partisan social isolation that has infiltrated the public generally also seems to have taken root among the youngest generation of potential voters. This finding is especially telling because many study participants live on campus and are potentially exposed to more diverse residential settings than they might be otherwise.

The preferences of partisans versus nonpartisans also reflected those of the general public. Study participants admitting a partisan preference, particularly Republican identifiers, were much more likely to say they preferred to live around those with the same political take on things than nonpartisans were. Whereas more than half of Democratic and more than two-thirds of Republican respondents reported agreement with the idea of living around their partisan comrades, a little fewer than half of the self-identified Independents did so (see Figure 7.2). Whereas nearly 13 percent of nonpartisans disagreed strongly with the idea of living around folks sharing their political beliefs, less than 5 percent of partisans of either persuasion felt this way.[1] The variation across the partisan spectrum evident in my sample is comparable to that reported in studies of the US electorate more widely. So, again, the preferences for partisan segregation many have highlighted among the general electorate apparently have not bypassed nascent voters.

When it came to the prospect of an immediate family member marrying into the out-party, students expressed far more neutral sentiments. About nine out of ten respondents claimed that it would not matter if they ended up with counterpartisan in-laws (see Figure 7.3). Though far more open to the idea of interparty marriage than the general public was, as reported by others, about 10 percent of the study participants still expressed some preference on this topic. Those saying

Figure 7.1 Preferences for Living Near Copartisans

Notes: Question wording: "It's important to me to live in a place where most people share my political views." Only 0.2 percent of all respondents chose not to answer this question.

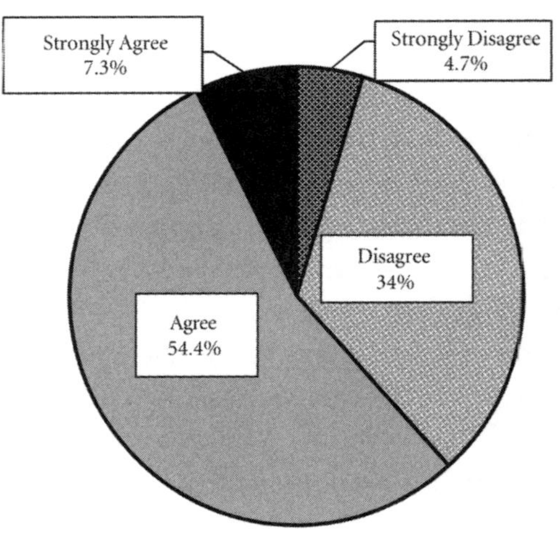

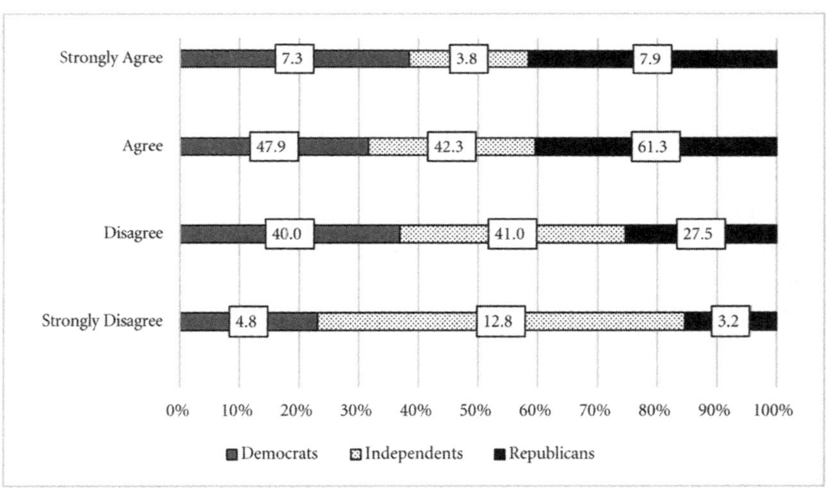

Figure 7.2 Preference for Living Near Copartisans, by Party Affiliation

Notes: Question wording: "It's important to me to live in a place where most people share my political views." Only 0.2 percent of all respondents chose not to provide an answer to this question.

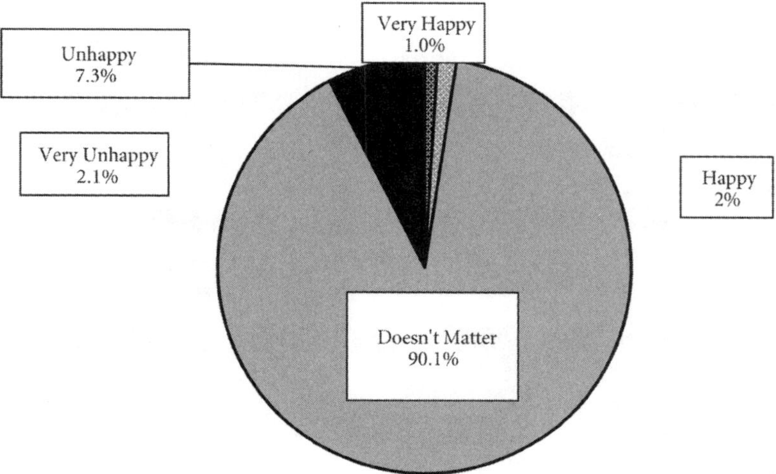

Figure 7.3 Reaction to Interparty Marriage

Notes: Question wording: "I would be upset if an immediate member of my family married a [Democrat/Republican/Democrat or Republican]." Only 0.2 percent of all respondents chose not to provide an answer to this question.

that such wedding nuptials would make them unhappy to some degree far outnumbered those who reported they would be celebrating such a union. Only about 3 percent of the sample said they would be happy or very happy to welcome counterpartisans into their families. More than three times that many (9.4 percent), in contrast, thought they would likely be unhappy or very unhappy about being asked to spend family time with out-party members. So, although the younger set of citizens under study here expressed less despair over the idea of interparty marriage than did the general public, there were still signs of budding regret about the possibility.

Although the distribution of preferences was similar across the partisan spectrum, Republican students were slightly more likely to express a preference on this topic and, when doing so, to report more negative sentiments (see Figure 7.4). Though nearly nine in ten partisans and nonpartisans alike were likely to say interparty marriage did not matter to them, about 4 percent fewer Republicans were likely to admit ambivalence.[2] For their part, nonpartisan students who expressed a preference were equally likely to say that the thought of adding a partisan to

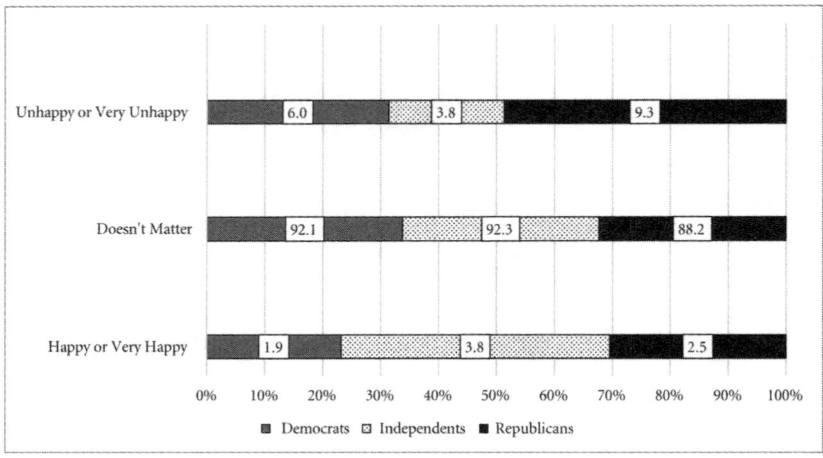

Figure 7.4 Reaction to Interparty Marriage, by Partisan Affiliation

Notes: Question wording: "I would be upset if an immediate member of my family married a [Democrat/Republican/Democrat or Republican]." Only 0.2 percent of all respondents chose not to provide an answer to this question.

the family pleased or displeased them. Partisans, meanwhile, showed a tendency to report negative feelings about the idea more often than positive ones. So, although study participants showed a generally accepting attitude toward mixed-party marriages, partisan identifiers expressed a little more disdain for the notion.

PARTISAN HATRED AND SENTIMENTS ON INTERPARTY SOCIAL INTERACTION

Taken together, these findings with regard to partisan preferences for social interaction with out-partisans revealed that my student sample exhibited, to some degree, the same tendencies as those reported for the public more generally. To more directly investigate questions of whether the observed partisan differences in attitudes about socially interacting with partisan opponents might be associated with feelings of partisan animosity, I tested for a correlation between feelings of physical, organizational, and interpersonal partisan hatred and opinions about living near and family marriage with partisan opponents. As expected, feelings of all three types of partisan hatred showed positive and statistically significant bivariate correlations with reported preferences for living near those sharing political views and acceptance of interpartisan marriage (see Table 7.1). Though I expected interpersonal hatred to show the strongest relationship with opinions about socially interacting with out-party members, feelings about knowing more members of the opposing party and socializing with them turned out to have weaker correlations than feelings of organizational and physical hatred, which showed associations of similar magnitude.

The unexpectedly weaker performance of the interpersonal hatred measure results from the variation in association across the partisan array. The Republican subsample of students who reported more intense feelings of interpersonal hatred showed the expected significantly positive relationships with both opinions about living around Democrats and having them marry into their families. Republican-identifying students who expressed more interpersonal hatred of their partisan foes registered a stronger desire not to live around them and not to have to call them family. In contrast, the interpersonal hatred expressed by students who reported Democratic leanings failed to show a significant relationship with either of the social interaction measures.

Among the Independent sample of students, those who reported feeling more physical revulsion about partisans also reported preferring not to live around them or have them marry into their families. At the same time, dislike of the party organizations showed an association only with sentiments about having partisans as neighbors. Independent-minded students' feelings about socializing with partisans, however, failed to show a relationship with attitudes about living near them. Most curiously, students who reported a lower desire to interact interpersonally with partisans reported more support for a partisan joining the familial ranks. So, to steal from a classic tune, the bivariate results suggest that nonpartisan study participants might well have felt like they had "clowns to the left of [them] and jokers to the right," but they still did not mind being "stuck in the middle" with them socially.[3] Of course, all of the associations examined thus far failed to consider

Table 7.1 Correlation between Partisan Hatred and Interparty Social Interaction

	Physical Hatred	*Organizational Hatred*	*Interpersonal Hatred*
All Respondents			
Homogenous residential preference	0.238**	0.297**	0.164**
Opposition to interparty marriage	0.283**	0.240**	0.099**
Democrats			
Homogenous residential preference	0.192**	0.222**	--0.021
Opposition to interparty marriage	0.306**	0.265**	--0.036
Independents			
Homogenous residential preference	0.234*	0.542**	0.144
Opposition to interparty marriage	0.239*	0.087	−0.405**
Republicans			
Homogenous residential preference	0.256**	0.280**	0.297**
Opposition to interparty marriage	0.278**	0.264**	0.298**

Notes: Cell entries are Pearson's r bivariate correlations. $^{*}p < 0.05$; $^{**}p < 0.01$ (two-tailed).

other possible correlates of partisan dislike that might modify the bivariate relationships I show here.

To account for the impact other attitudinal as well as demographic factors might play in shaping opinions about living around and introducing into the family those with conflicting views, I once again performed a series of multivariate regression analyses.[4] As before, I ran separate models for Democrats, Republicans, and Independents and controlled for partisan strength, ideology, ideological strength, political interest, and respondent sex, race, and ethnicity. Taking these additional characteristics into account helped to clarify the relationships at play in the nonpartisan segment of the sample and largely confirmed those heretofore for partisans.

Partisan Hatred and Preference for Residential Homogeneity

The first column of results presented in Table 7.2 corroborates the previously observed relationships between Democrats' desire to avoid living near Republicans and their physical and organizational hatred of them. The magnitude of these relationships is among the strongest in the model. With an odds ratio of 1.99, feelings of physical hatred exhibited the second-strongest magnitude of effect of all the factors in the model, eclipsed only by the single significant control variable of race, which had an odds ratio of similar magnitude (2.12).[5] Even partisan and ideological strength (with odds ratios of 1.59 and 1.92, respectively) showed slightly weaker relationships with residential preference. Although only marginally significant, organizational hatred also showed a positive relationship, with a healthy odds ratio (1.45). Taken together, these findings suggest that Democratic students who held the GOP in contempt and expressed more immediate, visceral hatred of counterpartisans were much more likely to register a desire to isolate themselves in like-minded communities than were other Democratically affiliated students. The performance of the control variables further suggests that a preference for residential homogeneity of viewpoints extends beyond mere matters of partisanship and ideology. Matters of race remained relevant even in the face of partisan hatred, though it is important to remember the strong relationship between race and partisanship.

The results for the right wing of my sample showed somewhat similar relationships, with all three forms of partisan hatred registering positive, and significant, relationships with a preference for living in communities of like-minded individuals. Further, as expected, feelings of interpersonal hatred among those who self-identified as Republicans showed a relationship with a magnitude on par with that of partisan strength (both registered odds ratios of 2.22). For their part, feelings of organizational and physical hatred demonstrated the next strongest connections with residential preference (with odds ratios of 1.88 and 1.80, respectively). And though the ideological orientation variables showed statistically significant relationships with residential preferences, the size of their effects were relatively small (0.452 and 0.489, respectively). On the whole, then, these findings suggest that GOP-affiliated students, particularly the stalwarts, who harbored the most hatred of all sorts toward Democrats also expressed a stronger preference to surround themselves with neighbors holding compatible views.

Using these multivariate results, I estimated the probability of expressing desire to live amid those with similar political outlooks. As illustrated in Figure 7.5, Democratic and Republican identifiers who

Table 7.2 Partisan Hatred and Preference for Living Near Copartisans

	Democrats	*Independents*	*Republicans*
Immediate hatred	0.690*	−0.098	0.590*
	(0.295)	(0.618)	(0.257)
Chronic personal hatred	0.374^	2.034**	0.631*
	(0.216)	(0.512)	(0.234)
Chronic social hatred	−0.170	0.897*	0.799**
	(0.213)	(0.416)	(0.189)
Strong partisan	0.467	—	0.799**
	(0.332)		(0.248)
Liberal	0.137	0.945	−0.793*
	(0.291)	(0.637)	(0.375)
Conservative	−0.243	0.984	−0.716*
	(0.390)	(0.806)	(0.308)
Strong ideologue	0.650	0.034	0.050
	(0.490)	(1.156)	(0.441)
Political interest	0.159	0.660*	0.286
	(0.139)	(0.291)	(0.121)
Male	−0.046	−0.394	−0.065*
	(0.262)	(0.532)	(0.225)
Hispanic/Latino	−0.079	1.092^	0.089
	(0.300)	(0.650)	(0.287)
Black/African American	0.753**	1.688*	0.474
	(0.284)	(0.760)	(0.612)
Cut 1	−0.905	6.429	1.226
	(0.880)	(1.929)	(0.738)
Cut 2	2.045	9.936	3.971
	(0.861)	(2.161)	(0.719)
Cut 3	5.079	13.560	7.869
	(0.917)	(2.464)	(0.834)
Pseudo R-squared	0.0621	0.2747	0.1194
Likelihood ratio (sig.)	38.95	43.35	94.33
	(0.000)	(0.000)	(0.000)
Number of cases	297	69	401

Notes: Cell entries are ordered logit regression coefficients. **$p < 0.01$; *$p < 0.05$; ^$p < 0.10$ (two-tailed).

expressed more physical hatred of their partisan opponents were more likely to agree or strongly agree that they preferred like-minded neighbors. Though those on the right were predicted to be more likely to prefer residential purity, the association between feelings of the gut-level aversion was calculated to be slightly stronger for those on the left.

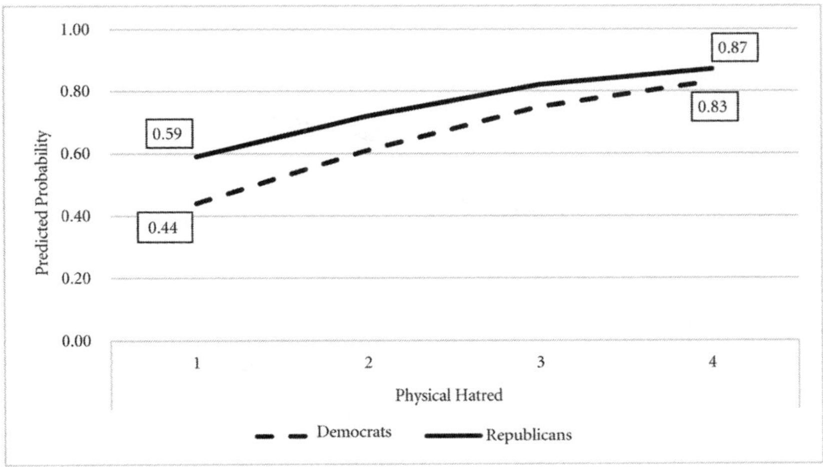

Figure 7.5 Physical Hatred and Predicted Probability of Preference for Living Near Copartisans

Notes: Predicted probabilities of agreeing or strongly agreeing to a desire for "living in a place where people sharing similar political views" were calculated using ordered logit regression coefficients shown in Table 7.2. All other hatred measures were set to their means, all control variables were set to their modal values, and hatred measure of interest was manipulated over the range of valid values.

Estimates suggest that GOP supporters who expressed the strongest physical repulsion against Democrats had about a 28 percent higher chance of stating a preference for living around those on the same political wavelength, their partisan peers who recorded the lowest level of instinctual hatred. In comparison, Democratic-affiliated study participants showed a predicted 39 percent increase across the physical hatred scale. These combined tendencies resulted in a partisan gap in residential preferences that narrowed when looking across physical hatred levels. Among partisans harboring the strongest feelings of physical contempt for their political opponents, both Democratic and Republican students alike were predicted to have a better than 80 percent chance of wanting to live in communities of political isolation. Importantly, these projections account for the effects of partisan strength, ideology, and important demographic characteristics.

The estimated effects of organizational hatred exhibited a similar pattern, though the predicted effects for the Republican subsample

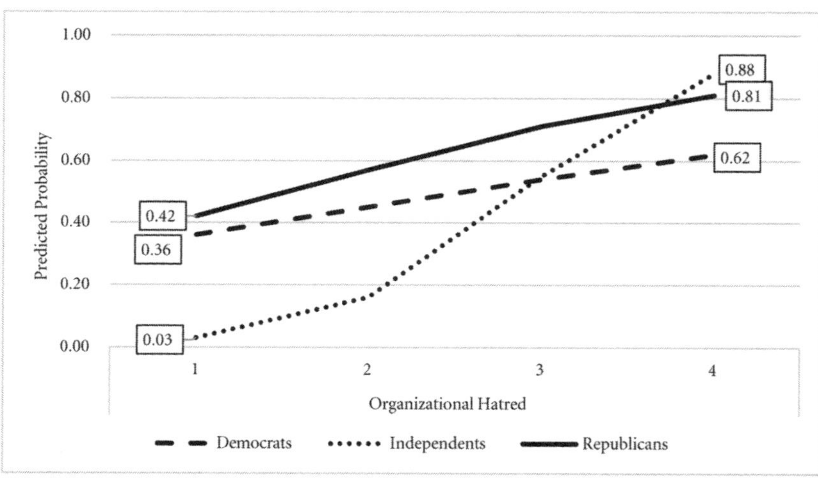

Figure 7.6 Organizational Hatred and Predicted Probability of Preference for Living Near Copartisans

Notes: Predicted probabilities of agreeing or strongly agreeing to a desire for "living in a place where people sharing similar political views" were calculated using ordered logit regression coefficients shown in Table 7.2. All other hatred measures were set to their means, all control variables were set to their modal values, and hatred measure of interest was manipulated over the range of valid values.

were stronger than they were for those on the left of the partisan spectrum (see Figure 7.6). Republican-affiliated respondents who expressed the highest level of disgust with the Democratic Party were estimated to have about a 39 percent higher chance of recording a preference for copartisan neighborhoods, whereas Democratic loyalists were predicted to have only about a 26 percent higher chance of doing so. Counter to the shrinking partisan gap in effects across the physical hatred scale, the combined trends for feelings of organizational hatred served to widen the gap in residential preferences between the parties. Respondents with Republican attachments were estimated to have about a 6 percent higher chance of stating a preference for residential uniformity of political opinions on the lowest end of the scale; those expressing the strongest level of disgust with the Democratic Party were predicted to be about 19 percent more likely to do so than their partisan adversaries. Once again, these results control for the simultaneous impacts of partisan strength, ideology, and demographic characteristics likely to also play a role in shaping residential preferences.

These predicted effects pale, however, in comparison with those for the Independents among my study participants. Nonpartisan students taking part in this study who reported the lowest levels of odium for the parties were predicted to have a mere 3 percent chance of yearning for a partisan-free community. In strong contrast, those expressing the most resentment of partisan organizations had nearly a 90 percent estimated chance of seeking such living arrangements. These results suggest that seeing organized party politics as repulsive might be angering the uncommitted portion of the electorate even more than it does those with ties to one of the two major parties.

Finally, those in the Republican subsample were calculated to show a stronger association between feelings of interpersonal hatred and desiring a politically consistent domestic context than were others (see Figure 7.7). Those affiliated with the Republican Party who registered the most interpersonal animosity toward Democrats were about 51 percent more likely to say they did not want to live around them than were their copartisans harboring the lowest level. In contrast, Independent-minded students taking part in this study were predicted to have about a 44 percent higher chance of wanting to avoid seeing partisans over their backyard fences across the interpersonal hatred scale. Meanwhile, the findings with regard to the Democratic subsample failed to establish even a probable relationship between feelings of interpersonal animosity and residential preference.

Taken altogether, the findings with regard to partisan hatred and residential preference suggest that animosities across party lines might indeed be connected to trends in the residential preferences of college students. Further, the effects of different sorts of partisan hatred might be operating differently for those on one side of the partisan spectrum, those on the other, and those in the middle. Although the estimated effects of partisan hatred were stronger for some groups than others, it is important to keep an eye on the absolute intensity of housing preferences among those expressing the strongest partisan hostilities, regardless of partisanship. Partisans expressing the highest levels of cross-party physical revulsion were predicted to be, on average,

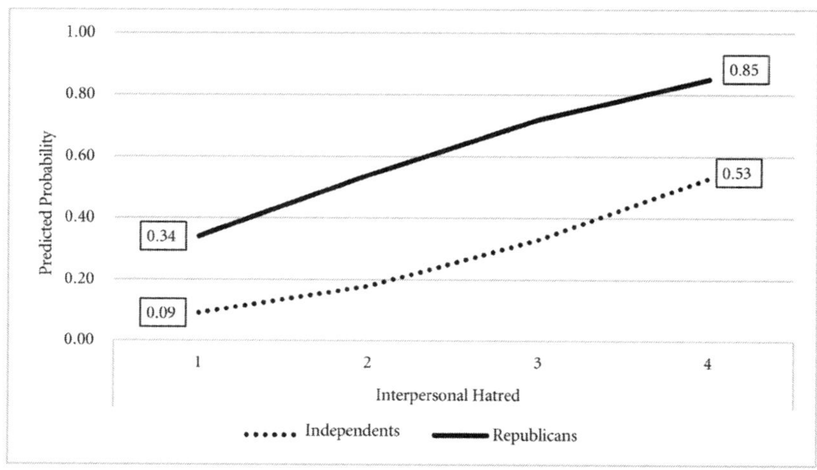

Figure 7.7 Interpersonal Hatred and Predicted Probability of Preference for Living Near Copartisans

Notes: Predicted probabilities of agreeing or strongly agreeing to a desire for "living in a place where people sharing similar political views" were calculated using ordered logit regression coefficients shown in Table 7.2. All other hatred measures were set to their means, all control variables were set to their modal values, and hatred measure of interest was manipulated over the range of valid values.

about 85 percent likely to say they desired partisan purity on their blocks. Similarly, no matter their partisan affiliation, those reporting the most dislike for competing party organizations were estimated to have about a 77 percent chance of doing so. When it came to feelings of interpersonal hatred, GOP supporters and their nonpartisan counterparts harboring the least desire to socialize with out-party members were calculated to have nearly a 70 percent higher chance of desiring to avoid seeing their partisan opponents in the neighborhood park. It appears that even among the youngest ranks of the electorate, partisan acrimony might be tied to a desire to for day-to-day living arrangements that offer insulation from contrary political opinions.

Partisan Hatred and Attitudes about Interparty Marriage

Much the same can be said about the connections between partisan hatred and attitudes about having a close family member choose a spouse with a competing political outlook. As the results presented in Table 7.3 illustrate, partisans harboring more physical and organizational hatred of their partisan opponents also say they would not be pleased if a close family member chose a spouse with conflicting partisan views. For Republican identifiers, their feelings of interpersonal hatred also correlated with their annoyance at the idea of welcoming a counterpartisan into the family. Once again, the magnitude of the relationships is among the strongest in the models. In the Democratic model, the odds ratios for the physical and organizational partisan hatred measures (1.54 and 1.42, respectively) were on par with that for ideological strength (1.97). Much the same is the case for the performance of the partisan hatred measures in the Republican model, where the odds ratios for physical, organizational, and interpersonal hatred (0.706, 0.856, and 0.905, respectively) were nearly as strong as those for ideological strength (1.18), conservative ideology (–1.09), and political interest (–0.100).

The association between partisan hatred and attitudes about partisan intermarriage turned out to be quite a bit different in the Independent model. Neither physical nor organizational hatred showed a significant relationship to opinions about mixed-party marriages. Although feelings of interpersonal hatred were significantly related to Independents' opinions about bringing a partisan into the family, the direction of the association was surprising. The results suggest that Independents holding stronger feelings of interpersonal hatred of partisans were less likely to express displeasure at the thought of a close family member marrying someone from one of the major parties. The magnitude of this effect is roughly equivalent to that of race and about half as strong as ideological strength. This might suggest that Independents separate their feelings about the two major parties from sentiments about family dynamics.

To put the nature of the relationships between partisan hatred and thoughts about cross-party marriage into better perspective, I once again calculated the predicted probability of being unhappy or very unhappy with the prospect of having an in-law from among the partisan opposition. As shown in Figure 7.8, feelings of physical revulsion are more strongly related to marriage attitudes for the Democratic subsample than for the Republican one. Whereas students claiming either

Table 7.3 Partisan Hatred and Dislike of Partisan Intermarriage

	Democrats	*Independents*	*Republicans*
Immediate hatred	1.542**	1.079	0.706*
	(0.483)	(1.334)	(0.353)
Chronic personal hatred	1.431**	-0.413	0.856*
	(0.436)	(0.856)	(0.374)
Chronic social hatred	-0.325	-2.561*	0.905**
	(0.387)	(1.004)	(0.290)
Strong partisan	0.151	—	0.963
	(0.624)		(0.436)
Liberal	-0.409	-1.302	-1.015
	(0.621)	(1.405)	(0.645)
Conservative	0.628	0.030	-1.085*
	(0.863)	(2.502)	(0.524)
Strong ideologue	1.965**	5.094	1.182*
	(0.734)	(4.903)	(0.504)
Political interest	-0.067	-0.090	-0.100**
	(0.271)	(0.594)	(0.185)
Male	0.465	-1.276	-0.053
	(0.526)	(1.162)	(0.359)
Hispanic/Latino	-0.771	5.208	0.035
	(0.654)	(4.553)	(0.529)
Black/African American	-0.908	2.541	-1.027
	(0.587)	(3.028)	(1.013)
Cut 1	-2.366	-10.412	-0.884
	(1.865)	(0.425)	(1.195)
Cut 2	-0.476	2.725	0.349
	(1.625)	(5.090)	(1.095)
Cut 3	7.912	—	7.679
	(1.833)		(1.225)
Cut 4	9.578	—	9.766
	(1.911)		(1.327)
Pseudo R-squared	0.237	0.452	0.200
Likelihood ratio (sig.)	52.25	22.19	77.81
	(0.000)	(0.014)	(0.000)
Number of cases	297	69	401

Notes: Cell entries are ordered logit regression coefficients. $^{**}p < 0.01$; $^{*}p < 0.05$ (two-tailed).

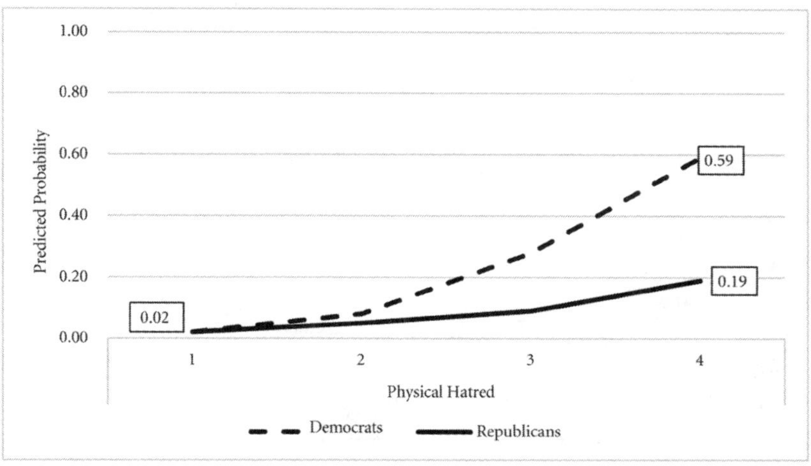

Figure 7.8 Physical Hatred and Predicted Probability of Being Unhappy about Interpartisan Marriage

Notes: Predicted probabilities of responding "unhappy" or "very unhappy" were calculated using ordered logit regression coefficients shown in Table 7.5. All other hatred measures were set to their means, all control variables were set to their modal values, and hatred measure of interest was manipulated over the range of valid values.

partisan identity who registered the lowest level of physical hatred had only about a 2 percent chance of saying they would be dissatisfied if a close family member married an out-party affiliate, those who reported the strongest disgust with their partisan opponents were calculated to be more likely to do so. The Democratic students expressing the strongest physical dislike of Republicans were predicted to have about a 59 percent chance of saying that having a Republican in-law would upset them. In comparison, the GOP supporters in my sample who said they had the strongest feelings of disgust with Democrats were predicted to have only about a 19 percent chance of being saddened about a mixed-party family marriage.

The connection between feelings of personal hatred and affect about interpartisan marriage was also slightly stronger for Democratic study participants than for Republicans (see Figure 7.9), though the predicted levels of dissatisfaction were relatively low for partisans from both sides. Democrats saying they had the lowest levels of organizational animosity toward the Republican Party were calculated to have

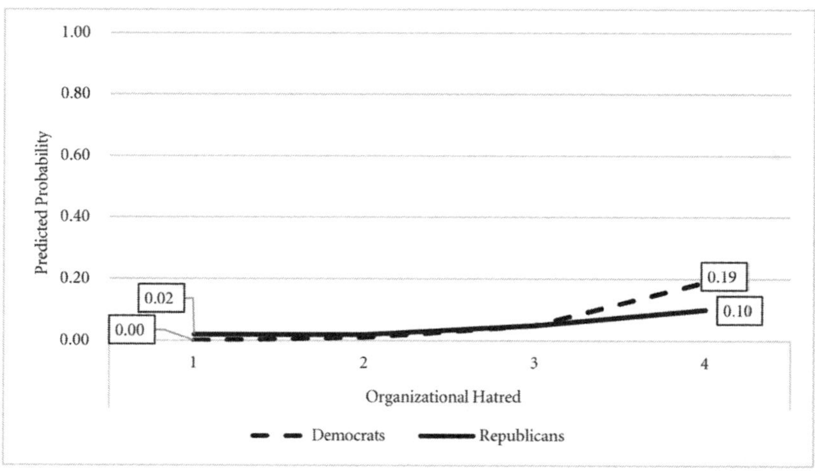

Figure 7.9 Organizational Hatred and Predicted Probability of Being Unhappy about Interpartisan Marriage

Notes: Predicted probabilities of responding "unhappy" or "very unhappy" were calculated using ordered logit regression coefficients shown in Table 7.5. All other hatred measures were set to their means, all control variables were set to their modal values, and hatred measure of interest was manipulated over the range of valid values.

almost no chance of saying they would be unhappy with a close relative marrying a Republican. Similarly, Republican students feeling equally low levels of organizational hatred had only about a 2 percent chance of expressing opposition to interparty marriage. Looking to the other end of the organizational hatred scale, Democrats expressing the strongest feelings of organizational hatred were calculated to have about a 19 percent chance, and Republicans about a 10 percent chance, of being upset with family nuptials involving an out-party member.

As I turn finally to the association between interpersonal partisan hatred and feelings about interparty marriage, Figure 7.10 shows the countervailing relationships for Republican identifiers and nonpartisans. Republican study participants who harbored the most interpersonal hatred toward Democrats had about a 10 percent higher predicted chance of saying they would be dismayed if a family member took a Democratic spouse. The predicted effect for Independents, on the other hand, showed the opposite pattern. Nonpartisan students who expressed the strongest interpersonal dislike for partisans were

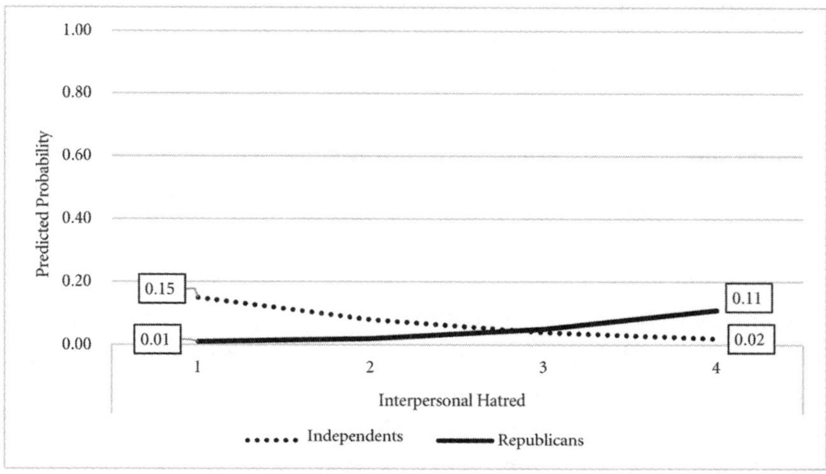

Figure 7.10 Interpersonal Hatred and Predicted Probability of Being Unhappy about Interpartisan Marriage

Notes: Predicted probabilities of responding "unhappy" or "very unhappy" were calculated using ordered logit regression coefficients shown in Table 7.5. All other hatred measures were set to their means, all control variables were set to their modal values, and hatred measure of interest was manipulated over the range of valid values.

about 13 percent less likely to say they would be upset about having a partisan in the family. Again, however, overall levels of opposition to interparty marriage remained low.

All in all, the results presented in this chapter suggest the same as in chapter 6—young voters look much like their elders. Feelings of hatred toward partisan opponents might indeed be connected to college students' distaste for interpartisan marriage and, especially, a preference for living alongside others with similar political outlooks. Like the results from chapter 6, should these relationships extend to the youth population more generally, it suggests that feelings of partisan animosity could affect the residential and marriage decisions of college students as they embark on their adult lives. Social isolation might lead to increased exposure to reinforcing political messages, which have been shown to further enhance feelings of out-party resentment.

8. A More Civil Political Future?

He who knows only his own side of the case, knows little of that.

—John Stuart Mill

"People, I just want to say, you know, can we all get along? Can we get along?" Rodney King posed this question during the 1992 Los Angeles riots that followed the acquittal of the police officers who had beaten him. In the years since, the US public has witnessed a rise in intergroup animosities. These contentious battles not only play out along the long-standing racial divide in the nation since its birth but also more and more along partisan lines. As Democrats and Republicans sorted themselves into increasingly homogenous parties during the late twentieth century, divisions across racial, class, and ideological lines more closely overlapped the partisan identities of those in office and the mass electorate alike. The resulting political landscape we face today is rife with cross-partisan sentiments that overlap with age-old antagonisms rooted in ideological, racial, and class-based identities. Thus, more than a quarter of a century after King posed his question, it has been repeatedly met with a resoundingly negative reply.

SOCIAL IDENTITY AND PARTISAN HATRED ON THE COLLEGE CAMPUS

In the preceding pages, I have argued that partisan identities operate much like other social identities to generate in-party loyalty and out-party hostility, examined the ways in which the youngest members of the electorate expressed hatred of their partisan enemies, and explored some of the political and social consequences of such cross-partisan sentiments. Much like their elders, college students divulged a good deal of contempt for those from the opposite party. The students studied here claimed to be offended by the opposing party's actions, expressed a desire to avoid social interaction with opposing party members, and admitted occasionally being physically repulsed by and feeling impulses to physically harm their partisan rivals. Further, the analyses presented herein suggest that such sentiments relate to feelings about presidential candidates and reluctance to engage in compromise with their partisan competitors. More generally, students expressing partisan hatred tended to be less likely to express a willingness to live near counterpartisans or welcome an in-law from the opposite party into their family. On the whole, then, the youngest segment of the electorate appeared to express much the same interpartisan distrust and anger as the general US public.

Despite arguments that the youngest segment of the electorate is far less likely to be knowledgeable about politics and current events and therefore to express more apathy about political goings on, it appears that at least some college students have partisan attachments and loyalties that can affect their political attitudes and behaviors even without very high levels of political interest. As I have argued, this is likely because partisanship acts much like social identities of other sorts, making it easy for even the uninformed, inattentive, and less-knowledgeable members of the public to be motivated by appeals to party labels. After all, "easy, gut-level" responses to emotional appeals are likely to resonate even with those who do not pay much attention to politics. As some have contended, "Although politics is generally thought to be outside everyday experience for most Americans, social identity is a deeply embedded psychological orientation toward all social interactions" (Mason 2018, 298). Consequently, a person need not be politically sophisticated for partisanship to affect his or her feelings and actions (Devine 2015, 511).

Further, the subtle ways in which social identities operate mean that people often remain unaware of the influence such identities have on their attitudes and behaviors. Combined with the effects of a media environment in which individuals can selectively expose themselves to information reinforcing their existing beliefs and political identities, even nascent ones, can provoke feelings of disgust and anger toward political opponents (see, e.g., Mason 2018). Online media consumption, especially, might build partisan enmities among college students.

As suggested by the findings presented earlier, college students tended to select online more than traditional print and broadcast media, and more exposure to online media tended to be associated with higher levels of expressed hatred of the opposite party.

Like any other study, though, a few caveats about the research I present here should be kept in mind. It is important to remember that my study focuses on a single sample of students at one university at a single point in time. Although the students I studied are typical of college students across the nation in many ways, it is possible they did not entirely mirror that population. Thus, replication of the research offered here on a more broadly representative sample of currently enrolled college students can potentially add to our knowledge about the ways in which partisan hatred operates. Similarly, studies of the general US population's feelings of hatred toward counterpartisans might lead to the discovery of important similarities and differences across generations. Another artifact of my study design is the inability to clearly establish causal order. Because I rely on a cross-sectional sample, I am limited in my ability to completely untangle the relationships between partisan hatred and media use as well as between partisan animosities and ratings of political candidates/officeholders. Although I present some evidence that sentiments about the opposing party more likely drive both, I also acknowledge the existence of reciprocal relationships. A longitudinal study examining the existence and operation of partisan hatred and/or an experimental design could more clearly establish the direction of causality between these as well as other potentially important factors. Still, my research suggests that college students exhibited much the same type of affective polarization that has become more prevalent in the US electorate more generally. And, though my findings reflect student attitudes expressed before the highly emotional and divisive 2016 presidential election, some have argued that since then, "the gap between liberal and conservative views on campus has become even more pronounced . . . with college campuses hitting record levels of polarization, which has sparked passionate and sometimes violent protests" (Bryant 2018). Campus conflicts of this sort might portend even more intense feelings of partisan hatred among college-aged voters after they leave college.

IRRESPONSIBLE RESPONSIBLE PARTIES?

With all the interpartisan rancor evident today, it is somewhat ironic that many bemoaned the similarity between the two major parties in the postwar era. In fact, the leading association of political scientists argued at the time that what the country needed were two parties more distinct from each other. In 1950, the American Political Science Association (APSA) convened a task force and endorsed the resulting report that outlined "the inability of parties to present clear alternatives to voters" (Brady and Han 2015, 142). The APSA task force concluded that the weak parties of the time were incapable of offering the public clear choices and were thus "a barrier to effective democratic leadership" (Schier and Eblery 2016, 90). The authors contended that "responsible, pragmatic parties would give the American public clearer policy choices than the umbrella parties did" and offered specific advice as to how such parties could be created (Paulson 2018, 120). Ironically, the suggested party changes, which have since come to fruition, align with contemporary criticisms about the party organizations.

First, the APSA committee called for parties "able to bring forth programs to which they commit themselves and . . . possess sufficient internal cohesion to carry out these programs" (American Political Science Association 1950, 17–18). That is, the parties needed to offer coherent platforms, and the parties' members should stridently work together toward implementing the policies those platforms entail. The task force further reasoned that the "fundamental requirement of accountability is a two-party system in which the opposition party acts as the critic of the party in power" (American Political Science Association 1950, 18). In effect, the authors called for parties to actively oppose and challenge each other's proposals. Finally, the report spoke to the electoral connection, calling for party leaders to be responsible to rank-and-file party members, "as enforced in primaries, caucuses, and conventions" (American Political Science Association 1950, 23). Parties, it seems, were asked to better reflect the desires of the most engaged portions of their memberships, who coincidentally, tend to be the more ideologically extreme (Abramowitz 2010; Barber and McCarty 2015; Carsey and Layman 2015).

Shortly after the report was issued, critics raised concerns (Key 1966; Kirkpatrick 1971; Ranney 1954). Some pointed to the "social realities and usefulness of umbrella parties" (Paulson 2018, 120; see also Manuel and Cammisa 1999; Paulson 2000, 2007; Sundquist 1992). In the years since, many of these critics have seen the task force's recommendations materialize. As suggested, the major parties sorted themselves along ideological lines and became more internally homogenous and coherent. The parties increasingly committed to proposing and fighting for passage of legislation supporting their fundamental platform stances and to opposing those of the other party. Party nomination practices were reformed in ways that increased the influence of party activists as well as rank-and-file voters.

Beginning in the late 1960s congressional rules and procedural changes also underwent change as the parties became more distinct from each other. Congressional leaders were given increased power (Rhode 1991). "And what do party leaders do with their power? It turns out they promote ideological division and polarization in Congress" (Schier and Eblery 2016, 97). The House speaker, in particular, gained authority in a number of ways. Using newly granted powers to determine the majority party members on the Rules Committee, speakers were better able to control floor debate. In addition, opportunities for offering amendments were limited, and the number of days in session and number of committees and subcommittees were reduced. Further, party leadership increasingly modified legislation outside of committees. Congressional leaders used their enhanced power to coerce their partisan opponents as well as their own party members to alter their voting behavior. Procedural changes related to the way in which votes in the Committee of the Whole were recorded, making it easier for leaders to attach amendments to a bill and force members from the opposition party into casting unpopular votes to begin consideration of the primary legislation itself (Roberts and Smith 2003; Theriault 2008). "This simple change led to a dramatic increase in the number of party-line recorded votes and therefore led to an increase in measured polarization for indices . . . such as the DW-NOMINATE scores" (Barber and McCarty 2015, 35; see also Roberts 2007). Minority parties responded with Senate filibusters to derail legislation and took advantage of recorded votes and television cameras in the chambers to force their partisan opponents, especially those in competitive districts, into casting unpopular votes (Schier and Eblery 2013). By 1975, this tactic had already become so common that the Senate lowered the proportion of votes needed to end a filibuster (from two-thirds to three-fifths). The US Congress became a place of intense partisan battles, with leaders on both sides of the aisle employing strategies to embarrass and defeat their partisan counterparts and rank-and-file members doing the same.

In many ways, the lack of compromise and cross-partisan animosities many criticize as obstructionist and harmful to the nation reflect party actions in line with the task force's recommendations. The nomination and election of more and more extreme candidates from both parties increased the ideological homogeneity within and distance between the parties. The resulting decline in bipartisan compromise "over the past five decades [further] promoted ideological polarization between our political parties" (Paulson 2018, 121). The increase of party-line voting, annual budget battles in which partisans stubbornly defend their own positions, acrimonious fights over legislative proposals such as both the Clinton- and Obama-era health-care reforms as well as the Trump border security imperative, and increasingly contentious clashes in the Senate confirmation process provide ready evidence of such tendencies. In the end, "the current state of high ideological definition of the parties stands as an example of 'be careful what you wish for' for political scientists" (Persily 2015, 5). The irresponsible parties earlier generations decried have been transformed into the responsible parties the APSA championed. The result, however, has been a responsible party system that many now see as irresponsible. It does indeed seem that, as Brady and Han (2015, 142) observed, "The grass is always greener."

A Revival of Reforms?

In the face of a highly polarized nation and rising hostilities across partisan lines, scholars have again begun offering suggestions about potential causes and solutions. Some view congressional polarization as the result of "both sincere ideological differences about policy means and ends and strategic behavior to exploit those differences to win election" (McCarty 2015, 6). Solutions have been offered that address both of these factors. Some argue we should reform electoral procedures to enable the election of more moderates to office (Persily 2015, 13). Others see the possibility of uniting "free-market conservatives with civil and social liberties-oriented liberals" in support of libertarian candidates (Noel 2013, 178). Either approach, they argue, would help to counter the intense partisan divide that exists between partisans in office as well as those in the mass electorate.

Relatedly, gerrymandered districts, party primary systems, and campaign finance patterns have all been suggested as causes of contemporary partisan divisions. Partisan gerrymandering has been argued to create a situation where safe candidates need cater only to the demands of the party base rather than compete for more moderate voters (Carson et al. 2007; Theriault 2008; Tufte 1973). The evidence in support of this argument, however, is rather weak (Barber and McCarty 2015). After all, the Senate, which is free of districts, shows increasing polarization as much as the district-based House (McCarty, Poole, and Rosenthal 2006). Similarly, though it might seem plausible to many that as the parties sorted along ideological lines, only liberal candidates could possibly secure Democratic nominations and only conservative office-seekers could expect Republican nominations, the evidence again suggests otherwise (Barber and McCarty 2015, 30; see also Brady, Han, and Pope 2007; Gerber and Morton 1998; Kaufman, Gimpel, and Hoffman 2003). Polarization has gone up in the same period that primaries were opened to nonpartisans (McCarty, Poole, and Rosenthal 2006), and existing research reveals only modest, at best, effects for a move to open-primary systems (Barber and McCarty 2015, 30; see also Bullock and Clinton 2011; Hirano et al. 2010; Masket et al. 2013). There also seems to be little evidence that ideologically motivated campaign donors are responsible for pushing the parties apart and fanning the flames of partisan hatred. Even though some argue that politicians are likely to cater to the extreme policy goals of special-interest funders (Lessig 2011) and accommodate ideologically extreme individual donors (Baron 1994; Ensley 2009; Moon 2004), little evidence arises to suggest this is the case (Barber and McCarty 2015). Even though ideologically motivated donors might not be a primary impetus for increased partisan bitterness, they might "have exacerbated the problem" (McCarty 2015, 6). All in all, then, though there is little evidence to support arguments that reforming political districting practices, party primary procedures, or campaign finance patterns would help mute the partisan rancor of contemporary US politics.

JUST DEAL WITH IT

Finding little potential benefit to making reforms in those areas, some view polarization, and the accompanying attitudes and behavior, as a fact of contemporary US politics that must be faced. After all, "competition for power . . . contributes to our confrontational politics" (Lee 2015, 78; see also Lee 2009), and the past thirty years have offered the nation an era of partisan parity near the level of that of the Civil War (Lee 2015). As was the case then, partisan competition tends to exaggerate the distance that exists between parties. Political identities become core to self-esteem considerations, and "even when the parties do not disagree in substantive terms, they still have political motivations to actively seek and find reasons to oppose one another" (Lee 2015, 78). Thus, political actors have little desire to pursue cross-partisan issue agreements or bipartisan negotiation and compromise.

US politics has a well-established history of partisan animosity. Consider the following comments: "A dangerous man . . . who ought not be trusted with the reins of government." He possesses an "exuberant vanity and insatiable egotism." His "egotism, vanity, and ungovernable temper" make him wrong for the presidency. He is a "lecherous beast," a "moral leper." He is "neurotic." He suffers from megalomania and paranoia. He is "ridiculous and a little scary: trigger-happy, a bomb-thrower." He is "wholly unqualified by education, habit, and temper for the station of President." Though reminiscent of remarks made about Donald Trump, these comments were in fact uttered about, respectively, Alexander Hamilton (the first two), John Adams, Theodore Roosevelt, Grover Cleveland, William Jennings Bryan, Barry Goldwater, and Andrew Jackson.

Only when compared to the relative partisan harmony of the mid-twentieth century does today's partisan divide seem astounding. As some have pointed out, "Polarization has deeper structural and historical roots . . . it may even be the norm in American politics" (Hopkins and Sides 2015, ix). In fact, congressional polarization has been the norm for most of US history, with the mid-twentieth century offering a respite. Consequently, as Hare, Poole, and Rosenthal (2015) point out, "perhaps it is more realistic to expect that congressional polarization may essentially stabilize at or near current levels for the foreseeable future" (149). Such a perspective leads some to suggest that the nation's current state of polarization and partisan anger should be dealt with using procedural reforms that help "to minimize the potential for government paralysis" (Persily 2015, 13).

Akin to the APSA task force, scholars have recently offered proposals for party reforms as a means to combat the current contentious climate. Frequently the reforms made following the APSA report are targeted for repeal. The enforcement of party-line voting by strong party leaders has been seen as the root cause of today's polarization (Barber and McCarty 2015), and, as discussed in this tome's opening chapter, even former and current members of Congress suggest that such pressures have increased (also see Edwards 2012). Academic investigation, though, offers only mixed findings, with some studies suggesting the presence of such pressures but unable to document the rise in such pressures over time (see Cox and Poole 2002; McCarty, Poole, and Rosenthal 1997; Snyder and Groseclose 2000). Thus, reforms targeted at rolling back the increased power of party leaders offer only limited chances of success in relieving partisan tensions. Interestingly, however, not all suggest that weakening the parties will remedy the situation. Pildes (2015), for instance, argues that we should accept polarization as a given and calls on strong party leaders committed to bipartisanship to step up and "help lessen negative governance problems of polarization" (157–159). Because partisan divides are likely to exist in US politics, he argues, effective leaders offer the best hope of political compromises that enable effective governance. Although reforms aimed at party organizations, legislative institutions, or electoral processes might prove successful, such changes would likely be slow to develop, and their potential effects on mass attitudes would likely develop even more sluggishly. Alongside any remedies attempted at the elite or institutional levels, partisan animosities and the behavioral consequences they breed might be effectively addressed at the level of the individual voter.

TODAY'S STUDENTS, TOMORROW'S LEADERS?

Because tomorrow's political leaders will come from, and be chosen by, the young voters of today, the findings presented in this treatise take on added significance. As others have noted and I document in this study, in many ways young voters reflect many of the same partisan attitudes their elders do. Given the issue positions of the millennial and iGen generations stabilizing where they are now, Shapiro (2015) contends that "there could well be no change in the existing pattern of partisan conflict" (153) unless one of the parties shifts significantly on key issues. The current political climate and empirical evidence suggest, however, that such a change is not likely to occur anytime soon. For, as Noel (2013) points out, "What seems particularly significant about the modern era is that ideology and party voting have come together, perhaps for the first extended period in U.S. history" (173). As long as this trend continues, it is likely young people will form their political identities in a polarized political context from socializing agents who harbor intense cross-partisan animosities.

The results I present in this book suggest that today's young voters have indeed inherited the cross-partisan animosities of the world that surrounded them in their formative years. Some people have suggested that dispelling myths about partisan opponents can help tamp down the partisan hatred evident among my sample of college students. Though it will likely be difficult to penetrate already ingrained partisan perceptions, there is some evidence that receiving factual information about the composition of the out-party is associated with "viewing that party as less extreme and feeling less socially isolated from the party's supporters" (Ahler and Sood 2018). Although somewhat hopeful, parties, candidates, and the media have few incentives for providing such information. As they compete for the attention and support of young voters, fueling negative sentiments across party lines continues to be a useful tactic for garnering votes and viewers. Similarly, childhood socialization holds little hope for reversing the partisan anger and hatred increasingly evident in recent years. Family members are not likely to expose children to an unbiased flow of information because their own partisan identities likely motivate them to filter information in a manner that favors their existing partisan allegiances.

Educating Tomorrow's Leaders?

As others have argued, and as I addressed in chapter 2, the college years offer perhaps the best opportunity for attitude change. My findings as well as those reviewed previously (see chapter 2), however, suggest this does not appear to be the case when it comes to tolerance of those who hold differing political views. Many argue that intolerance of conflicting opinions on college campuses began with changes in the culture of higher education that occurred in the late 1980s and 1990s (Chong 2006; Sides 2017). During that era, those in higher education engaged in debates about whether derogatory speech on college campuses, especially but not limited to speech targeting racial minorities, merited First Amendment protections (Chong 2006; Lawrence 1990; Matsuda, Delgado, and Crenshaw 1993; Walker 1994). In response, many colleges and universities adopted speech codes that sought to regulate and punish offensive speech (Heumann and Church 1997; Kolowich 2018; Shiell 1998; Walker 1994), prompting some to claim that college campuses were becoming "islands of repression" (d'Souza 1991; Finn 1989) where the expression of unpopular ideas was verboten.[1]

Though the courts eventually struck down many of the speech codes as overly broad and conflicting with constitutional protections of free speech, university administrators continued to be supportive of restricting the airing of unpopular, and potentially hurtful, speech on their campuses (Kolowich 2018). In fact, estimates suggest that between one-third and one-half of colleges and universities in the United States have regulations against group-targeted speech (Chong 2006; Korwar 1995). It would seem that the American preference for equality over liberty that de Tocqueville (2012) identified nearly a century ago is alive and well.[2]

Some claim the change in campus culture that resulted from the speech code debates has created an "illiberal" dynamic in which students seek to silence, rather than engage with, those holding opposing viewpoints (Stevens and Haidt 2018). Recent research showing that those with higher levels of education tend to exhibit more ideological prejudice than those with less education (Henry and Napier 2017) add support to such a contention, as does evidence that the relationship between educational attainment and intolerance of differing viewpoints changed in important ways after the speech code debates of the late 1980s. Younger generations of college students tend to express more support for "blasphemy laws" that mandate punishment for insulting or disrespectful speech. Almost half of the millennial and iGen cohorts favor such laws, in contrast with about one-third of Boomers (Stevens and Haidt 2018). Likewise, Chong (2006) documents a strong negative relationship between support for multiculturalism and tolerance of a person who believes blacks are genetically inferior for those educated since 1986 but the opposite for those educated before then. In just one year, Stevens and Haidt (2018) found that support for an "open learning environment," in which students are exposed to all types of speech and viewpoints, over a "positive environment," in which certain speech or expression is prohibited, shrank by about 15 percent. Similarly, Villasenor (2017) found that about half of the postmillennial college students he studied felt that silencing a speaker they found offensive was acceptable, and they preferred a campus environment that sheltered them from offensive views. On the whole, the contemporary US academy seems less of a "place to 'find oneself' and learn from others" than "a place where already-formed citizens clash, stay with like-minded others, or avoid politics altogether" (Herbst 2010, 111).

Those on the forefront of research in this area express pessimism about the possibility of a sea change in the willingness of young people to tolerate contrary opinions. Pointing out that younger generations have not witnessed effective political institutions or norms in their lives and seem less able to handle political disagreement, as well as the fact that the campus "call-out" culture seems to be spreading quickly into business and other institutions, Johnathan Haidt argues that Americans' "dysfunction and anger will worsen" (Edsall 2019). All in all, then, recent empirical research does not bode well for the possibility that today's college students will reverse the trend of rising partisan polarization and cross-partisan hatred so many bemoan.

Changes to higher-education policies regarding speech that current and upcoming students find disagreeable are not likely to be made rapidly, if at all. Based on my findings, it also appears that today's college students might likely continue to isolate themselves from their partisan opponents in both the political and social spheres and socialize their children into the same partisan attitudes they hold. Consequently, if we are to hope for a downturn in partisan polarization and cross-partisan animosities, we might want to consider other possible sources of such change. As Levendusky (2017) suggests, the mass media might play some role by emphasizing a common social identity as Americans instead of accentuating political and sociodemographic differences. Should the public, especially younger generations, come to view themselves as members of the same in-group of US citizens rather than as members of competing groups of liberal Democrats and conservative Republicans, perhaps cross-partisan compromises might be found and fewer angry words (and fists) might be hurled across the partisan divide. Unfortunately, the media tend to present such a perspective only in times the nation faces a crisis, such as the terrorist attacks of September 11, 2001. A highly visible event that serves to unify the citizenry against a common out-group enemy might lead to the same kind of "unity that seemed to well up everywhere" for a brief period after that day (Peltz 2016). However, as much of the research related to rally effects tells us, such reenvisioning of our social identities dissipates rather quickly in the face of political decision making. Thus, holding out hope for redefining social identities seems to offer little, if any, direction for decreasing the level of virulence in today's political world.

A NATION OF INCIVILITY?

As my evidence and that of others suggests, students entering college bring with them a set of socialized political beliefs that tend to be reinforced in their college years, along with habits regarding the ways in which they interact with those holding contrary viewpoints. Many contend that much of the incivility seen on contemporary college campuses stems from the development of a culture that protects young people from controversial conversations and uncomfortable situations from their earliest years (Furedi 2017; Lukianoff and Haidt 2018). The US education system, it seems, might be failing to teach younger generations how to critically engage in conversations with those who express contrary opinions.

A study conducted by the Southern Poverty Law Center in the context of the 2016 presidential election offers some perspective on the latter (Costello 2016). Results from a nationwide survey of K–12 teachers show that more than half of the respondents reported an increase in uncivil discourse in their classrooms. Teachers reported that students often expressed anger and displayed inability to engage in civil discourse, resorting instead to "shouting matches, verbal hostility, and sometimes even fights" (11). Explaining how words can intensify existing animus between students, one high school teacher reported that a student who disagreed with another yelled, "What is the matter with you? This is why I HATE people" (11). A middle school teacher reported, "Students [were] quick to become accusatory and condemn others for having a different point of view" (11). Even in elementary schools, teachers reported the use of campaign rhetoric as part of students' bullying vocabulary, and students were "crying in the classroom and having meltdowns at home" because of political conversations at school (5). The same study reports that more than 40 percent of teachers said they were hesitant to teach about the 2016 election. Instead, concerned with "maintaining both objectivity and order," they avoided political conversations altogether (12). Some of those who chose to bring such conversations into the classroom often said that when "faced with the choice between maintaining neutrality and denouncing rhetoric that's counter to their values, many respondents indicated they would abandon neutrality" (13), choosing instead to espouse one side of a political argument to be "allies" with some of their students. With little education and training in how to critically engage in discussions about controversial issues from the time they enter school, it is little wonder coeds on college campuses struggle with contentious political debates.

Still, academics with personal political beliefs on both the left and right are expressing distress at the "fragility of 21st-century students" (Nichols 2017). As university faculty and administrators attempt to balance a tradition of campus free speech with verbal complaints and threats of physical violence (Noddings 2018), they worry they are creating "a citizenry unprepared for its duties in the public sphere and . . . instead are engaging in relentless conflict on social media, taking offense at everything while believing anything" (Nichols 2017). Though administrative policies and norms regarding conflictual political discussions on college campuses might be difficult and slow to change, all hope is not necessarily lost. Educators at all levels of the educational system, but especially university faculty, can work to enhance student ability to become more critical and open-minded thinkers in their classrooms. After all, if those charged with educating future generations "are not teaching [their] students how to talk civilly about politics, where are they going to learn how to do so?" (Plane 2016, 5).

Civil Discourse 101

The university holds an important, though not exclusive, responsibility for the development of citizens capable of engaging in contentious debates about important issues. John Henry Newman (1852) argued that the goal of higher education was the

> training of good members of society. . . . It is the education which gives a man a clear, conscious view of his own opinions and judgements, a truth in developing them, an eloquence in expressing them, and a force in urging them. It teaches him to see things as they are, to go right to the point, to disentangle a skein of thought to detect what is sophistical and to discard what is irrelevant. (178)

His assertion that students should be taught to understand their own opinions, seek truth in developing those opinions, and express them clearly to others reflects well the traditional vision of what those holding college degrees should look like. If we accept his argument, it seems reasonable to assume that those who choose to become university students would enjoy engaging in challenging cognitive tasks, be willing to persevere through four years of rigorous academic challenges, and be unsatisfied with arriving at conclusions they do not feel are fully informed. As the arguments and evidence I present in this volume suggest, however, these characteristics might not be on ready display in the contemporary US student body. This does not necessarily mean that university faculty should heed the warning Dante encountered in his journey through hell, "Lasciate ogne speranza, voi ch'intrate," each time they walk into their classrooms.

An increasing number of resources for building opportunities to teach students how to critically and civilly engage in discussions of controversial issues have recently been made available to those in teaching roles. Many of these include lists of practical tips (Plane 2016), strategies (National Council for the Social Studies 2019), and steps (Sacramento State Center for Teaching and Learning 2019). Offering advice such as avoiding the use of loaded terms; avoiding inflammatory language; employing active listening; avoiding interrupting others; seeking understanding; committing to learning, not debating; acknowledging others' viewpoints; showing respect; avoiding antagonizing others; containing emotional reactions; and starting small and building up, as well as specific classroom procedures and activities, these self-help guides might prove useful to many. Still, they do little to explain how to ingrain such habits in students or how to take a more holistic approach to changing habits of thought and norms of uncivil discourse.

Seeking to better understand the psychological roots of such habits and norms in an effort to address their behavioral consequences, scholars have been working to develop strategies for countering ingrained ways of responding to contrary viewpoints. For instance, some researchers focus on developing the habit of actively open-minded thinking (AOT) as a remedy, or least a salve, for incivility in politics. AOT involves teaching students (and others) to seek out reasons their initial conclusions about a topic might be incorrect, argued to help "students to think on their own . . . [and] understand the nature of expert knowledge, and, more generally, the nature of academic disciplines" (Baron 1993, 191). This type of thinking requires students to exhibit several characteristics. First, they need to develop an affinity for engaging in and enjoying cognitive tasks that require effort (Cacioppo, Petty, and Kao, 1984). People who develop this propensity have been shown to be less likely to assert conclusions unsupported by evidence (Kardash and Scholes 1996). Second, they need to exhibit "perseverance and passion for long-term goals," what some have called "grit" (Duckworth et al. 2007; Haran, Ritov, and Mellers 2013, 190). Third, they need to become maximizers, not satisficers. That is, they should seek out more information before deciding they are informed enough to decide (Haran, Ritov, and Mellers 2013). Instead of seeking a conclusion that is "good enough," they need to aim at achieving the highest expected utility (the most accurate conclusion) from their decision.

Though they might not accurately describe today's university students, these three attributes reflect well the classical image of a well-educated college graduate as well as that of an actively open-minded thinker. If we are concerned with educating people to be Newman's "good members of society," we might want to better focus our efforts on building habits of open-minded thinking alongside our attempts to educate our students in the content of our disciplines. After all, some argue that the absence of such thinking "contributes to the political problems in today's world" (Baron 2019). Recent empirical research offers some evidence that creating a context within which an actively open-minded approach is rewarded can improve the quality of debates and encourage epistemic humility (recognition of the limits of one's knowledge). Using forecasting tournaments, in which participants on competing teams attempted to arrive at the most accurate prediction of the occurrence of future events, Tetlock and colleagues (2014) showed that these competitions "nudge players in polarized debates toward the right epistemic direction" (293). That is, participation in tournaments that rewarded arriving at the most accurate answer, not necessarily the most personally preferred one, helped combat common psychological tendencies that can impede sound decision making. Because participants face the possibility of publicly visible falsification of their predictions, they "learn to make more circumspect claims" (Tetlock et al. 2014, 293). The possibility of public accountability tends to "suppress self-justification and stimulate self-critical thinking" (Lerner and Tetlock 1999). In effect, tournaments create a context in which debiasing factors operate so that "ideological thinking will . . . translate into worse performance," and people are pressured "to acknowledge opposing arguments . . . as well as gaps in their knowledge" and "engage in perspective taking" to do well (Mellers, Tetlock, and Arkes 2019), all of which can counter overconfidence and tamp down affective preferences. Such findings support well John Stuart Mill's argument that "the whole strength and value . . . of human judgment [is] that it can be set right when it is wrong; reliance can be placed on it only when the means of setting it right are kept constantly at hand."[3] Incorporating similar techniques in academic exercises and activities might serve to train students to become more critical and civil participants in controversial political dialogues and help them reach Mill's ideal form of human judgment.

Relatedly, researchers have highlighted the psychological need for cognitive closure as a potential impediment to critical thinking and civil discourse (Tetlock et al. 2014). Individuals who show a high need for closure tend to behave more like Berlin's (1954) hedgehogs than foxes. They prefer to view the world through the lens of a single defining idea rather than draw on a wide array of perspectives. Luttig (2018) has recently documented a connection between a need for closure and partisan strength, affective polarization, and partisan sorting. His findings support viewing partisanship as a social identity that encourages viewing the world through an "us-versus-them" lens that can lead to extremism. Incorporating pedagogical strategies that combat (or least require recognition of) the tendency to favor cognitive closure might help encourage the development of more critical and civil political engagement.

Thus, those making university curricular decisions might want to consider the potential benefits of providing students a well-rounded liberal arts education that exposes them to a variety of perspectives on how to view and understand the world (Noddings 2018). Doing so might serve well not only college students but society more generally. The central importance of free speech in such an endeavor should not be overlooked. Stressing the importance of keeping one's "mind open to criticism of his opinions and conduct," Mill advised "listen[ing] to all that could be said against him; to profit by as much of it as was just, and expound to himself, and upon occasion to others, the fallacy of what was fallacious."[4] A university environment open to the expression of a diversity of viewpoints will enable students to practice the advice Mill offered and can bring the university closer to Newman's (1852) vision of an institution that "educates the intellect to reason well in all matters, to reach out towards truth, and to grasp it" (125–126). If the university holds as its telos the pursuit of truth (veritas), then college campuses should be places for the exploration of a variety of beliefs and arguments and, as Hamilton suggested in the first Federalist Paper, the "passions and prejudices little favorable to the discovery of truth" should occupy little territory in the academy.

Appendix: Measures and Coding

Immediate Physical Partisan Hatred: Index of six measures: "When you are in the presence of [Democrats/Republicans/Democrats and Republicans], how often do you:" 1 = almost never; 2 = sometimes; 3 = frequently; 4 = almost all the time. See Table 3.4 for descriptive statistics. Cronbach's alpha = 0.863.

(1) experience unpleasant physical feelings (e.g., increased blood flow or pulse rate, sweating, muscle tension, chest pains).

(2) have extreme feelings toward [Democrats/Republicans/Democrats and Republicans].

(3) have thoughts of a desire to get rid of or destroy [Democrats/Republicans/Democrats and Republicans] in any kind of manner.

(4) feel a desire to take action in order to take revenge on [Democrats/Republicans/Democrats and Republicans] and their leaders.

(5) imagine a violent action against [Democrats/Republicans/Democrats and Republicans].

(6) feel negative and hard feelings toward [Democrats/Republicans].

Chronic Organizational Partisan Hatred: Index of the following four measures: "How much do you agree with each of the following statements?" 1 = strongly agree; 2 = agree; 3 = disagree; 4 = strongly disagree. See Table 3.4 for descriptive statistics. Cronbach's alpha = 0.784.

(1) "The actions of the [Democratic/Republican/Democratic and Republican] Party have offended me and/or members of my party over a long period of time." (reverse coded)

(2) "Some of the actions of the [Democratic/Republican/Democratic and Republican] Party and its leaders are a result of a 'bad' internal character." (reverse coded)

(3) "Some of the actions of the [Democratic/Republican/Democratic

and Republican] Party and its leaders are a result of an intentional desire to harm me and members of your party." (reverse coded)

(4) "The thought of the [Democratic/Republican/Democratic and Republican] Party gives rise to negative feelings in me." (reverse coded)

Chronic Interpersonal Partisan Hatred: Index of the following two measures: "How much do you agree with each of the following statements?" 1 = strongly agree; 2 = agree; 3 = disagree; 4 = strongly disagree. See Table 3.4 for descriptive statistics. Cronbach's alpha = 0.720.

(1) "I would be glad to socialize more with members of the [Democratic/Republican/ Democratic and Republican] Party."

(2) "I would be glad to know more [Democrats/Republicans/Democrats and Republicans]."

Chronic National Partisan Hatred: Index of the following two measures: "How much do you agree with each of the following statements?" 1 = strongly agree; 2 = agree; 3 = disagree. 4 = strongly disagree. See Table 3.4 for descriptive statistics. Cronbach's alpha = 0.275.

(1) "[Democrats/Republicans/Democrats and Republicans/Democrats and Republicans] are a threat to the nation's well-being." (reverse coded)

(2) "The actions of [Democrats/Republicans/Democrats and Republicans] and leaders of their party are just and legitimate."

Feeling Thermometers: "I'd like to get your feelings toward some of our political leaders and groups who are in the news these days. Using a 100-point scale, where ratings between 50 degrees and 100 degrees mean that you feel favorable and warm toward the person/group. Ratings between 0 degrees and 50 degrees mean that you don't feel favorable toward the person/group and that you don't care too much for that person/group. You would rate the person at the 50-degree mark if you don't feel particularly warm or cold toward the person/group."

(1) President Barack Obama (mean = 43.9; s.d. = 31.3; median = 50.0)

(2) Former President George W. Bush (mean = 54.1; s.d. = 28.2; median = 50.0)

(3) The Republican Party (mean = 56.9; s.d. = 27.4; median = 51.0)

(4) The Democratic Party (mean = 48.3; s.d. = 27.4; median = 50.0)

Partisan Identification: Derived from answers to the following questions: (a)"Generally speaking, do you usually think of yourself as a Democrat, a Republican, an independent, or what?"; If Democrat or Republican: "Would you call yourself a strong [Democrat/Republican] or a not very strong [Democrat/Republican]?"; If Independent: "Do you think of yourself as closer to the Republican Party or to the Democratic Party?" 1 = Strong Democrat (7.5 percent; 62); 2 = Weak Democrat (20.4 percent; 169); 3 = Lean Democrat (10.5 percent; 87); 4 = Independent (9.4 percent; 78); 5 = Lean Republican (10.7 percent; 89); 6 = Weak Republican (19.4 percent; 161); 7 = Strong Republican (22.1 percent; 183).

Ideology: "When it comes to politics, would you describe yourself as . . ." 1 = extremely liberal (3.1 percent; 25); 2 = moderately liberal (16.8 percent; 135); 3 = slightly liberal (15.2 percent; 122); 4 = neither liberal nor conservative (22.5 percent; 181); 5 = slightly conservative (15.4 percent; 124); 6 = moderately conservative (22.4 percent; 180); extremely conservative (4.5 percent; 36).

Political Interest: "How interested are you in information about what's going on in government and politics?" 1 = not at all interested (7.5 percent; 62); 2 = slightly interested (30.1 percent; 249); 3 = moderately interested (44.6 percent; 369); 4 = very interested (13.5 percent; 112); 5 = extremely interested (4.2 percent; 35).

Media Consumption: "How often do you get information about politics from each of the following sources?" 1 = never; 2 = less than once a month; 3 = one to three times a month; 4 = almost every week; 5 = three times a week or more; 6 = every day.

(1) paper newspapers (mean = 1.97; s.d. = 1.15; median = 2.00)

(2) magazines (mean = 1.84; s.d. = 0.98; median = 2.00)

(3) television (mean = 3.82; s.d. = 1.34; median = 4.00)

(4) radio (mean = 2.93; s.d. = 1.45; median = 3.00)

(5) internet news sites (mean = 4.03; s.d. = 1.49; median = 4.00)

(6) internet blogs (mean = 2.86; s.d. = 1.72; median = 3.00)

Male: Respondent sex: 0 = female (65.8 percent; 528); 1 = male (34.2 percent; 275)

Race/Ethnicity: “Which of the following racial/ethnic categories best describes you—White (Anglo); Black (African American); Hispanic (Latino/Latina); Asian American; Other?” Coded as dichotomous variables. See Table 3.1 for descriptive statistics.

Residential Preference: “How much do you agree with each of the following statements? “It is important to me to live in a place where most people share my political views.” 1 = strongly disagree (4.7 percent; 39); 2 = disagree (33.5 percent; 277); 3 = agree (54.5 percent; 450); 4 = strongly agree (7.3 percent; 60).

Marital Preference: “How would you react if an immediate family member were to marry a [Democrat/Republican/Democrat or Republican]? Would you be . . .” 1 = very happy (1.0 percent; 8); 2 = happy (1.5 percent; 12); 3 = doesn't matter (90.0 percent; 743); 4 = unhappy (5.4 percent; 45); 5 = very unhappy (2.1 percent; 17).

Compromise: “Thinking about how Republican and Democratic politicians should address the most important issues facing the country, imagine a scale from zero to 100 where 100 means Republicans get everything they want, 0 means Democrats get everything they want, where do you think things should end up?” Ranges 0 to 100; mean = 55.37; s.d. = 18.38; median = 50.00.

Notes

CHAPTER ONE: INCIVILITY AND POLARIZATION

1. "These are things that people threw at candidate for president." *Life Magazine* 9, no. 19 (November 4, 1940): 86–88.

2. Though party organizations remained intact, President Roosevelt took direct aim at Southern conservative senators in his own party (the "Copperheads among us," as he called them in his June 24, 1938, Fireside Chat), allowing them little influence on his policy decisions and seeking to influence their electoral defeat. Internal partisan battles of this sort continued through the 1960s and perhaps even until the early 2000s when Zell Miller took aim at Ted Kennedy and John Kerry, his fellow partisans in the Senate chamber.

3. The nation has, however, had a history of vigilante violence against minorities seeking access to the voting booth (see Kropf 2016).

4. In the earlier era, John Tyler, James Buchanan, Andrew Johnson, and Ulysses S. Grant faced impeachment threats. In the later century, only Franklin D. Roosevelt and Jimmy Carter did not face impeachment threats. Most impeachment threats, though, ended well before official charges were filed. Only Andrew Johnson, Bill Clinton, and Donald Trump have been formally charged by the House and tried in the Senate.

5. Although much scholarly consensus exists about the Reagan era ushering in an overtly partisan presidency, some have argued that this trend began with a type of "subrosa" partisanship under Dwight Eisenhower, Richard Nixon, and Gerald Ford (Galvin 2013).

6. See the Vote View website, https://voteviewblog.com for details of this measure.

7. The fact that the House typically showed more polarization than the Senate might be construed as evidence that candidates facing more frequent elections were driven to polarization more quickly as a result of electoral imperatives.

8. At the same time, however, it is important to note that the candidates preferred by the more ideological activists fail frequently to receive party nominations.

9. Though some have contended that much of the trend identified by these authors was more an artifact of survey question wording changes (e.g., Bishop, Tuchfarber, and Oldendick 1978; Sullivan, Pierson, and Marcus 1978).

10. Such opposition represents well the Responsible Party model championed by reformers more than a half century ago (see chapter 8 for more details).

11. Results are based on data from the Pew Research Center, Political Typology Survey, conducted June 8–18 and June 27–July 9, 2017.

CHAPTER TWO: AFFECTIVE POLARIZATION AND SOCIAL IDENTITIES

1. Because leaning partisans have been shown to think and behave more like weak partisans than "pure" Independents, leaners are considered partisans throughout this book.

2. *Democracy in America,* vol. 1, Part 2, chap. 7.

3. The "nonconformist" ideas and lifestyles included in these studies included being an admitted homosexual or communist, believing that blacks are genetically inferior, opposing all churches and religions, or advocating for nonelected, militaristic government.

4. The millennial generation typically includes those born in the 1980s and early 1990s and entering college early in the twenty-first century, whereas those in the iGen (sometimes also called Gen Z) cohort have been born since about 1995 and started entering college in about 2013.

5. There were some differences across the partisan spectrum, with Democratic-affiliated students reporting slightly higher levels of preference of environments that sheltered students from offensive views, but nearly half of Independents and Republicans were reported to have felt the same way.

6. Pew Research Center, Political Typology Survey, conducted June 8–18 and June 27–July 9, 2017.

CHAPTER THREE: STUDYING PARTISAN HATRED ON THE COLLEGE CAMPUS

1. The US Department of Education, National Center for Education Statistics reports that 76 percent of undergraduate college students were enrolled in public colleges and universities in 2015.

2. See the Appendix and chapter 4 for the question wording and details.

3. The US Department of Education, National Center for Education Statistics reports that in the same year, 56 percent of undergraduate students were female.

4. Summary statistics for all thermometer targets are available in the Appendix.

5. Following the research that shows leaning partisans hold attitudes and behave in ways similar to partisan identifiers (see, e.g., Theodoridis 2017) I code leaning partisans as partisan affiliates throughout this book.

6. These two dimensions might be viewed as similar to attitudinal intensity and stability, respectively.

7. I again consider those who reported a leaning, weak, or strong preference for a major party as partisans. Only those who reported complete independence from both parties are considered Independents.

8. Though not presented, I also tested all the models discussed in subsequent chapters with the national partisan hatred measure included. The models with only three hatred measures (physical, organizational, and interpersonal) included showed better fit statistics (r-squared values and f-statistics) and present fewer collinearity problems (as indicated by Tolerance/VIF statistics) than models with the national hatred index measure included as well.

CHAPTER FOUR: WHO HATES? CORRELATES OF PARTISAN HATRED

1. Reported radio consumption might be higher than expected for this age group because many of the students on the SHSU campus are commuters who listen to either radio (or podcasts) during their travel to and from campus.

2. Though not asked in this survey, the proportion of the sample who accessed social media outlets would likely be higher than that for blogs.

3. For each type of media, reported consumption rates for both formats were averaged.

CHAPTER FIVE: MEDIA MESSAGES AND PARTISAN HATRED

1. Along with the argument that selective exposure contributes to media reinforcement rather than conversion power are arguments that consumers also selectively interpret the media messages they receive in light of their preexisting attitudes (e.g., Campbell et al. 1960).

2. But see Garrett (2009) for contrary evidence.

3. Pearson's r bivariate correlations for the two forms of print, broadcast, and online media were 0.465, 0.486, and 0.523, respectively, whereas television and internet news use correlated at 0.495 (all statistically significant at $p < 0.001$, two-tailed).

4. My arguments about media use and partisan sentiments assume a causal flow that runs from the media to public opinion. Although there are good

theoretical reasons for making such an assumption, it is important not to forget that the opposite might also be the case. That is, those who harbor outparty animosities might seek different types of media than those who are less upset with their partisan competitors. To test for this possibility, I also modeled the relationship between media use and political attitudes as a nonrecursive one using simultaneous equation modelling (SEM). The SEM results suggested that partisan hatred did indeed help predict the consumption of media, particularly online media, to some degree. Importantly, though, the predictive power media exerted on partisan hatred remained. Further, the substantive impact the media variables exerted on partisan hatred was consistently stronger than the impact the partisan hatred variables exerted on reported media use.

5. Ordered logit analyses were also performed for all regression results presented here. The statistical and substantive results were unchanged from those presented here. Because OLS regression coefficients are more directly interpreted, I present only the OLS results here.

6. Standardized betas are estimated changes in the value of the dependent variable for each single standard deviation change in the independent variable. Standardizing the raw regression coefficients presented in the tables here transforms them so that they range from −1 to +1. Standardized coefficients can be directly compared and allow for a comparison of the strength of impact the independent variables have on the dependent variable. Values closer to zero indicate weak relationships, and those closer to either positive one or negative one indicate stronger relationships.

7. All control variables were held at their modal values, the media measure of interest was manipulated over the range of valid values, and all other media usage measures were held at their means.

8. The predicted levels of physical hatred across the magazine usage scale showed a similar range, from 1.10 at the lowest level of magazine readership and 2.04 at the highest.

CHAPTER SIX: THE POLITICAL CONSEQUENCES OF PARTISAN HATRED

1. As with the question of media influence examined earlier, it is possible that the analyses I have presented thus far might incorrectly model the causal flow between feelings of partisan hatred and thermometer ratings. Although I assumed that feelings of partisan hatred preceded thermometer ratings of the parties and their presidential officeholders, it is possible that the opposite

is the case. Perhaps students form more global sentiments about the parties first, and their affect toward partisan opponents evolve thereafter. After all, scholars have long argued that individuals form judgments about political parties in their early years that remain fairly stable over the life span. Impressions of other political objects, whether made through rational calculations, heuristics, online processing, or some other means, are subsequently made as they are encountered but likely remain influenced by earlier impressions. If such were the case, then the relationship would be better modeled by using thermometer ratings to predict feelings of partisan hatred. To test for this possibility, I also modeled the relationship between thermometer rating and partisan hatred as a nonrecursive one using simultaneous equation modelling (SEM). The SEM results suggest that partisan hatred did indeed help predict the thermometer ratings to a small degree. Importantly, though, the predictive power partisan hatred exerted on ratings remained. Further, the substantive impact the partisan hatred exerted on ratings was consistently stronger than the impact the thermometer ratings exerted on partisan hatred.

2. For Independents, the likelihood ratios for all four models fail to reach traditional levels of statistical significance, and none of the partisan hatred measures exhibit a statistically significant relationship with thermometer ratings.

3. As with the earlier analyses, however, the potential direction of causality for these relationships must not be overstated. Though I presumed a causal flow from feelings of partisan hatred to extreme thermometer ratings, arguably the reverse is true. I again explored that possibility by modeling all the relationships discussed here, taking thermometer ratings as predictors of the different sorts of partisan hatred. The results from those analyses replicate those discussed earlier. The models assuming reversed causation show worse overall model fits and fewer significant relationships between the variables in the models.

4. I did so by calculating the absolute value of the difference between an even split (of fifty) and the raw numeric point offered by each respondent (i.e., compromise point—fifty), creating a measure of the distance from an equal compromise point each reported point represented.

CHAPTER SEVEN: THE SOCIAL CONSEQUENCES OF PARTISAN HATRED

1. Further, the seven-point political partisanship scale is positively and significantly correlated with the preference for living near copartisans measure (Pearson's $r = 0.138$, $p < 0.000$, two-tailed).

2. Still, it is important to note that partisanship and opinions on interparty marriage fail to show a correlation at traditional levels of statistical significance (Pearson's $r = 0.051$, $p = 0.147$, two-tailed).

3. Stealers Wheel. *Stealers Wheel.* Apple Studio AMLS 68121, 1972, LP Album.

4. Unlike the media models I presented in chapter 6, ordered logistic models of residential proximity and interpartisan marriage returned different results from those performed using OLS regression. Consequently, I present and interpret the logistic models here.

5. An odds ratio is a measure of association between the independent predictor and the dependent outcome that ranges from zero to infinity. The odds ratio represents the odds that an outcome will occur given a particular value of the predictor, compared with the odds of the outcome occurring with a one-unit higher value of the predictor. An odds ratio of 1.00 indicates that there is neither an increase nor a decrease in the odds of the outcome variable occurring. When the odds ratio is greater than 1, it describes a positive relationship; and an odds ratio less than 1 describes a negative relationship.

CHAPTER EIGHT: A MORE CIVIL POLITICAL FUTURE?

1. Many contended that "the range of ideas circulating in the academy [had] narrowed and American universities [had] grown increasingly intolerant toward dissenting voices" (Chong 2006). Others defended the speech codes as necessary to combat serious incidents of racial harassment and to protect the right of minority groups to fully engage in campus activities (Delgado 1982, 1991; Heumann and Church 1997; MacKinnon 1993; Matsuda 1989). The argument was that without the codes in place, "universities may become hostile educational environments in which some students are deprived of an equal opportunity to thrive" (Chong 2006, 33).

2. de Tocqueville (2012), vol. 2, pt. 2, chap. 1.

3. Mill (2002), chap. 2.

4. Mill (2002), chap. 2.

References

Abelson, R. P. 1995. "Attitude Extremity." In *Attitude Strength: Antecedents and Consequences*, edited by R. E. Petty and J. A. Krosnick, 25–42. Mahwah, NJ: Lawrence Erlbaum.

Abramowitz, A. I. 2010. *The Disappearing Center: Engaged Citizens, Polarization, and American Democracy*. New Haven, CT: Yale University Press.

———. 2015. "How Race and Religion Have Polarized Americana Voters." In *Political Polarization in American Politics*, edited by Daniel J. Hopkins and John Sides. New York: Bloomsbury Academic.

Abramowitz, A. I., and K. L. Saunders. 2005. "Why Can't We All Just Get Along? The Reality of a Polarized America." *Forum: A Journal of Applied Research in Contemporary Politics* 3, no. 2: 1.

———. 2008. "Is Polarization a Myth?" *Journal of Politics* 70: 542–555.

Abramowitz, A. I., and Steven Webster. 2016. "The Rise of Negative Partisanship and the Nationalization of U.S. Elections in the 21st Century." *Electoral Studies* 41: 12–22.

Abrams, Dominic. 1994. "Political Distinctiveness: An Identity Optimizing Approach." *European Journal of Social Psychology* 24, no. 3: 357–365. https://doi.org/10.1002/ejsp.2420240305.

Abrams, Dominic, and Nicholas Emler. 1992. "Self-Denial as a Paradox of Political and Regional Social Identity: Findings from a Study of 16- and 18-Year-Olds." *European Journal of Social Psychology* 22: 279–295.

Abrams, Dominic, Margaret Wetherell, Sandra Cochrane, Michael A. Hogg, and John C. Turner. 1990. "Knowing What to Think by Knowing Who You Are: Self-Categorization and the Nature of Norm Formation, Conformity and Group Polarization." *British Journal of Social Psychology* 29, no. 2: 97–119. https://doi.org/10.1111/j.20448309.1990.tb00892.x.

Achen, Christopher, and Larry Bartels. 2016. "Democracy for Realists: Holding Up a Mirror to the Electorate." *Juncture* 22, no. 4: 269–275. https://doi.org/10.1111/j.20505876.2016.00873.x.

Ahler, Douglas J. 2014. "Self-Fulfilling Misperceptions of Public Polarization." *Journal of Politics* 76, no. 3: 607–620.

Ahler, Douglas J., and Gaurav Sood. 2018. "The Parties in Our Heads: Misperceptions about Party Composition and Their Consequences." *Journal of Politics* 80, no. 3: 964–981.

Aldrich, J., and R. Niemi. 1996. "The Sixth American Party System." In S.C. Craig, *Broken Contract: Changing Relationships between Americans and Their Government*. Boulder, CO: Westview Press.

Alford, John R., Peter K. Hatemi, John R. Hibbing, Nicholas G. Martin, and Lindon J. Eaves. 2011. "The Politics of Mate Choice." *Journal of Politics* 73, no. 2: 362–379.

Allegheny College. 2013. "Allegheny Commends Two Senators with Civility Award." *Campus*, March 8. https://alleghenycampus.com/8305/news/allegheny-commends-senators-civility-award/?print=true

Allen, Cooper. 2016. "Trump on Clinton: 'She has tremendous hate in her heart.'" *USA Today*, October 9. https://www.usatoday.com/story/news/politics/onpolitics/2016/10/09/hillary-clinton-donald-trump-debate/91830944/.

Allen, Karma, and Emily Shapiro. 2017. "What We Know about the Congressional Baseball Shooting." *ABC News*, June 15. http://abcnews.go.com/US/congressional-baseball-shooting/story?id=48051222.

Allen, Vernon L., and David A. Wilder. 1975. "Categorization, Belief Similarity, and Intergroup Discrimination." *Journal of Personality and Social Psychology* 32, no. 6: 971–977. https://doi.org/10.1037/00223514.32.6.971.

Allport, Gordon. 1954. *The Nature of Prejudice*. Cambridge, MA: Addison-Wesley.

Alwin, D. F., R. L. Cohen, and T. M. Newcomb. 1991. *Political Attitudes over the Life Span: The Bennington Women after Fifty Years*. Madison: University of Wisconsin Press.

American Political Science Association. 1950. "Toward a More Responsible Two-Party System: A Report of the Committee on Political Parties." *American Political Science Review* 44, no. 3: 99.

Andrighetto, Luca, Cristina Baldissarri, Sara Lattanzio, Steve Loughnan, and Chiara Volpato. 2014. "Humanitarian Aid? Two Forms of Dehumanization and Willingness to Help after Natural Disasters." *British Journal of Social Psychology* 53, no. 3: 573–584. https://doi.org/10.1111/bjso.12066.

Ansolabehere, Stephen, and Shanto Iyengar. 1995. *Going Negative*. New York: Free Press.

Ansolabehere, Stephen, Jonathan Rodden, and James M. Snyder. 2006. "Purple America." *Journal of Economic Perspectives* 20, no. 2: 97–118.

Antle III, W. James. 2017. "How American Politics Became Consumed with Hate." *Week*, June 14. https://theweek.com/articles/705728/how-american-politics-became-consumed-hate.

Asch, Solomon. 1951. "Effects of Group Pressure upon the Modification and Distortion of Judgment." In *Groups, Leadership and Men*, edited by H. Guetzkow. Pittsburgh, PA: Carnegie Press.

Bafumi, Joseph, and Michael C. Herron. 2010. "Leapfrog Representation and Extremism: A Study of American Voters and Their Members in Congress." *American Political Science Review* 88, no. 1: 519–542.

Banaji, Mahzarin R., and Larisa Heiphetz. 2010. "Attitudes." In *Handbook of Social Psychology*, edited by S. T. Fiske, D. T. Gilbert, & G. Lindzey, 353–393. Hoboken, NJ: Wiley.

Bandura, A. 2016. *Moral Disengagement: How People Do Harm and Live with Themselves*. New York: Worth.

Barabak, Mark Z. 2017. "Reaction to Shooting at Congressional Baseball Practice Reveals a Nation That Doesn't Just Disagree. It Hates." *Los Angeles Times*, June 14. http://www.latimes.com/politics/la-na-pol-shooting-politics-20170614-story.html.

Barber, Michael, and Nolan McCarty. 2015. "Causes and Consequences of Polarization." In *Political Negotiation: A Handbook*, edited by Jane Mansbridge and Cathie Jo Mart. Washington, DC: Brookings Institution.

Baron, David P. 1994. "'Electoral Competition with Informed and Uninformed Voters." *American Political Science Review* 88, no. 1: 33–47.

Baron, Jonathan. 1993. "Why Teach Thinking? An Essay." *Applied Psychology: An International Review* 42, no. 3: 191–214. https://doi.org/10.1111/j.146405 97.1993.tb00731.x.

———. 2019. "Actively Open-Minded Thinking in Politics." *Cognition* 188: 8–18.

Bartels, Larry M. 2002. "Beyond the Running Tally: Partisan Bias in Political Perceptions." *Political Behavior* 24, no. 2: 117–150.

Bawm, Kathleen, Martin Cohen, David Koral, Seth Market, Hans Noel, and John Zaller. 2012. "A Theory of Political Parties: Groups, Policy Demands, and Nominations in American Politics." *Perspectives on Politics* 10, no. 3: 571–597.

Bayh, Evan. 2010. "Why I'm Leaving the Senate." *New York Times*, February 20.

Beck, Paul Allen. 1977. "Partisan Dealignment in the Postwar South." *American Political Science Review* 71, no. 2: 477–496.

Benhabib, S. 1996. "Toward a Deliberative Model of Democratic Legitimacy." In *Democracy and Difference*, edited by S. Benhabib. Princeton, NJ: Princeton University Press.

Bennett, W. L., and R. Entman. 2000. *Mediated Politics: Communication in the Future of Democracy*. Cambridge, UK: Cambridge University Press.

Bennett, W. L., and S. Iyengar 2008. "A New Era of Minimal Effects? The Changing Foundations of Political Communication." *Journal of Communication* 58, no. 4: 707–731.

Benson, T. Lloyd. 2004. *The Caning of Senator Sumner.* Belmont, CA: Wadsworth.

Berelson, B. R., P. F. Lazarsfeld, and W. N. McPhee. 1954. *Voting: A Study of Opinion Formation in a Presidential Campaign*. Chicago, IL: University of Chicago Press.

Berlin, Isaiah. 1954. *The Hedgehog and the Fox.* Princeton, NJ: Princeton University Press.

Billig, Michael, and Henri Tajfel. 1973. "Social Categorization and Similarity in Intergroup Behaviour." *European Journal of Social Psychology* 3, no. 1: 27–52. https://doi.org/10.1002/ejsp.2420030103.

Bimber, B. A., and R. Davis. 2003. *Campaigning Online: The Internet in U.S. Elections*. New York: Oxford University Press.

Binder, A. R., E. Kasja, D. B. Dalrymple, and D. A. Scheufele. 2009. "The Soul of a Polarized Democracy: Testing Theoretical Linkages between Talk and Attitude Extremity During the 2004 Presidential Election." *Communication Research* 36: 315–340.

Bishop, B. 2008. *Big Sort Maps*. http://www.thebigsort.com/maps.php.

———. 2009. *The Big Sort: Why the Clustering of Like-Minded America Is Tearing Us Apart*. Boston: Mariner.

Bishop, George F., Alfred J. Tuchfarber, and Robert W. Oldendick. 1978. "Change in the Structure of American Political Attitudes: The Nagging Question of Question Wording." *American Journal of Political Science* 22, 2: 250–269.

Blake, Aaron. 2016a. "Why American Politics Is All about Whom You Hate, in 3 Charts." *Washington Post,* June 22. https://www.washingtonpost.com/news/the-fix/wp/2016/06/22/why-american-politics-is-all-about-who-you-hate-in-3-charts/.

———. 2016b. "Did Hillary Clinton Just Make Her Own '47 Percent' Gaffe?" *Jewish World Review,* September 12. http://www.jewishworldreview.com/0916/blake091216.php3.

Bobo, Lawrence, and Frederick C. Licari. 1989. "Education and Political Tolerance: Testing the Effects of Cognitive Sophistication and Target Group Affect." *Public Opinion Quarterly* 53: 285–308.

Bond, Jon R., and Richard Fleisher. 2000. *Polarized Politics: Congress and the President in a Partisan Era*. Washington, DC: Congressional Quarterly Press.

Borhek, J. T. 1965. "A Theory of Incongruent Experience." *Pacific Sociological Review* 8, no. 1: 89–95.

Boyd, Richard W. 1972. "Popular Control of Public Policy: A Normal Vote Analysis of the 1968 Election." *American Political Science Review* 66, no. 2: 429–449.

Brader, Ted. 2006. *Campaigning for Hearts and Minds*. Chicago, IL: University of Chicago Press.

Brady, David W., and Hahrie Han. 2015. "Our Politics May Be Polarized, but That Is Nothing New." In *Political Polarization in American Politics*, edited by Daniel J. Hopkins and John Sides. New York: Bloomsbury Academic.

Brady, David W., Hahrie Han, and Jeremy C. Pope. 2007. "Primary Elections and Candidate Ideology: Out of Step with the Primary Electorate?" *Legislative Studies Quarterly* 32, no. 1: 79–105.

Brewer, Marilynn B. 2001. "The Many Faces of Social Identity: Implications for Political Psychology." *Political Psychology* 22, no. 1: 115–125.

———. 2005. "The Rise of Partisanship and the Expansion of Partisan Conflict within the American Electorate." *Political Research Quarterly* 58: 219–229.

Brewer, Marilynn B., and Madelyn Silver. 1978. "Ingroup Bias as a Function of Task Characteristics." *European Journal of Social Psychology* 8, no. 3: 393–400. https://doi.org/10.1002/ejsp.2420080312.

Broockman, David. 2015. "Are Politicians and Activists Reliably 'More Extreme' Than Voters? A Skeptical Perspective." In *Political Polarization in American Politics*, edited by Daniel J. Hopkins and John Sides. New York: Bloomsbury Academic.

Brooks, David M. 2014. "Why Partyism Is Wrong." *New York Times*, October 28, 2014.

Brownstein, R. 2007. *The Second Civil War: How Extreme Partisanship Has Paralyzed Washington and Polarized America*. New York: Penguin.

Bryant, Christa Case. 2018. "At College Decision Time, Conservatives Face Tough Choices." *Christian Science Monitor*, April 23. https://www.csmonitor.com/EqualEd/2018/0423/At-college-decision-time-conservatives-face-tough-choices.

Bullock, Will, and Joshua D. Clinton. 2011. "More a Molehill than a Mountain: The Effects of the Blanket Primary on Elected Officials' Behavior from California." *Journal of Politics* 73, no. 3: 915–930.

Burns, James MacGregor. 1984. *The Power to Lead: The Crisis of the American Presidency*. New York: Simon and Schuster.

Cacioppo, John T., Richard E. Petty, and Chuan F. Kao. 1984. "The Efficient Assessment of Need for Cognition." *Journal of Personality Assessment* 48, no. 3: 306–307. https://doi.org/10.1207/s15327752jpa4803_13.

Cadinu, Maria Rosaria, and Marcella Cerchioni. 2001. "Compensatory Biases after Ingroup Threat: 'Yeah, but We Have a Good Personality.'" *European Journal of Social Psychology* 31, no. 4: 353–367. https://doi.org/10.1002/ejsp.46.

Campbell, A., P. E. Converse, W. E. Miller, and D. E. Stokes. 1960. *The American Voter*. Hoboken, NJ: Wiley.

Campbell, S. W., and N. Kwak. 2010. "Mobile Communication and Civic Life: Linking Patterns of Use to Civic and Political Engagement." *Journal of Communication* 60, no. 3: 536–555.

Campus, D., G. Pasquino, and C. Vaccari. 2008. "Social Networks, Political Discussion, and Voting in Italy: A Study of the 2006 Election." *Political Communication* 25: 423–444.

Carmines, Edward G., and James A. Stimson. 1989. *Issue Evolution: Race and the Transformation of American Politics*. Princeton, NJ: Princeton University Press.

Carsey, Thomas, and Geoffrey Layman. 2015. "Our Politics Is Polarized on More Issues Than Ever Before." In *Political Polarization in American Politics*, edited by Daniel J. Hopkins and John Sides. New York: Bloomsbury Academic.

Carson, Jamie L., Michael H. Crespin, Charles J. Finocchiaro, and David W. Rhode. 2007. "Redistricting and Party Polarization in the U.S. House of Representatives." *American Politics Research* 35, no. 6: 878–904.

Carvacho, Héctor, Andreas Zick, Andrés Haye, Roberto Gonzáles, Jorge Manzi, Caroline Kocik, and Melanie Bertl. 2013. "On the Relation between Social Class and Prejudice: The Roles of Education, Income, and Ideological Attitudes." *European Journal of Social Psychology* 43: 272–285.

Cassese, Erin C. 2019. "Partisan Dehumanization in American Politics." *Political Behavior* (April). https://doi.org/10.1007/s1110901909545-w.

Chan, Jimmy, and Daniel F. Stone. 2013. "Media Proliferation and Partisan Selective Exposure." *Public Choice* 156, nos. 3–4: 467–490.

Chan, Jimmy, and Wing Suen. 2008. "A Spatial Theory of News Consumption and Electoral Competition." *Review of Economic Studies* 75, no. 3: 699–728.

Chancellor, J., and W. R. Mears. 1995. *The New News Business: A Guide to Writing and Reporting*. New York: HarperCollins.

Chen, M. Keith, and Ryne Rohla. 2018. "The Effect of Partisanship and Political Advertising on Close Family Ties." *Science*, June 1, 1020–1024.

Chong, Dennis. 2006. "Free Speech and Multiculturalism in and out of the Academy." *Political Psychology* 27, no. 1: 29–54.

Claassen, Christopher, Patrick Tucker, and Steven Smith. 2015. "Ideological Labels in America." *Political Behavior* 37, no. 2: 253–278.

Clark, Russell D., and Anne Maass. 1988. "Social Categorization in Minority

Influence: The Case of Homosexuality." *European Journal of Social Psychology* 18, no. 4: 347–364.

Cohen, Michael A. 2016. *American Maelstrom: The 1968 Election and the Politics of Division.* New York: Oxford University Press.

Conover, Pamela Johnston, and Stanley Feldman. 1981. "The Origins and Meaning of Liberal/Conservative Self-Identifications." *American Journal of Political Science* 25, no. 4: 617–645.

Converse, Philip E. 1964. "The Nature of Belief Systems in Mass Publics." In *Ideology and Discontent*, ed. David Apter. New York: The Free Press of Glencoe.

Coser, Lewis A. 1956. *The Functions of Social Conflict*. New York: Free Press.

Costello, Maureen B. 2016. "Teaching the 2016 Election: The Trump Effect—the Impact of the Presidential Campaign on Our Nation's Schools." Southern Poverty Law Center. https://www.splcenter.org/sites/default/files/splc_the_trump_effect.pdf.

Cowan, G., and J. Mettrick. 2002. "The Effects of Target Variables and Setting on Perceptions of Hate Speech." *Journal of Applied Social Psychology* 32: 277–299.

Cox, Gary W., and Keith T. Poole. 2002. "On Measuring Partisanship in Roll-Call Voting: The US House of Representatives, 1877–1999." *American Journal of Political Science* 46, no. 3: 477–489.

Crotty, William. 2013. *Winning the Presidency 2012*. Boulder, CO: Paradigm Publishers.

Cummins, Joseph. 2007. *Anything for a Vote: Dirty Tricks, Cheap Shots, and October Surprises in U.S. Presidential Elections.* Philadelphia, PA: Quirk Books.

D'Alessio, D. 2012. *Media Bias in Presidential Election Coverage, 1948–2008.* Lanham, MD: Lexington.

D'Allesio, D., and M. Allen. 2000. "Media Bias in Presidential Elections: A Meta-Analysis." *Journalism and Mass Communication Quarterly* 50: 133–156.

Dalton, R. 2013. *The Apartisan American*. Thousand Oaks, CA: Sage.

Delgado, R. 1982. "Words That Wound: A Tort Action for Racial Insults, Epithets, and Name-Calling." *Harvard Civil Rights-Civil Liberties Law Review* 17: 133.

———. 1991. "Campus Anti-Racism Rules: Constitutional Narratives in Collision." *Northwestern University Law Review* 85: 343.

DePinto, Jennifer, Fred Backus, Kabir Khanna, and Anthony Salvanto. 2017. "Poll: Americans ay U.S. Political Debate Is Increasingly Uncivil." *CBS News,* June 20. https://www.cbsnews.com/news/poll-americans-say-u-s-political-debate-is-increasingly-uncivil/.

de Tocqueville, Alexis. 2012. *Democracy in America,* edited by Harvey C. Mansbridge and Delba Winthrop. Chicago, IL: University of Chicago Press.

Devine, Christopher J. 2015. "Ideological Social Identity: Psychological Attachment to Ideological In-Groups as a Political Phenomenon and a Behavioral Influence." *Political Behavior* 37, no. 3: 509–535.

Dilliplane, Susanna. 2011. "All the News You Want to Hear: The Impact of Partisan News Exposure on Political Participation" *Public Opinion Quarterly* 75, no. 2: 287–316.

DiMaggio, P., J. Evans, and B. Bryson. 1996. "Have Americans' Social Attitudes Become More Polarized?" *American Journal of Sociology* 102: 690–755.

Dinas, Elias. 2013. "Opening 'Openness to Change': Political Events and the Increased Sensitivity of Young Adults." *Political Research Quarterly* 66, no. 4: 868–882.

Doherty, C. 2014. "7 Things to Know about Polarization in America." *Pew Research Center Report.* http://www.pewresearch.org/fact-tank/2014/06/12/7-things-to-know-about-polarization-in-america/.

Doise, Willem, and Anne Sinclair. 1973. "The Categorization Process in Intergroup Relations." *European Journal of Social Psychology* 3, no. 2: 145–157. https://doi.org/10.1002/ejsp.2420030204.

Domke, D., D. P. Fan, M. Fibison, D. V. Shah, S. S. Smith, and M. D. Watts. 1997. "News Media, Candidates and Issues, and Public Opinion in the 1996 Presidential Campaign." *Journalism and Mass Communication Quarterly* 74: 718–737.

Douthat, Ross. 2010. "The Partisan Mind." *New York Times,* November 29. https://www.nytimes.com/2010/11/29/opinion/29douthat.html.

———. 2015. "Fear and Loathing in American Politics: On the Roots and Possible Consequences of Negative Partisanship." *New York Times,* April 21. https://douthat.blogs.nytimes.com/2015/04/21/fear-and-loathing-in-american-politics/?searchResultPosition=4.

d'Souza, Dinesh. 1991. *Illiberal Education: The Politics of Race and Sex on Campus.* New York: Free Press.

Duck, J., M. Hogg, and D. Terry. 1995. "Me, Us and Them: Political Identification and the Third-Person Effect in the 1993 Australian Federal Election." *European Journal of Social Psychology* 25: 195–215.

Duckworth, Angela L., Christopher Peterson, Michael D. Matthews, and Dennis R. Kelly. 2007. "Grit: Perseverance and Passion for Long-Term Goals." *Journal of Personality and Social Psychology* 92, 6: 1087–1101. https://doi.org/10.1037/00223514.92.6.1087.

Edgerly, Stephanie, Emily K. Vraga, Leticia Bode, Kjerstin Thorson, and

Esther Thorson. 2018. "New Media, New Relationship to Participation? A Closer Look at Youth News Repertoires and Political Participation." *Journalism and Mass Communication Quarterly* 95, no. 1: 192–212. https://doi.org/10.1177/1077699017706928.

Edsall, Thomas B. 2018. "What Motivates Voters More Than Loyalty? Loathing." *New York Times,* March 1. https://www.nytimes.com/2018/03/01/opinion/negative-partisanship-democrats-republicans.html.

———. 2019. "No Hate Left Behind: Lethal Partisanship Is Taking Us into Dangerous Territory." *New York Times,* March 13. https://www.nytimes.com/2019/03/13/opinion/hate-politics.html.

Edwards, Mickey. 2012. *The Parties Versus the People: How to Turn Republicans and Democrats into Americans.* New Haven, CT: Yale University Press.

Eilperin, Juliet. 2007. *Fight Club Politics: How Partisanship Is Poisoning the House of Representatives.* Lanham, MD: Rowman and Littlefield.

Ekman, P. 1992. "An Argument for Basic Emotions." *Cognition and Emotion* 6: 169–200.

Elazar, Daniel J. 1966. *American Federalism: A View from the States.* New York: Crowell.

Ellemers, Naomi. 2017. *Morality and the Regulation of Social Behavior: Groups as Moral Anchors.* New York: Psychology.

Ellemers, Naomi, and Kees van den Bos. 2012. "Morality in Groups: On the Social-Regulatory Functions of Right and Wrong." *Social and Personality Psychology Compass* 6, no. 12: 878–889. https://doi.org/10.1111/spc3.12001.

Ellis, Christopher, and James A. Stimson. 2012. *Ideology in America.* New York: Cambridge University Press.

Ensley, Michael J. 2009. "Individual Campaign Contributions and Candidate Ideology." *Public Choice* 138, no. 1: 221–238.

Entman, R. M. 1989. "How the Media Affect What People Think: An Information Processing Approach." *Journal of Politics* 51: 347–370.

Esman, M. J. 2004. *An Introduction to Ethnic Conflict.* Cambridge: Polity.

Evans, J. H., B. Bryson, and P. DiMaggio. 2001. "Opinion Polarization: Important Contributions, Necessary Limitations." *American Journal of Sociology* 106: 944–959.

Eveland Jr., William P., and Dhavan V. Shah. 2003. "The Impact of Individual and Interpersonal Factors on Perceived News Media Bias." *Political Psychology* 24, no. 1: 101–117.

Finkel, Steven. 1993. "Reexamining the 'Minimal Effects' Model in Recent Presidential Elections." *Journal of Politics* 55: 1–21.

Finn, C. E. 1989. "The Campus: An Island of Repression in a Sea of Freedom."

Commentary Magazine (September). https://www.commentarymagazine.com/articles/chester-finn-2/the-campus-an-island-of-repression-in-a-sea-of-freedom/.

Fiorina, Morris P. 2013. "America's Missing Moderates: Hiding in Plain Sight." *American Interest.* http://www.the-american-interest.com/articles/2013/02/12/americas-missing-moderates-hiding-in-plain-sight/.

Fiorina, Morris P., and Samuel J. Abrams. 2008. "Political Polarization in the American Public." *Annual Review of Political Science* 11: 563–588.

———. 2009. *Disconnect: The Breakdown of Representation in American Politics.* Norman: University of Oklahoma Press.

———. 2015. "Americans Are Not Polarized, Just Better Sorted." In *Political Polarization in American Politics,* edited by Daniel J. Hopkins and John Sides. New York: Bloomsbury Academic.

Fiorina, Morris P., Samuel J. Abrams, and Jeremy C. Pope. 2005. *Culture War? The Myth of a Polarized America.* Boston: Pearson Longman.

———. 2006. *Culture War? The Myth of a Polarized America,* 2nd ed. Boston: Pearson Longman.

Fleisher, R., and J. R. Bond. 2001. "Evidence of Increasing Polarization among Ordinary Citizens." In *American Political Parties: Decline or Resurgence?,* edited by J. E. Cohon, R. Fleisher, and P. Kantor. Washington, DC: Congressional Quarterly Press.

Freeman, Joanne B. 2001. *Affairs of Honor: National Politics in the New Republic.* New Haven, CT: Yale University Press.

French, David. 2019. "Partisan Hate Is Becoming a National Crisis." *National Review.*

Frijda, N. H., B. Mesquita, J. Sonnemans, and S. Van Goozen. 1991. "The Duration of Affective Phenomena or Emotions, Sentiments, and Passions." *International Review of Studies of Emotions,* edited by K.T. Strongman, 187–226. Chichester, UK: Wiley.

Furedi, Frank. 2017. *What's Happened to the University? A Sociological Exploration of Its Infantalisation.* Abingdon, UK: Routledge.

Galvin, Daniel T. 2013. "Presidential Partisanship Reconsidered: Eisenhower, Nixon, Ford, and the Rise of Polarized Politics." *Political Research Quarterly* 66, no. 1: 46–60.

Garner, A., and H. Palmer. 2010. "Polarization and Issue Consistency over Time." *Political Behavior* 33: 225–246.

Garrett, R. Kelly. 2009. "Politically Motivated Reinforcement Seeking: Reframing the Selective Exposure Debate." *Journal of Communication* 59: 676–699.

Geiger, Abigail. 2016. "For Many Voters, It's Not Which Presidential Candidate They're for but Which They're Against." Pew Research Center. http://www.pewresearch.org/fact-tank/2016/09/02/for-many-voters-its-not-which-presidential-candidate-theyre-for-but-which-theyre-against/.

Gelman, Andrew. 2015. "How Better Educated Whites Are Driving Polarization." In *Political Polarization in American Politics*, edited by Daniel J. Hopkins and John Sides. New York: Bloomsbury Academic.

Gentzkow, Matthew, and Jesse M. Shapiro. 2011. "Ideological Segregation Online and Offline." *Quarterly Journal of Economics* 126, no. 4: 1799–1839.

Gerber, A., and D. Green. 1998. "Rational Learning and Partisan Attitudes." *American Political Science Review* 42, 3: 794–818.

Gerber, A., G. Huber, D. Doherty, and C. Dowling. 2012. "Personality and the Strength and Direction of Partisan Identification." *Political Behavior* 34: 653–688.

Gerber, Alan, and Rebecca B. Morton. 1998. "Primary Election Systems and Representation." *Journal of Law, Economics, and Organization* 14, no. 2: 304–324.

Gergen, K. J. 2003. "Self and Community in the New Floating Worlds." In *Mobile Democracy: Essays on Society, Self, and Politics*, edited by K. Nyiri, 103–114. Vienna, Austria: Passagen Verlag.

———. 2008. "Communication and the Transformation of the Democratic Process." In *Handbook of Mobile Communication Studies*, edited by J. Katz, 297–310. Cambridge: Massachusetts Institute of Technology Press.

Gibson, J. L. 2006. "Do Strong Group Identities Fuel Intolerance? Evidence from the South African Case." *Political Psychology* 27, no. 5: 665–705.

Gilmour, John B. 1995. *Strategic Disagreement: Stalemate in American Politics.* Pittsburgh, PA: University of Pittsburgh Press.

Graber, D. 1980. *Mass Media and American Politics.* Washington, DC: Congressional Quarterly Press.

Graham, Jesse, Jonathan Haidt, and Brian A. Nosek. 2009. "Liberals and Conservatives Rely on Different Sets of Moral Foundations." *Journal of Personality and Social Psychology* 96, no. 5: 1029–1046.

Green, Donald P. 1988. "On the Dimensionality of Public Sentiment Toward Partisan and Ideological Groups." *American Journal of Political Science* 32, no. 3: 758–780.

Green, Donald, B. Palmquist, and E. Schickler. 2002. *Partisan Hearts and Minds.* New Haven, CT: Yale University Press.

Greene, S. 1999. "Understanding Party Identification: A Social Identify Approach." *Political Psychology* 20, no. 2: 393–403.

Groseclose, Timothy, and Nolan McCarty. 2001. "The Politics of Blame:

Bargaining Before an Audience." *American Journal of Political Science* 45, no. 1: 100–119.

Grossman, Matt, and David A. Hopkins. 2016. *Asymmetric Politics: Ideological Republicans and Group Interest Democrats*. Oxford, UK: Oxford University Press.

Hacker, J. S., and P. Pierson. 2006. *Off Center: The Republican Revolution and the Erosion of American Democracy*. New Haven, CT: Yale University Press.

Haidt, Jonathan. 2012. *The Righteous Mind: Why Good People Are Divided by Politics and Religion*. New York: Vintage.

Haidt, J., E. Rosenberg, and H. Hom. 2003. "Differentiating Diversities: Moral Diversity Is Not Like Other Kinds." *Journal of Applied Social Psychology* 33: 1–36.

Halperin, E. 2011. "Emotional Barriers to Peace: Negative Emotions and Public Opinion about the Peace Process in the Middle East." *Peace and Conflict: Journal of Peace Psychology* 17: 22–45.

Halperin, E., D. Canetti, and S. Kimhi. 2012. "In Love with Hatred: Rethinking the Role Hatred Plays in Shaping Political Behavior." *Journal of Applied Social Psychology* 42, no. 9: 2231–2256.

Halperin, E., and J. J. Gross. 2011. "Intergroup Anger in Intractable Conflict: Long-Term Sentiments Predict Anger Responses During the Gaza War." *Group Processes and Intergroup Relations* 14: 477–488.

Halperin, E., A. Russell, C. S. Dweck, and J. J. Gross. 2011. "Anger, Hatred, and the Quest for Peace: Anger Can Be Constructive in the Absence of Hatred?" *Journal of Conflict Resolution* 55: 274–291.

Haran, Uriel, Ilana Ritov, and Barbara A. Mellers. 2013. "The Role of Actively Open-Minded Thinking in Information Acquisition, Accuracy, and Calibration." *Judgment and Decision Making* 8, no. 3: 188–201.

Hare, Christopher, and Keith T. Poole. 2015. "How Politically Moderate Are Americans? Less Than It Seems." In *Political Polarization in American Politics*, edited by Daniel J. Hopkins and John Sides. New York: Bloomsbury Academic.

Hare, Christopher, Keith T. Poole, and Howard Rosenthal. 2015. "Polarization in Congress Has Risen Sharply. Where Is It Going Next?" In *Political Polarization in American Politics*, edited by Daniel J. Hopkins and John Sides. New York: Bloomsbury Academic.

Haslam, N., and S. Loughnan. 2016. "How Dehumanization Promotes Harm." In *The Social Psychology of Good and Evil*, edited by A. G. Miller, 140–158. New York: Guilford.

Hays, Samuel P. 1957. *The Response to Industrialism, 1885–1914*. Chicago, IL: University of Chicago Press.

Henry, P. J., and Jaime L. Napier. 2017. "Education Is Related to Greater Ideological Prejudice." *Public Opinion Quarterly* 81, no. 4: 930–942.

Herbst, Susan. 2010. *Rude Democracy: Civility and Incivility in America*. Philadelphia, PA: Temple University Press.

Herszenhorn, David M. 2009. "In Senate Health Care Vote, New Partisan Vitriol." *New York Times*, December 24. https://www.nytimes.com/2009/12/24/us/politics/24assess.html.

Hetherington, M. J. 2001. "Resurgent Mass Partisanship: The Role of Elite Polarization." *American Political Science Review* 95, no. 3: 619–631.

Hetherington, M. J., M. T. Long, and T. J. Rudolph. 2016. "Revisiting the Myth: New Evidence of a Polarized Electorate." *Public Opinion Quarterly* 80: 321–350.

Hetherington, M. J., and T. J. Rudolph. 2014. "The Emergence of Polarized Trust." In *Annual Meeting of the American Political Science Association Proceedings*. Washington, DC: American Political Science Association.

Heumann, M., and T. W. Church, eds. 1997. *Hate Speech on Campus*. Boston: Northeastern University Press.

Hibbing, John R., Kevin B. Smith, and John R. Alford. 2014. *Predisposed: Liberals, Conservatives, and Biology of Political Differences*. New York: Routledge.

Hill, Seth J., and Chris Tausanovitch. 2015. "A Disconnect in Representation? Comparison of Trends in Congressional and Public Polarization." *Journal of Politics* 77, no. 4: 1058–1075.

Hirano, Shigeo, James M. Snyder, Jr., Stephen Ansolabehere, and John Mark Hansen. 2010. "Primary Elections and Partisan Polarization in U.S.: *Congressional Elections*." *Quarterly Journal of Political Science* 5, no. 2: 169–191.

Hoffer, William, and James Hull. 2010. *The Caning of Charles Sumner: Honor, Idealism, and the Origins of the Civil War*. Baltimore, MD: Johns Hopkins University Press.

Hopkins, Daniel J., and John Sides, eds. 2015. *Political Polarization in American Politics*. New York: Bloomsbury Academic.

Huckfeldt, R., P. E. Johnson, and J. Sprague. 2004. *Political Disagreement: The Survival of Diverse Opinions within Communication Networks*. New York: Cambridge University Press.

Huddy, Leonie, Stanley Feldman, and Christopher Weber. 2007. "The Political Consequences of Perceived Threat and Felt Insecurity." *Annals of the American Academy of Political and Social Sciences* 614(1): 131–153.

Huddy, Leonie, and Lilliana Mason. 2010. "Measuring Partisanship as a Social Identity, Predicting Political Activism." Paper presented at the annual meeting of the International Society for Political Psychology, San Francisco, CA, July 7–10.

Huddy, Leonie, Lilliana Mason, and Lene Aarøe. 2015. "Expressive Partisanship: Campaign Involvement, Political Emotion, and Partisan Identity." *American Political Science Review* 109, no. 1: 1–17. https://doi.org/10.1017/S0003055414000604.

Hunter, James Davison. 1991. *Culture Wars: The Struggle to Define America.* New York: Basic Books.

———. 1995. *Before the Shooting Begins: Searching for Democracy in America's Culture War.* New York: Free Press.

Hyman, Herbert. 1959. *Political Socialization: A Study in the Psychology of Political Behavior.* Glencoe, IL: Free Press.

Hyman, Herbert H., and Paul B. Sheatsley. 1947. "Some Reasons Why Information Campaigns Fail." *Public Opinion Quarterly* 11, no. 3: 412–423.

Iyengar, Shanto. 1991. *Is Anyone Responsible? How Television Frames Political Issues.* Chicago, IL: University of Chicago Press.

Iyengar, S., and D. R. Kinder. 1987. *News That Matters.* Chicago, IL: University of Chicago Press.

Iyengar, Shanto, and Masha Krupenkin. 2018. "The Strengthening of Partisan Affect." *Political Psychology* 39, no. 1: 201–218. https://doi.org/10.1111/pops.12487.

Iyengar, Shanto, Gaurav Sood, and Yphtach Lelkes. 2012. "Affect, Not Ideology Social Identity Perspective on Polarization." *Public Opinion Quarterly* 76, no. 3: 405–431. https://doi.org/10.1093/poq/nfs038.

Iyengar, Shanto, and Sean J. Westwood. 2015. "Fear and Loathing across Party Lines: New Evidence on Group Polarization." *American Journal of Political Science* 59, no. 3: 690–707. https://doi.org/10.1111/ajps.12152.

Jacobs, Tom. 2018. "Political Polarization Shortened Thanksgiving Dinners." *Pacific Standard Magazine.* https://psmag.com/news/bickering-on-thanksgiving-is-fowl-play.

Jacobson, G. C. 2004. "Partisan and Ideological Polarization in the California Electorate." *State Politics and Policy Quarterly* 4, no. 1: 113–139.

Jaffe, Alexandra. 2016. "Marco Rubio Claims Donald Trump Wet His Pants, Reads Misspelled Tweets Aloud." *Week,* February 26. https://theweek.com/speedreads/608726/marco-rubio-claims-donald-trump-wet-pants-reads-misspelled-tweets-aloud.

Jenssen, Anders Todal, and Heidi Engesbak. 1994. "The Many Faces of

Education: Why Are People with Lower Education More Hostile Toward Immigrants Than People with Higher Education?" *Scandinavian Journal of Educational Research* 38: 33–50.

Jerit, Jennifer, and Jason Barabas. 2012. "Partisan Perceptual Bias and the Information Environment." *Journal of Politics* 74 (July): 672–684.

Jesse, N. G., and K. P. Williams. 2011. *Ethnic Conflict: A Systematic Approach to Cases of Conflict*. Washington, DC: Congressional Quarterly Press.

Jetten, Jolanda, Nyla R. Branscombe, Michael T. Schmitt, and Russell Spears. 2001. "Rebels with a Cause: Group Identification as a Response to Perceived Discrimination from the Mainstream." *Personality and Social Psychology Bulletin* 27, no. 9:1204–1213.

Jonas, E., S. Schulz-Hardt, and D. Frey. 2005. "Giving Advice or Making Decisions in Someone Else's Place: The Influence of Impression, Defense, and Accuracy Motivation on the Search for New Information." *Personality and Social Psychology Bulletin* 31, no. 1: 977–990.

Kalmoe, Nathan, and Lilliana Mason. 2018. "Lethal Mass Partisanship: Prevalence, Correlates, and Electoral Contingencies." In *Annual Meeting of the American Political Science Association Proceedings*. Washington, DC: American Political Science Association.

Kamisar, Ben. 2016. "Sanders Supporters Chant 'Lock Her Up' at Philadelphia Rally: Report." *Hill*, July 25. https://thehill.com/blogs/ballot-box/presidential-races/289078-sanders-supporters-chant-lock-her-up-at-philadelphia.

Kardash, CarolAnne M., and Roberta J. Scholes. 1996. "Effects of Preexisting Beliefs, Epistemological Beliefs, and Need for Cognition on Interpretation of Controversial Issues." *Journal of Educational Psychology* 88, no. 2: 260–271. https://doi.org/10.1037/00220663.88.2.260.

Kaufman, Karen M., James G. Gimpel, and Adam H. Hoffman. 2003. "A Promise Fulfilled? Open Primaries and Representation." *Journal of Politics* 65, no. 2: 457–476.

Kelly, C. 1988. "Intergroup Differentiation in a Political Context." *British Journal of Social Psychology* 27: 319–332.

———. 1989. "Political Identity and Perceived Intragroup Homogeneity." *British Journal of Social Psychology* 28: 239–250.

———. 1990a. "Identity and Intergroup Perceptions in Minority-Majority Contexts." *Human Relations* 43: 583–599.

———. 1990b. "Identity and Levels of Influence: When a Political Minority Fails." *British Journal of Social Psychology* 29: 289–301.

Key Jr., V. O. 1966. *The Responsible Electorate: Rationality in Presidential Voting, 1936–1960*. Cambridge, MA: Harvard University Press.

Kimball, David C., Bryce Summary, and Eric C. Vorst. 2013. Paper presented at the State of the Parties: 2012 and Beyond conference, November 7, 2013, Akron, OH.

Kinder, Donald R. 2003. "Communication and Politics in the Age of Information." In *The Oxford Handbook of Political Psychology*, edited by D. O. Sears, L. Huddy, and R. Jervis, 357–393. Oxford, UK: Oxford University Press.

Kinder, Donald R., and Nathan P. Kalmoe. 2017. *Neither Liberal nor Conservative: Ideological Innocence in the American Public*. Chicago, IL: University of Chicago Press.

Kirkpatrick, Evron M. 1971. "Toward a Responsible Two-Party System: Political Science, Policy Science, or Pseudo Science?" *American Political Science Review* 65: 965–990.

Klapper, Joseph. 1960. *The Effects of Mass Communication*. Glencoe, IL: Free Press.

Klar, Samara. 2013. "The Influence of Competing Identity Primes on Political Preferences." *Journal of Politics* 75, no. 4: 1108–1124.

———. 2018. "When Common Identities Decrease Trust: An Experimental Study of Partisan Women." *American Journal of Political Science* 62, no. 3: 610–622.

Klein, Ezra. 2010. "With His Health-Care Summit, Obama Could Make Partisanship Worse." *Washington Post,* February 21. https://www.washingtonpost.com/wp-dyn/content/article/2010/02/19/AR2010021902050.html.

Knight, J., and J. Johnson. 1994. "Aggregation and Deliberation: On the Possibility of Democratic Legitimacy." *Political Theory* 22: 277–296.

Kolowich, Steve. 2018. "State of Conflict." *Chronicle of Higher Education,* April 27. https://www.chronicle.com/interactives/state-of-conflict.

Korwar, A. R. 1995. *War of Words: Speech Codes at Public Colleges and Universities*. Nashville, TN: The Freedom Forum First Amendment Center.

Krieg, Gregory. 2016. "Donald Trump Defends Size of His Penis." *CNN Politics,* March 4. https://www.cnn.com/2016/03/03/politics/donald-trump-small-hands-marco-rubio/index.html.

Kropf, Martha. 2016. *Institutions and the Right to Vote in America*. New York: Palgrave-Macmillan.

Krosnick, J. A., and D. F. Alwin. 1989. "Aging and Susceptibility to Attitude Change." *Journal of Personality and Social Psychology* 57, no. 3: 416–425.

Kteily, N., and E. Bruneau. 2017. "Backlash: The Politics and Real-World Consequences of Minority Group Dehumanization." *Personality and Social Psychology Bulletin* 43, no. 1: 87–104.

Lasswell, Harold D. 1927. *Propaganda Technique in the World War*. New York: Knopf.

Lau, Richard R., David J. Anderson, Tessa M. Ditonto, Mona S. Kleinberg, and David P. Redlawsk. 2016. "Effect of Media Environment Diversity and Advertising Tone on Information Search, Selective Exposure, and Affective Polarization." *Political Behavior* 39: 231–255.

Lauter, David. 2017. "Trump's Standing in Polls Has Dropped: How Significant Is the Slide?" *Los Angeles Times*, May 23. https://www.latimes.com/politics/la-na-pol-app-trump-poll-drop-20170523-story.html.

Lawrence III, C. R. 1990. "If He Hollers Let Him Go: Regulating Racist Speech on Campus." *Duke Law Journal* 39, no. 3: 431–483.

Layman, G. C., and T. M. Carsey. 2002. "Party Polarization and 'Conflict Extension' in the American Electorate." *American Journal of Political Science* 46: 786–802.

Lazarsfeld, Paul F., Bernard Berelson, and Hazel Gaudet. 1944. *The People's Choice*. New York: Columbia University Press.

Leach, C. W., N. Ellemers, and M. Barreto. 2007. "Group Virtue: The Importance of Morality (vs. Competence and Sociability) in the Positive Evaluation of In-Groups." *Journal of Personality and Social Psychology* 93, no. 2: 234–249.

Lee, Frances E. 2009. *Beyond Ideology: Politics, Principles, and Partisanship in the U.S. Senate*. Chicago, IL: University of Chicago Press.

———. 2015. "American Politics Is More Competitive Than Ever, and That Is Making Partisanship Worse." In *Political Polarization in American Politics*, edited by Daniel J. Hopkins and John Sides. New York: Bloomsbury Academic.

Lee, Kurtis. 2016. "Hillary Clinton Says Trump 'Taking a Hate Movement Mainstream.'" *Los Angeles Times*, August 24. https://www.latimes.com/nation/politics/trailguide/la-na-trailguide-updates-08242016-htmlstory.html.

Lenz, Gabriel S. 2012. *Follow the Leader? How Voters Respond to Politicians' Policies and Performance*. Chicago, IL: Chicago University Press.

Lerner, Jennifer S., and Dacher Keltner. 2000. "Beyond Valence: Toward a Model of Emotion-Specific Influences on Judgement and Choice." *Cognition and Emotion* 14, no. 4: 473–493. https://doi.org/10.1080/026999300402763.

Lerner, Jennifer S., and Philip E. Tetlock. 1999. "Accounting for the Effects of Accountability." *Psychological Bulletin* 125, no. 2: 255–275.

Lessig, Lawrence. 2011. *Republic, Lost: How Money Corrupts Congress—and a Plan to Stop It*. New York: Hachette.

Levendusky, Matthew. 2009. *The Partisan Sort: How Liberals Became Demo-*

crats and Conservatives Became Republicans. Chicago, IL: Chicago University Press.

———. 2017. "Americans, Not Partisans: Can Priming American National Identity Reduce Affective Polarization?" *Journal of Politics* 80, no. 1: 59–70.

Levendusky, Matthew, Jeremy C. Pope, and Simon D. Jackman. 2008. "Measuring District-Level Partisanship with Implications for Analysis of US Elections." *Journal of Politics* 70, no. 3: 736–753.

Levine, J. M., and E. Russo. 1995. "Impact of Anticipated Interaction on Information Acquisition." *Social Cognition* 13, no. 3: 293–317.

Levine, Robert A., and Donald T. Campbell. 1972. *Ethnocentrism: Theories of Conflict, Ethnic Attitudes, and Group Behavior*. Hoboken, NJ: Wiley.

Levitin, Teresa E., and Warren E. Miller. 1979. "Ideological Interpretations of Presidential Elections." *American Political Science Review* 73, no. 3: 751–771.

Lindaman, K., and D. P. Haider-Markel. 2002. "Issue Evolution, Political Parties, and the Culture Wars." *Political Research Quarterly* 55, no. 1: 91–110.

Longo, Nicholas B., and Ross P. Meyer. 2006. "College Students and Politics: A Literature Review." Center for Information and Research on Civic Learning & Engagement (CIRCLE) Working Paper. https://www.civicyouth.org/PopUps/WorkingPapers/WP46LongoMeyer.pdf.

Lublin, G. 2010. "Jimmy Carter Says US Is More Polarized Now Than During Civil War." *Business Insider*. http://www.businessinsider.com/jimmy-carter-says-us-is-more-polarized-than-during-civil-war-2010-9.

Lukianoff, Greg, and Jonathon Haidt. 2018. *The Coddling of the American Mind*. New York: Penguin.

Luttig, Matthew D. 2018. "The 'Prejudiced Personality' and the Origins of Partisan Strength, Affective Polarization, and Partisan Sorting." *Advances in Political Psychology* 39, no. 1: 239–256.

Mackie, Diane M., Thierry Devos, and Eliot R. Smith. 2000. "Intergroup Emotions: Explaining Offensive Action Tendencies in an Intergroup Context." *Journal of Personality and Social Psychology* 79, no. 4: 602–616. https://doi.org/10.1037/00223514.79.4.602.

MacKinnon, C. 1993. *Only Words*. Cambridge, MA: Harvard University Press.

Malka, Ariel, and Yphtach Lelkes. 2010. "More Than Ideology: Conservative-Liberal Identity and Receptivity to Political Cues." *Social Justice Research* 23, nos. 2–3: 156–188. https://doi.org/10.1007/s1121101001143.

Mann, Thomas, and Norman J. Ornstein. 2012. *It's Even Worse Than It Looks: How the American Constitutional System Collided with the New Politics of Extremism*. New York: Basic Books.

Manuel, Paul Christopher, and Anne Marie Cammisa. 1999. *Checks and*

Balances? How a Parliamentary System Could Change American Politics. Boulder, CO: Westview Press.

Maoz, I., and C. McCauley. 2005. "Psychological Correlates of Support for Compromise: A Polling Study of Jewish-Israeli Attitudes Toward Solutions to the Israeli-Palestinian Conflict." *Political Psychology* 26: 791–808.

Marcus, George, W. Russell Neuman, and Michael MacKuen. 2000. *Affective Intelligence and Political Judgment.* Chicago, IL: University of Chicago Press.

Markus, Gregory B. 1988. "The Impact of Personal and National Economic Conditions on the Presidential Vote: A Pooled Cross-Sectional Analysis." *American Journal of Political Science* 32: 137–154.

Marques, José, Dominic Abrams, and Rui G. Serôdio. 2001. "Being Better by Being Right: Subjective Group Dynamics and Derogation of In-Group Deviants When Generic Norms Are Undermined." *Journal of Personality and Social Psychology* 81, no. 3: 436–447. https://doi.org/10.1037/00223514.81.3.436.

Masket, Seth, Boris Shor, Steven Rogers, and Nolan McCarty. 2013. "A Primary Cause of Partisanship? Nomination Systems and Legislator Ideology." In *Typescript.* Princeton, NJ: Princeton University.

Mason, Lilliana. 2015a. "'I Disrespectfully Agree': The Differential Effects of Partisan Sorting on Social and Issue Polarization." *American Journal of Political Science* 59, no. 1: 128–145.

———. 2015b. "Party Polarization Is Making Us More Prejudiced." In *Political Polarization in American Politics*, edited by Daniel J. Hopkins and John Sides. New York: Bloomsbury Academic.

———. 2018. "Ideologues Without Issues: The Polarizing Consequences of Ideological Identities." *Public Opinion Quarterly* 82, no. S1: 866–887. https://doi.org/10.1093/poq/nfy005.

Matsuda, M. J. 1989. "Public Response to Racist Speech: Considering the Victim's Story." *Michigan Law Review* 87: 2320–2381.

Matsuda, M. J., C. Lawrence, R. Delgado, and K. Crenshaw, eds. 1993. *Words That Wound: Critical Race Theory, Assaultive Speech, and the First Amendment.* Boulder, CO: Westview.

McCarty, Nolan. 2015. "What We Know and Do Not Know about Our Polarized Politics." In *Political Polarization in American Politics*, edited by Daniel J. Hopkins and John Sides. New York: Bloomsbury Academic.

McCarty, Nolan, Keith T. Poole, and Howard Rosenthal. 1997. *Income Redistribution and the Realignment of American Politics.* Washington, DC: American Enterprise Institute.

———. 2006. *Polarized America: The Dance of Ideology and Unequal Riches.* Cambridge: Massachusetts Institute of Technology Press.

McConnell, Christopher, Yotam Margalit, Neil Malhoarta, and Matthew Levendusky. 2018. "The Economic Consequences of Partisanship in a Polarized Era." *American Journal of Political Science* 62, no. 1: 5–18.

McDonald, Jonathan Ladd, and Gabriel S. Lenz. 2009. "Exploiting a Rare Communication Shift to Document the Persuasive Power of the News Media." *American Journal of Political Science* 53, no. 2: 394–410.

McGuire, William J. 1986. "The Myth of Massive Media Impact." In *Public Communication and Behavior*, edited by George Comstock, 173–257. New York: Academic Press.

McLeish, Kendra N., and Robert J. Oxoby. 2008. "Social Interactions and the Salience of Social Identity." Institute of Labor Economics Discussion Papers 3354. https://www.iza.org/publications/dp/3554/social-interactions-and-the-salience-of-social-identity.

McPhee, W. N., R. B. Smith, and J. Ferguson. 1963. "A Theory of Informal Social Influence." In *Formal Theories of Mass Behavior*, edited by W. N. McPhee. New York: Free Press.

Mellers, Barbara, Philip Tetlock, and Hal R. Arkes. 2019. "Forecasting Tournaments, Epistemic Humility, and Attitude Depolarization." *Cognition* 188: 19–26.

Milkis, Sidney M. 1993. *The President and the Parties: The Transformation of the American Party System since the New Deal.* Oxford, UK: Oxford University Press.

Milkis, Sidney M., and Jesse H. Rhodes. 2007. "George W. Bush, the Republican Party, and the 'New' American Party System." *Perspectives on Politics* 5: 461–488.

Mill, John Stuart. 2002. *On Liberty*, edited by Kathy Casey. Detroit, MI: R. R. Donnelly.

Miller, Arthur H., and Warren E. Miller. 1976. "Ideology in the 1972 Election: Myth or Reality—a Rejoinder." *American Political Science Review* 70, no. 3: 832–849.

Miller, Arthur H., Warren E. Miller, Alden S. Raine, and Thad A. Brown. 1976. "A Majority Party in Disarray: Policy Polarization in the 1972 Election." *American Political Science Review* 70, no. 3: 753–778.

Miller, Steven D., and David O. Sears. 1986. "Stability and Change in Social Tolerance: A Test of the Persistence Hypothesis." *American Journal of Political Science* 30, no. 1: 214–236.

Mitchell, Amy, Jeffrey Gottfried, Michael Barthel, and Elisa Shearer. 2016. "The

Modern News Consumer: News Attitudes and Practices in the Digital Era." Pew Research Center. Cited in http://www.journalism.org/2016/07/07/pathways-to-news/.

Mitchell, G. 2000. "Bird in the Hand for Bush?" In *Mass Media Effects Research: Advances Through Meta-analysis*, edited by Raymond W. Preiss, Barbara Mae Gayle, Nancy Burrell, Mike Allen, and Jennings Bryant, 24–27. New York: Routledge.

Moon, Woojin. 2004. "Party Activists, Campaign Resources and Candidate Position Taking: Theory, Tests and Applications." *British Journal of Political Science* 34, no. 4: 611–633.

Moscovici, S., and M. Zavalloni. 1969. "The Group as a Polarizer of Attitudes." *Journal of Personality and Social Psychology* 12: 125–135.

Mullainathan, Sendhil, and Andrei Shleifer. 2005. "The Market for News." *American Economics Review* 95: 1031–1053.

Mullen, E., and L. J. Skitka. 2006. "Exploring the Psychological Underpinnings of the Moral Mandate Effect: Motivated Reasoning, Group Differentiation, or Anger?" *Journal of Personality and Social Psychology* 90: 629–643.

Mutz, D. C. 2002. "Cross-Cutting Social Networks: Testing Democratic Theory in Practice." *American Political Science Review* 96, no. 2: 111–126.

Mutz, D. C., and P. S. Martin. 2001. "Facilitating Communication Across Lines of Political Difference: The Role of Mass Media." *American Political Science Review* 95, no. 1: 97–114.

Mutz, D.C., and J. J. Mondak. 2006. "The Workplace as a Context for Cross-Cutting Political Discourse." *Journal of Politics* 68, no. 1: 140–155.

Nagar, R., and I. Maoz. 2017. "Predicting Jewish-Israeli Recognition of Palestinian Pain and Suffering." *Journal of Conflict Resolution* 61, no. 2: 372–397.

National Council for the Social Studies. 2019. "Setting the Stage for Civil Discourse." *Social Education* 80, no. 5: 272–275.

Negroponte, N. 1995. *Being Digital*. New York: Knopf.

Nelson, Jacqueline K., Kevin M. Dunn, and Yin Paradies. 2011. "Bystander Anti-Racism: A Review of the Literature." *Analyses of Social Issues and Public Policy* 11, no. 1: 263–284.

Newman, John Henry. 1852. *The Idea of a University*. Pittsburgh, PA: National Institute for Newman Studies. http://www.newmanreader.org/works/idea/.

Nichols, Tom. 2017. "Our Graduates Are Rubes." *Chronicle of Higher Education*, January 15. https://www.chronicle.com/article/Our-Graduates-Are-Rubes/238865.

Nicholson, Stephen P. 2005. "The Jeffords Switch and Public Support for Divided Government." *British Journal of Political Science* 35: 343–356.

Nie, Norman H., and Kristi Andersen. 1974. "Mass Belief Systems Revisited: Political Change and Attitude Structure." *Journal of Politics* 36, no. 3: 540–591.

Nie, Norman H., Jane Junn, and Kenneth Stehlik-Barry. 1996. *Education and Democratic Citizenship in America*. Chicago, IL: University of Chicago Press.

Nie, Norman H., Darwin W. Miller III, Saar Golde, Daniel M. Butler, and Kenneth Winneg. 2010. "The World Wide Web and the U.S. Political News Market." *American Journal of Political Science* 54, no. 2: 428–439.

Nie, Norman, Sidney Verba, and John R. Petrocik. 1976. *The Changing American Voter*. Cambridge, MA: Harvard University Press.

Noddings, Nel. 2018. "Making Connections in the School Curriculum." *Theory into Practice* 57: 333–338.

Noel, Hans. 2013. *Political Ideologies and Political Parties in America*. New York: Cambridge University Press.

———. 2014. "Polarization Is about More Than Just Sorting, but Sorting Is Polarization Anyway." http://www.mischiefsoffaction.com/2014/06/polarization-is-aboutmore-than-just.html/.

———. 2015. "How Ideological Activists Constructed Our Polarized Parties." In *Political Polarization in American Politics*, edited by Daniel J. Hopkins and John Sides. New York: Bloomsbury Academic.

Norpoth, Helmut, and Jerrold G. Rusk. 1982. "Partisan Dealignment in the American Electorate: Itemizing the Deductions since 1964." *American Political Science Review* 76, no. 3: 522–537.

Parker, M. T., and R. Janoff-Bulman. 2013. "Lessons from Morality-Based Social Identity: The Power of Outgroup 'Hate,' Not Just Ingroup 'Love.'" *Social Justice Research* 26: 81–96.

Patterson, T. E., and W. Donsbach. 1996. "New Decisions: Journalists as Partisan Actors." *Political Communication* 13: 455–468.

Paulson, Arthur. 2000. *Realignment and Party Revival: Understanding Americana Electoral Politics at the Turn of the Twenty-First Century*. Westport, CT: Praeger.

———. 2007. *Electoral Realignment and the Outlook for American Democracy*. Boston: Northeastern University Press.

———. 2018. *Donald Trump and the Prospect for American Democracy: An Unprecedented President in an Age of Polarization*. Lanham, MD: Lexington Books.

Pearson-Merkowitz, Shanna, Alexandra Filindra, and Joshua J. Dyck. 2016.

"When Partisans and Minorities Interact: Interpersonal Contact, Partisanship, and Public Opinion Preferences on Immigration Policy." *Social Science Quarterly* 97, no. 2: 311–324. https://doi.org/10.1111/ssqu.12175.

Peltz, Jennifer. 2016. "15 Years after Sept. 11: How the Unity We Forged Broke Apart." *Associated Press*, September 6. https://apnews.com/c2ca34c161144108969c8f1b8ae704fd/how-american-unity-forged-after-sept-11-broke-apart.

Persily, Nathaniel. 2015. *Solutions to Political Polarization in America.* New York: Cambridge University Press.

Peters, G., ed. 2012. *Political Party Platforms of Parties Receiving Electoral Votes: 1840–2012.* American Presidency Project. http://www.presidency.ucsb.edu/platforms.php.

Pettigrew, Thomas F. 1979. "The Ultimate Attribution Error: Extending Allport's Cognitive Analysis of Prejudice." *Personality and Social Psychology Bulletin* 5, no. 4: 461–476. https://doi.org/10.1177/014616727900500407.

Pew Research Center. 2004. "Cable and Internet Loom Large in Fragmented Political News Universe: Perceptions of Partisan Bias Seen as Growing, Especially by Democrats." *Pew Research Center Report,* January 11. https://www.pewresearch.org/internet/2004/01/11/cable-and-internet-loom-large-in-fragmented-political-news-universe/.

———. 2009. "Partisanship and Cable News Audiences." *Pew Research Center Report,* October 30. http://www.pewresearch.org/2009/10/30/partisanship-and-cable-news-audiences/politic.

———. 2014. "Political Polarization in the American Public." *Pew Research Center Report,* June 12. http://www.people-press.org/2014/06/12/al-polarization-in-the-american-public/.

———. 2016. "As Election Nears, Voters Divided Over Democracy and 'Respect.'" *Pew Research Center Report,* October 27. http://www.people-press.org/2016/10/27/as-election-nears-voters-divided-over-democracy-and-respect/.

Pfiffner, James P. 2006. "Partisan Polarization, Politics, and the Presidency: Structural Sources of Conflict." In *Rivals for Power*, edited by J. A. Thurber, 33–58. Lanham, MD: Rowman and Littlefield.

Pildes, Richard. 2015. "How to Fix Our Polarized Politics? Strengthen Political Parties." In *Political Polarization in American Politics*, edited by Daniel J. Hopkins and John Sides. New York: Bloomsbury Academic.

Plane, Dennis. 2016. "Practical Tips for Civil Discourse in the Era of Polarized Politics: Talking about the Racist and the Crook." Diversity and

Democracy Series. *Juniata Voices* 17, September 28. https://www.juniata.edu/offices/juniata-voices/media/volume-17/vol17-Plane.pdf.

Poole, Keith T., and Howard Rosenthal. 1997. *Congress: A Political-Economic History of Roll-Call Voting.* New York: Oxford University Press.

———. 2001. "D-Nominate after 10 Years: A Comparative Update to Congress—a Political-Economic History of Roll-Call Voting." *Legislative Studies Quarterly* 26, no. 1: 5–29.

Popp, Elizabeth, and Thomas J. Rudolph. 2011. "A Tale of Two Ideologies: Explaining Public Support for Economic Interventions." *Journal of Politics* 73, no. 3: 808–820.

Poushter, Jacob. 2015. "40% of Millennials OK with Limiting Speech Offensive to Minorities." *Pew Research Center Fact Tank,* November 20. http://www.pewresearch.org/fact-tank/2015/11/20/40-of-millennials-ok-with-limiting-speech-offensive-to-minorities/.

Price, V., J. N. Cappella, and L. Nir. 2002. "Does Disagreement Contribute to More Deliberative Opinions?" *Political Communication* 19: 95–112.

Prior, Markus. 2007. *Post-Broadcast Democracy: How Media Choice Increases Inequality in Political Involvement and Polarizes Elections.* New York: Cambridge University Press.

Puleo, Stephen. 2013. *The Caning: The Assault That Drove America to Civil War.* Yardley, PA: First Westholme.

Ranney, Austin. 1954. *The Doctrine of Responsible Party Government: Its Origins and Present State.* Urbana: University of Illinois Press.

Redlawsk, David P. 2002. "Hot Cognition or Cool Consideration? Testing the Effects of Motivated Reasoning on Political Decision Making." *Journal of Politics* 64, no. 4: 1021–1044. https://doi.org/10.1111/14682508.00161.

Reilly, Katie. 2016. "Hillary Clinton Says She Regrets Part of Her 'Deplorables' Comment." *Time,* September 10. https://time.com/4486601/hillary-clinton -donald-trump-basket-of-deplorables-half/.

Reiter, Howard L., and Jeffrey Stonecash. 2011. *Counter Realignment: Political Change in the Northeastern United States.* Cambridge, UK: Cambridge University Press.

Rhode, David W. 1991. *Parties and Leaders in the Postreform House.* Chicago, IL: University of Chicago Press.

Rhodes, J. 2012. "The Ties That Divide: Bonding Social Capital, Religious Friendship Networks, and Political Tolerance among Evangelicals." *Sociological Inquiry* 82, no. 2: 163–186.

Roberts, Jason M. 2007. "The Statistical Analysis of Roll-Call Data: A Cautionary Tale." *Legislative Studies Quarterly* 32, no. 3: 341–360.

Roberts, Jason M., and Steen S. Smith. 2003. "Procedural Contexts, Party Strategy, and Conditional Party Voting in the US House of Representatives." *American Journal of Political Science* 47, no. 2: 305–317.

Robinson, M. J., and M. Clancey. 1985. "Teflon Politics." *Public Opinion* 17: 14–18.

Robinson, M. J., and M. Sheehan. 1983. *Over the Wire and on TV*. New York: Russell Sage Foundation.

Roccas, Sonia, and Marilynn B. Brewer. 2002. "Social Identity Complexity." *Personality and Social Psychology Review* 6: 88–106.

Rodgers, Daniel T. 1982. "In Search of Progressivism." *Review in American History* 10, no. 4: 113–132.

Rohde, David W. 1991. *Parties and Leaders in the Post-Reform House*. Chicago, IL: University of Chicago Press.

Rokeach, Milton. 1973. *The Nature of Human Values*. New York: Free Press.

Rosenstone, Steven J., and John Mark Hansen. 1993. *Mobilization, Participation, and Democracy in America*. New York: Longman.

Rothgerber, Hank, and Stephen Worchel. 1997. "The View from Below: Intergroup Relations from the Perspective of the Disadvantaged Group." *Journal of Personality and Social Psychology* 73, no. 6: 1191–1205.

Rudolph, Susanne Hoeber, and Lloyd I. Rudolph. 1993. "Modern Hate." *New Republic*, March 22.

Russell, Bertrand. 1928. *Sceptical Essays*. London: Allen and Unwin.

Sacramento State Center for Teaching and Learning. 2019. "Difficult Conversations: Strategies for Civil Discourse." *Civil Discourse Handout*. https://www.csuchico.edu/diversity/_assets/documents/resources-civil-discourse.pdf.

Scheufele, D. A., M. C. Nisbet, D. Brossard, and E. C. Nisbet. 2004. "Social Structure and Citizenship: Examining the Impacts of Social Setting, Network Heterogeneity, and Informational Variables on Political Participation." *Political Communication* 21: 315–338.

Schier, Sten E., and Todd E. Eblery. 2013. *American Government and Popular Discontent: Stability Without Success*. New York: Routledge.

———. 2016. *Polarized: The Rise of Ideology in American Politics*. Lanham, MD: Rowman and Littlefield.

Schlueter, Elmar, Peter Schmidt, and Ulrich Wagner. 2008. "Disentangling the Causal Relations of Perceived Group Threat and Outgroup Derogation: Cross-National Evidence from German and Russian Panel Surveys." *European Sociological Review* 24, no. 5: 567–581.

Schmitt, Carl. 1963. *The Theory of the Partisan: A Commentary/Remark on the Concept of the Political*. Berlin: Duncker and Humblot.

Schrek, Carl. 2016. "In U.S. Election, a 'Dirty' Campaign of Historic Proportions." *Radio Free Europe Radio Liberty,* October 29. https://www.rferl.org/a/us-presidential-election-clinton-trump-dirty-campaign/28082392.html.

Schwartz, J. 2002. *Associated Press Reporting Handbook.* Boston: McGraw-Hill.

Scott, Eugen. 2018. "The 'Value Divide' between Democrats and Republicans Is Getting Bigger and Bigger." *Washington Post,* March 18. https://www.washingtonpost.com/news/the-fix/wp/2018/03/18/americans-generally-dont-think-their-political-opponents-share-their-values/.

Sears, D. O., and C. L. Funk. 1999. "Evidence of Long-Term Persistence of Adults' Political Predispositions." *Journal of Politics* 61, no. 1: 1–28.

Sears, D. O., and N. A. Valentino. 1997. "Politics Matters: Political Events as Catalysts for Preadult Socialization." *American Political Science Review* 91, no. 1: 45–65.

Selnow, G. W. 1998. *Electronic Whistle-Stops: The Impact of the Internet on American Politics.* Westport, CT: Praeger.

Shafer, Byron E. 1997. "Foundation Stones of Present Discontents: The American Political Nation, 1776–1945." In *Present Discontents: American Politics in the Very Late Twentieth Century* by Byron Shafer. Chatham, NJ: Chatham House.

Shafer, Byron E., and Richard Johnston. 2009. *The End of Southern Exceptionalism: Class, Race, and Partisan Change in the Postwar South.* Cambridge, MA: Harvard University Press.

Shah, D. V., M. D. Watts, D. Domke, D. P. Fan, and M. Fibison. 1999. "News Coverage, Economic Cues, and the Public's Presidential Preferences: 1984–1996." *Journal of Politics* 61: 914–943.

Shapiro, Robert Y. 2015. "Can Young Voters Break the Cycle of Polarization?" In *Political Polarization in American Politics,* edited by Daniel J. Hopkins and John Sides. New York: Bloomsbury Academic.

Sharp, David. 2012. "Snowe Won't Miss Partisanship: Retiring Senator Plans to Nurture Centrists with Books, Speeches, and PAC." *Washington Times,* December 31, 895–917.

Shaw, Daron. 2012. "If Everyone Votes Their Party, Why Do Presidential Election Outcomes Vary So Much?" *Forum* 3, no. 1: Article 1.

Shearer, Elisa. 2018. "Social Media Outpaces [*sic*] Print Newspapers in the U.S. as a News Source." *Pew Research Center Report,* December 10. https://www.pewresearch.org/fact-tank/2018/12/10/social-media-outpaces-print-newspapers-in-the-u-s-as-a-news-source/.

Sherif, Muzafer. 1966. *The Psychology of Social Norms.* Oxford, UK: Harper.

Sherif, Muzafer., O. J. Harvey, B. J. White, W. R. Hood, and C. W. Sherif. 1961. *Intergroup Conflict and Cooperation: The Robbers Cave Experiment*. Scranton, PA: Harper and Row.

Shiell, T. C. 1998. *Campus Hate Speech on Trial*. Lawrence: University Press of Kansas.

Shor, Boris. 2015. "How US State Legislatures Are Polarized and Getting More Polarized." In *Political Polarization in American Politics*, edited by Daniel J. Hopkins and John Sides. New York: Bloomsbury Academic.

Sidanius, James, Shana Levin, Colette Laar, and David O. Sears. 2008. "The Diversity Challenge: Social Identity and Intergroup Relations on the College Campus." *Washington Monthly*, September 21. https://washington monthly.com/2012/09/21/your-do-nothing-congress-in-one-graph/.

Sides, John. 2017. "The 40-Year Decline in the Tolerance of College Students, Graphed." *Washington Post*, March 9. https://www.washingtonpost.com /news/monkey-cage/wp/2017/03/09/the-40-year-decline-in-the-toler ance-of-college-students-graphed/?utm_term=.acd8661fc260.

Silbey, Joel H. 1991. *The American Political Nation, 1838–1893*. Palo Alto, CA: Stanford University Press.

Sinclair, Barbara. 2006. *Party Wars: Polarization and the Politics of National Policy Making*. Norman: University of Oklahoma Press.

Skinner, Richard. 2012. "Barack Obama and the Partisan Presidency: Four More Years?" *Society* 49, no. 5: 423–429.

Skitka, L. J., C. W. Bauman, and E. G. Sargis. 2005. "Moral Conviction: Another Contributor to Attitude Strength or Something More?" *Journal of Personality and Social Psychology* 88, no. 6: 895–917.

Snyder, Jr., James M., and Tim Groseclose. 2000. "Estimating Party Influence in Congressional Roll-Call Voting." *American Journal of Political Science* 44, no. 2: 193–211.

Sowell, Thomas. 2007. *A Conflict of Visions: Ideological Origins of Political Struggles*. Revised ed. New York: Basic Books.

Specter, Arlen. 2010. "Text of Senator Specter's 'Closing Argument.'" *Philadelphia Inquirer*, December 21. https://www.inquirer.com/philly/news/break ing/20101221_Text_of_Sen__Specters_Closing_Argument.html

Stanton, Steven J., Jacinta C. Beehner, Ekjyot K. Saini, Cynthia M. Kuhn, and Kevin S. LaBar. 2009. "Dominance, Politics, and Physiology: Voters' Testosterone Changes on the Night of the 2008 United States Presidential Election." *PLoS ONE*, October 21. https://journals.plos.org/plosone /article?id=10.1371/journal.pone.0007543.

Steele, C. M. 2010. *Whistling Vivaldi*. New York: Norton.

Steeper, Frederick T., and Robert M. Teeter. 1976. "Comment on 'A Majority Party in Disarray.'" *American Political Science Review* 70, no. 3: 806–813.

Stephenson, Crocker, Cary Spivak, and Patrick Marley. 2011. "Justices' Feud Gets Physical." *Milwaukee Journal Sentinel,* June 25.

Stevens, Sean, and Jonathan Haidt. 2018. "The Skeptics Are Wrong Part 1: Speech Culture on Campus Is Changing." *Heterodox Academy.* https://heterodoxacademy.org/skeptics-are-wrong-about-campus-speech/.

Stoker, Laura, and M. Kent Jennings. 2008. "Of Time and the Development of Partisan Polarization." *American Journal of Political Science* 52, no. 3: 619–635. https://doi.org/10.1111/j.15405907.2008.00333.x.

Stonecash, Jeff. 2015. "The Two Key Factors Behind Our Polarized Politics." In *Political Polarization in American Politics*, edited by Daniel J. Hopkins and John Sides. New York: Bloomsbury Academic.

Stonecash, J. M., M. D. Brewer, and M. D. Marianai. 2003. *Diverging Parties: Social Change, Realignment, and Party Polarization*. Boulder, CO: Westview Press.

Stroud, Natalie Jomini. 2008. "Media Use and Political Predispositions: Revisiting the Concept of Selective Exposure." *Political Behavior* 30, no. 3: 341–366.

———. 2010. "Polarization and Partisan Selective Exposure." *Journal of Communication* 60: 556–576.

———. 2011. *Niche News: The Politics of News Choice.* Oxford, UK: Oxford University Press.

Suhay, Elizabeth. 2015. "Explaining Group Influence: The Role of Identity and Emotion in Political Conformity and Polarization." *Political Behavior* 37, no. 1: 221–251. https://doi.org/10.1007/s1110901492691.

Sullivan, John L., James E. Pierson, and George E. Marcus. 1978. "Ideological Constraint in the Mass Public: A Methodological Critique and Some New Findings." *American Journal of Political Science* 22, no. 2: 233–249.

Sundquist, James L. 1983. *Dynamics of the Party System: Alignment and Realignment of Political Parties in the United State*. Washington, DC: Brookings Institution.

———. 1992. *Constitutional Reform and Effective Government*. Washington, DC: Brookings Institution.

Sunstein, C. R. 2001. *Republic.Com*. Princeton, NJ: Princeton University Press.

———. 2007. *Republic.Com 2.0*. Princeton, NJ: Princeton University Press.

———. 2009. *Going to Extremes: How Like Minds Unite and Divide*. New York: Oxford University Press.

Tajfel, Henri. 1978. "Social Categorization, Social Identity, and Social

Comparisons." In *Differentiation between Social Groups*, edited by H. Tajfel, 27–60. London: Academic Press.

———. 1981. *Human Groups and Social Society: Studies in Social Psychology*. Cambridge, UK: Cambridge University Press.

Tajfel, Henri, M. G. Billig, R. P. Bundy, and C. Flament. 1971. "Social Categorization and Intergroup Behavior." *European Journal of Social Psychology* 1, no. 2: 149–178.

Tajfel, H., and J. C. Turner. 1979. "An Integrative Theory of Intergroup Conflict," in *The Psychology of Intergroup Relations*, edited by W. G. Austin and S. Worchel. Monterey, CA: Brooks Cole.

———. 1986. "The Social Identity Theory of Intergroup Behavior." In *The Psychology of Intergroup Relations*, 2nd ed., by S. Worchel and W. G. Austin. Chicago, IL: Nelson-Hall.

Terry, Deborah J., and Michael A. Hogg. 1996. "Group Norms and the Attitude-Behavior Relationship: A Role for Group Identification." *Personality and Social Psychology Bulletin* 22, no. 8: 776–793. https://doi.org/10.1177/0146167296228002.

Terry, Deborah J., Michael A. Hogg, and Katherine M. White. 1999. "The Theory of Planned Behaviour: Self-Identity, Social Identity and Group Norms." *British Journal of Social Psychology* 38, no. 3: 225–244. https://doi.org/10.1348/014466699164149.

Tetlock, Philip E., Barbara A. Mellars, Nick Rohrbaugh, and Eva Chen. 2014. "Forecasting Tournaments: Tools for Increasing Transparency and Improving the Quality of Debate." *Association for Psychological Science* 23, no. 4: 290–295.

Tewksbury, D. 2006. "Exposure to the Newer Media in a Presidential Primary Campaign." *Political Communication* 23, no. 3: 313–332.

Theiss-Morse, Elizabeth. 2009. *Who Counts as an American? The Boundaries of National Identity*. https://doi.org/10.1017/CBO9780511750717.

Theodoridis, Alexander G. 2017. "Me, Myself, and (I), (D), or (R)? Partisanship and Political Cognition Through the Lens of Implicit Identity." *Journal of Politics* 79, no. 4: 1253–1267. https://doi.org/10.1086/692738.

Theriault, Sean M. 2008. "The Procedurally Polarized Congress." Presentation at the Annual Meeting of the American Political Science Association.

———. 2015. "Partisan Warfare Is the Problem." In *Political Polarization in American Politics*, edited by Daniel J. Hopkins and John Sides. New York: Bloomsbury Academic.

Thompson, Hunter S. 1973. *Fear and Loathing: On the Campaign Trail, '72*. San Francisco: Straight Arrow.

Tufte, Edward R. 1973. "The Relationship between Seats and Votes in Two-Party Systems." *American Political Science Review* 67, no. 2: 540–554.

Turner, John C. 1985. "Social Categorization and Self-Concept: A Social Cognitive Theory of Group Behavior." In *Advances in Group Process: Theory and Research*, edited by E. J. Lawler, 77–121. Greenwich, CT: JAI Press.

———. 1991. *Social Influence*. Social Influence. Belmont, CA, US: Thomson Brooks/Cole Publishing Co.

Turner, J. C., M. A. Hogg, P. J. Oakes, S. D. Reicher, and M. S. Wetheral. 1987. *Rediscovering the Social Group: A Self-Categorisation Theory*. Oxford, UK: Blackwell.

US Congress. 1856. *Register of Debates*, 19th Cong., 1st sess., 1546.

US Senate. 1856. *Speech of Hon. Charles Sumner in the Senate of the United States, 19th and 20th May*. Boston: John P. Jewett.

Valentino, Nicholas A., Antoine J. Banks, Vincent L. Hutchings, and Anne K. Davis. 2009. "Selective Exposure in the Internet Age: The Interaction between Anxiety and Information Utility." *Political Psychology* 30, no. 4: 591–613.

Van Zomeren, Martijn, Colin Wayne Leach, and Russell Spears. 2010. "Does Group Efficacy Increase Group Identification? Resolving Their Paradoxical Relationship." *Journal of Experimental Social Psychology* 46, no. 6: 1055–1060. https://doi.org/10.1016/j.jesp.2010.05.006.

Viki, G. T., D. Osgood, and S. Phillips. 2013. "Dehumanization and Self-Reported Proclivity to Torture Prisoners of War." *Journal of Experimental Psychology* 49, no. 3: 325–328.

Villasenor, John. 2017. "Views among College Students Regarding the First Amendment: Results from a New Survey." Washington, DC: Brookings Institution. https://www.brookings.edu/blog/fixgov/2017/09/18/views-among-college-students-regarding-the-first-amendment-results-from-a-new-survey/.

Vucci, Evan, and Susan Walsh. 2013. "The Civil Senators, Feinstein and Graham: They've Won This Year's Prize for Civility in Public Life, Something We Must Encourage." *Pittsburgh Post-Gazzette,* March 16. https://www.post-gazette.com/opinion/Op-Ed/2013/03/13/The-civil-senators-Feinstein-and-Graham/stories /201303130248.

Waldman, P., and J. Devitt. 1998. "Newspaper Photographs and the 1996 Presidential Election: The Question of Bias." *Journalism and Mass Communication Quarterly* 75: 302–311.

Walker, S. 1994. *Hate Speech*. Lincoln: University of Nebraska Press.

Warner, B. 2010. "Segmenting the Electorate: The Effects of Exposure to Political Extremism Online." *Communication Studies* 61, no. 4: 430–444.

Wattenberg, Martin P. 2015. *Is Voting for Young People?* 4th ed. New York: Routledge.

Weaver, D. H., R. A. Beam, B. J. Brownlee, P. S. Vokes, and G. C. Wilhoit. 2007. *The American Journalist in the 21st Century: U.S. News People at the Dawn of a New Millennium.* Mahwah, NJ: Lawrence Erlbaum.

Weaver, P. H. 1972. "Is Television News Biased?" *Public Interest* 26: 57–74.

Weldon, S. A. 2006. "The Institutional Context of Tolerance for Ethnic Minorities: A Comparative, Multilevel Analysis of Western Europe." *American Journal of Political Science* 50, no. 2: 331–349.

White, J. K. 2003. *The Values Divide.* Chatham, NJ: Chatham House.

Wiebe, Robert H. 1967. *The Search for Order, 1877–1920.* New York: Hill and Wang.

Wilmer, F. 2002. *The Social Construction of Man, the State, and War: Identity, Conflict, and Violence in the Former Yugoslavia.* New York: Routledge.

Wood, Wendy, Gregory J. Pool, Kira Leck, and Daniel Purvis. 1996. "Self-Definition, Defensive Processing, and Influence: The Normative Impact of Majority and Minority Groups." *Journal of Personality and Social Psychology* 71, no. 6: 1181–1193. https://doi.org/10.1037/00223514.71.6.1181.

Zaller, J. 1992. *The Nature and Origins of Mass Opinion.* Cambridge, UK: Cambridge University Press.

Zaller, J. R., and S. Feldman. 1992. "A Simple Theory of the Survey Response." *American Journal of Political Science* 36: 579–616.

Zogby Analytics. 2016. "2016 Presidential Campaign Reveals Chilling Trend Lines for Civility in U.S. Politics." *Zogby Analytics.* https://zogbyanalytics.com/news/757-2016-presidential-campaign-reveals-chilling-trend-lines-for-civility-in-u-s-politics.

Zukin, C., S. Ketter, M. Andolina, K. Jenkins, and M. X. Delli Carpi. 2006. *A New Engagement? Political Participation, Civic Life, and the Changing American Citizen.* New York: Oxford University Press.

Index

Note: page numbers followed by *f* and *t* refer to figures and tables respectively. Those followed by n refer to notes, with note number.